Wealth
in
Western
Thought

Wealth in Western Thought

THE CASE FOR AND AGAINST RICHES

Edited by Paul G. Schervish

PRAEGER

Westport, Connecticut
London

Library of Congress Cataloging-in-Publication Data

Wealth in western thought : the case for and against riches / edited
by Paul G. Schervish.
    p. cm.
    Papers from an interdisciplinary seminar held at Boston College in
1989 and 1990, and sponsored by the T. B. Murphy Foundation
Charitable Trust.
    Includes bibliographical references and index.
    ISBN 0–275–94677–0 (alk. paper)
    1. Wealth—Moral and ethical aspects—Congresses. I. Schervish,
Paul G.
HC79.W4W42 1994
330.1′6—dc20   93–23469

British Library Cataloguing in Publication Data is available.

Library of Congress Catalog Card Number: 93–23469
ISBN: 0–275–94677–0

First published in 1994

Praeger Publishers, 88 Post Road West, Westport, CT 06881
An imprint of Greenwood Publishing Group, Inc.

Printed in the United States of America

∞™

The paper used in this book complies with the
Permanent Paper Standard issued by the National
Information Standards Organization (Z39.48–1984).

10 9 8 7 6 5 4 3 2 1

Copyright Acknowledgments

The editor and publisher gratefully acknowledge permission for use of the following material:

Lisa Sowle Cahill, "The New Testament and Ethics: Communities of Social Change," *Interpretations*, Volume 44 (October 1990), pages 383–95. Reprinted by permission of the publisher.

From *To Herland and Beyond* by Ann Lane. Compilation and introduction copyright © 1980 by Ann J. Lane. Reprinted by permission of Pantheon Books, a division of Random House, Inc.

Women and Economics by Charlotte Perkins Gilman, Introduction and Notes by Carl N. Degler. Introduction and Notes copyright © 1966 by Carl N. Degler. Reprinted by permission of HarperCollins Publishers.

Elizabeth Gurley Flynn, *The Rebel Girl: An Autobiography, My First Life* (New York: International Publishers, 1955, revised, 1973). Reprinted by permission of the publisher.

Robert L. Heilbroner, *The Essential Adam Smith* (New York: W.W. Norton, 1986). Reprinted by permission of the author and publisher.

Charlotte Perkins Gilman, *The Living of Charlotte Perkins Gilman: An Autobiography* (New York: D. Appleton-Century, 1935). Reprinted by permission of Schlesinger Library, Radcliffe College.

Michael O'Higgins, Guenther Schmaus, and Geoffrey Stephenson, "Income Distribution and Redistribution: A Microdata Analysis for Seven Countries," *The Review of Income and Wealth* 35, no. 2 (June 1989): table 2.

Timothy Smeeding, Barbara Torrey, and Martin Rein, "Patterns of Income and Poverty: The Economic Status of Children and the Elderly in Eight Countries," in Smeeding, Torrey and Rein, eds., *The Vulnerable* (Washington, D.C.: The Urban Institute Press, 1988): table 5–2.

To
Thomas B. Murphy

Happy the one who finds Wisdom,
the one who gains understanding.
For her profit is better than profit in silver,
and better than gold is her revenue.
The Book of Proverbs 3: 13–14

Contents

Preface

This book presents a set of contributions by scholars from a range of disciplines. Each chapter explores some aspect of the complex and often contradictory matrix of sentiments, feelings, and beliefs that frames the social doctrine of wealth in contemporary North America. The volume is the fruit of an experimental interdisciplinary seminar at Boston College in 1989 and 1990 sponsored by the T. B. Murphy Foundation Charitable Trust. In addition to exploring various dimensions of our Western view of wealth, a goal of the two-year seminar was to help resurrect in this age of specialization the concept of the university as the unit of research. To this end, the seminar gathered faculty from a broad range of disciplines to study and write about a common topic. The seven Boston College faculty members whose writings constitute this volume are professors of classics, economics, ethics, history, literature, scripture, and sociology.

During the first year we met regularly to read and discuss various historical, theological, literary, and sociological writings on economic life, and to determine the general seminar topic on which each of us would write. At the end of this initial year of reading, we agreed to focus on the Western cultural inheritance of normative sentiments about wealth and the wealthy. We chose this topic for several reasons. It is of course a subject that reveals much about contemporary modes of consciousness and behavior. What could be more central to the current controversies surrounding the issues of poverty, income distribution, consumer culture, and economic morality than the case for and against wealth that has preoccupied Western thought from its origins? "There is nothing on which [the world] is so hard as poverty," says Ebenezer Scrooge, feeling caught in the web of a major contradiction, "and there is nothing it professes to condemn with such severity as the pursuit of wealth!"[1] In addition to being pivotal, the topic of wealth (pro and con) was broad enough to be investigated from a number of different viewpoints, but sufficiently focused to enable us to learn from each other and to contribute to a joint publication. Finally, by examining the cultural meanings surrounding the production, distribution, and consumption of wealth, we obtain a lens onto many of the underlying convictions that shape contemporary moral discourse and public policy debates.

During the second year we devoted the seminar meetings to discussion of the drafts that became the chapters in this volume. These seminars turned out to be far more provocative than we had anticipated. Our exchanges, to use the language of diplomacy, were frank and constructive. While respecting each other's theoretical starting points, subjective predispositions, and scholarly perspectives, we pressed each other for clarity and consistency. We sought to sharpen the distinct thesis of each chapter and to expose any concealed arguments and assumptions. We reflected on the relevance of our colleagues' arguments for our own contributions and worked to locate the themes that tied the writings together. The title of this volume, *Wealth in Western Thought: The Case for and against Riches*, captures much of that common ground.

I view the work represented in this volume as a function of reading and writing. It presents a reading in two senses or, better, at two levels. At one level, each chapter takes as its data a number of ancient, medieval, modern, or contemporary texts that depict a reading of the meaning and morality of wealth during a particular era. At a second level, each chapter, while portraying what other documents say about wealth and the wealthy, constitutes a text in its own right and, as such, calls for a reading. But where there is a reading, there first has been a writing. As such, each chapter is also about writing, again in two senses. Most obviously, the volume is a set of texts expressing what we individually have to say about what others have said. Each chapter creates a local truth—a considered view—argued coherently about the meaning of wealth during a particular epoch at a particular place. But these writings are not completely independent. Taken together, they explore many of the common themes linked to the unfurling of Western consciousness and conscience about wealth. This more general array of meanings and emotions that circumscribes the moral sentiments of individuals within and across eras I refer to as the cultural scripture of wealth. The volume, then, to continue the metaphor, is an exegesis of some key chapters in this cultural scripture.

Substantively, what we have to say is captured by the subtitle of the book. What we study as well as what we have written is all part of "the talk for and against wealth," as David Gill, one of the contributors to this book, puts it. The documents we study and the papers we have written make a case that wealth is either good or bad or, more subtly argued, that wealth *may* be good or bad, opportunity or temptation, depending on how it is managed. Obviously, the adulation of and attack on riches in Western consciousness continues to the present. Like those who write biographies, one tends, regarding wealth, to make a relatively strong case for or against the subject.

Apart from this broad motif, we do not provide a common outlook on wealth in Western thinking, nor has this been our ambition. It can be tempting of course for members of an interdisciplinary seminar to pressure each other to abandon the methods of individual disciplines or ideological predispositions. Fortunately, we never allowed our diversity to be diluted. At the same time, we also avoided the opposite pitfall of reifying academic boundaries. It turns out that the economist undertook a history of ideas; the professors of ethics and literature drew heavily on their training in theology and scriptural studies; the scripture scholar and classicist employed sociological concepts; the historian and sociologist turned to literary analysis. The approach taken in this book is thus in many respects similar to that of *Reading Material Culture*, edited by Christopher Tilley,[2] which contains a series of essays by anthropologists and archaeologists undertaking critical assessments of dominant figures in cultural studies. We concur in the four "refusals" cited by Tilley: rigid disciplinary allegiance; divorce of theoretical from practical concern; separation of investigator from what is being investigated; and relegation of multifaceted topics to narrowly demarcated realms of research such as ideology, economics, or politics. In the end, one lesson may be that the success of an interdisciplinary project of this sort depends not on whether the participants water down their viewpoints or induce conformity. Rather, it depends on how multifaceted, intellectually curious, and personally generous are the researchers at the table.

To whatever extent this book advances the understanding of wealth, I am grateful to the members of the seminar who so faithfully and competently contributed to our joint endeavor. I especially appreciate the dedication of my colleagues to making the seminar work, particularly at those times when we were struggling to discover where we were going and how to proceed. I also want to thank Thomas B. Murphy for recognizing the importance of this venture and for his insightful participation in the seminar. Finally, I am grateful to Carol Ann Grimm and Elizabeth L. Byrne Radlo for their conscientious coordination of the seminars and to Mary C. Picarello for assembling the index.

Paul G. Schervish

NOTES

1. Charles Dickens, *A Christmas Carol* (1843; reprint, New York: Airmont Publishing, 1963), 55.

2. Christopher Tilley, ed., *Reading Material Culture* (Oxford: Basil Blackwell, 1990).

Wealth
in
Western
Thought

1

Introduction

PAUL G. SCHERVISH

When in the eighteenth century Adam Smith wrote *The Theory of Moral Sentiments* and *The Wealth of Nations*, he captured much of what long before and now long since has been the Western world's unique struggle with the moral and institutional infrastructure for dealing with wealth. In *Moral Sentiments*, Smith searches for the underlying purpose that mobilizes individuals into a relatively coherent social fabric. What are the motivating desires that provide the minimum standard for personal direction and social decorum? His answer: the universal search for approbation. And what induces such approbation? Dedicated commitment to the personal discipline and organizational framework surrounding the entrepreneurial quest for opulence and its attendant freedoms. In *The Wealth of Nations*, Smith explores the historical question of what has led to the dramatic change not just in a society's aggregate wealth or in the personal treasure of its elite, but in the fundamental well-being of whole populations. Again, his answer is that the new dispensation of capitalism provides for a productive ethic among the economically well-to-do such that they constructively reinvest rather than avariciously consume their newly created fortune. As a result, their abundance redounds to the benefit of the masses.

Karl Marx, the other intellectual titan at the crossroads of industrial capitalism, urged a different view. The sociocultural dispensation that according to Smith generated benefit for the masses, according to Marx generated domination. What for Smith was an institutionally infused convergence of interests between capital and labor, for Marx was an institutionally engendered contradictory and exploitative relationship between these same two classes. The innovations of capitalist relations that Smith viewed as unleashing the productive capacities of a nation had become for

Marx systematic fetters on the expanded reproduction of wealth and a source of increasing impoverishment for the masses. Ultimately, for Marx as for Smith, economic existence was both an institutional practice and a cultural awareness—a way of organizing social relations, ordering consciousness, and defining virtue.[1] But for Marx, Smith's tribute to the new order of enterprise, liberty, and virtue was merely the "language of the still revolutionary bourgeoisie." Writing after capitalism had advanced for an additional hundred years, Marx argued that such praise of capitalism's revolutionary capacity had now become the utterance of "lackeys and jesters maintained by the bourgeoisie and by idle wealth."[2] Smith's cultural icons were Marx's antiheroes.

It is not necessary to rehearse further the debate that pitted these two prodigious intellects of the Enlightenment against each other at a distance of three generations. Important, rather, is the simple but compelling insight that the Marx-Smith debate is only one episode of an enduring controversy in Western culture that can best be summarized as the "talk for and against wealth."[3] The controversy assumes a different form of discourse from era to era. And thanks to the West's traditional valuation of writing, the controversies of an earlier period often directly inform subsequent debates. Despite the historical imbrication of the assertions by moral philosophers, theologians, social scientists, and rulers, and their claims that they have provided the last word, there has been no resolution of the debate. Marx claims to have superseded Smith and Ricardo, just as Weber, Marshall, and Keynes claim to have superseded Marx. But the fact is, despite current events in Eastern Europe and the former Soviet Union, both discourses continue to the present,[4] offering still vital, conflicting views for reading wealth.

This book is about some of these other conflicting views. With perhaps the exception of Dayton Haskin's chapter on the parable of the talents, it is not an effort to read and write a systematic review of the twists and turns of the discourse of wealth. Rather, it offers a series of discrete readings of particularly important texts of the Western heritage by researchers from an array of disciplines. What follows are seven snapshots, as it were, of what the talk for and against wealth sounds like in a variety of contexts, at different points in time, from different points of view. These snapshots explore the meaning, responsibilities, justifications, and snares of wealth expressed in: the classical tradition of Greece; the social life and Biblical texts of first-century Christians; various interpretations of the parable of the talents from the second century to the present; the economic strengths and weaknesses of modern capitalism; writings by three early twentieth-century American women activists; the biographical narratives of contemporary American millionaires; and the principles of contemporary ethical thinking.

Simon Shama's analysis of the affluent Dutch at the beginning of their republic in the sixteenth and seventeenth centuries provides one such snapshot: "Just who, exactly, did the Dutch think they were?"[5] are Shama's first words in his chapter surveying the "discovery of a 'national genealogy' "[6] and national destiny by the wealthy Dutch. Just who they were, argues Shama, can be learned by discerning how the Dutch were both object and subject of what he calls a "patriotic scripture"—the compilation of oral pronouncements, written texts, visual artifacts, and musical forms telling the Dutch who they were in the eyes of Providence. The purpose of this patriotic scripture was not "to swallow up the secular world within the sacred, but rather to attribute to the vagaries of history . . . the flickering light of providential direction."[7]

For the Dutch, as for others throughout Western history, patriotic scriptures elucidate the privileges and responsibilities of wealth for the rich as well as the non-rich. Harold Beaver's review of Shama's book is appropriately titled, "Healthy, Wealthy and Worried Too."[8] As is the experience with any scripture, the Dutch found themselves invited to consolation and confronted by historical mission. According to Shama, "the greatest test of *standvastigheid* (steadfastness) which the Lord had laid on His people was, ironically, their own success. . . . If the end of gold was to be the Golden Calf, then the covenant would be broken, divine protection withdrawn and the errant people returned to the primal element from which they had been drained." Wealth, Shama contends, "far from being the reassuring symptom of the predestined Elect, as Weber argued, acted on contemporary consciences as a moral agitator.[9] Without it the Republic would collapse; with it, the Dutch could fall prey to false gods, Mammon and Baal, and engineer their own downfall. What was needed was a set of rules and conventions by which wealth could be absorbed in ways compatible with the godly purposes for which the Republic had been created."[10]

Although Shama portrays but one panel of the Western migration in the morality of wealth, it is instructive in two ways. First, by being situated in the transition from the classical and medieval epoch to the modern period, his analysis captures many themes we identify in this volume. Second, by portraying the variegated pattern of wealth's meanings at one time, he alerts us to equally complex meanings at other times. As Shama concludes,

For all this, Dutch society in its prime was hardly the sink of iniquity that the most incensed preachers liked to portray. While there was no formal set of controls regulating social ethics, an extensive array of informal, vernacular and domestic morals acted as the containing membranes of the busy, energetic organism. Some of these had classical origins, some scriptural; many were rooted in ancient Low Country folk fetishes; most were given a dusting of Calvinism for contemporary needs. All had to deal with what was peculiarly a Dutch problem: how to create a moral order within a terrestrial paradise.[11]

Like Shama, each of the seven authors in this book examines some particular text about the "agitation" of wealth in Western culture. By text, I mean not some demarcated artistic, written, or verbal document—although such texts in this narrow sense are part of what each of us studies. Rather, I use the term in the sense of a cultural text or scripture, an extended symbolic representation of a relatively coherent set of meanings. A text is thus a terrain of representations, a more or less tightly bound book of cultural expressions which captures the social story or cultural logic of a particular era or specific group within an era. It embodies the existential, normative, and utopian elements of culture and practice. That is, each text embeds and imparts a practical consciousness (Giddens, 1984) about what is, what ought to be, and how things will unfold. Each has a public and a private existence. Publicly, a text lives as social structure. According to Anthony Giddens, social structure is the allocative (regarding control of material forces) and authoritative (regarding control of human beings) rules and resources that condition human agency and result from it. As such, a text is a cultural scripture of common purposes and practices within which individual variation occurs. The private life of a text is agency and identity. According to Giddens, agency is the active capacity of individuals that both reproduces and transforms social structure. Thus, a text is also the normative orientation of personalized sentiments ("memory traces," as Giddens would phrase it) and conduct resulting from the internalization of a cultural scripture. As cultural scriptures of normative orientation, then, the texts that each of us studies provide moral discipline: an invitation to virtue and a prohibition on vice. Michel de Certeau (1984: 139) describes the inscription of culture on identity by saying that "from birth to mourning after death, law 'takes hold of' bodies in order to make them its text. Through all sorts of initiations (in rituals, at school, etc.), it transforms them into tables of the law, into living tableaux of rules and customs, into actors in the drama organized by a social order." In this way, this book is a reading of the Western drama of history and biography as it concerns, to paraphrase Shama, that recurring question of how to create a moral order within a terrestrial setting.

But not only are we reading various cultural texts in a search for their prescriptions and proscriptions about wealth, we are also thoroughly implicated writers. We propose our own reading of how others have read wealth, becoming additional voices in the talk for and against it. Everyone that writes, says Thomas Carlyle, "is writing a new Bible; or a new Apocrypha; to last for a week, or for a thousand years."[12] Each of us has a "scriptural" case to make about the case we study. Each of us, however, makes our case in two voices—what Zygmunt Bauman refers to as "legislator and interpreter."[13]

For Bauman, the legislator role of intellectuals is typically connected to a modern view of the world, while the interpreter role is connected to a postmodern view. "In referring to intellectual practices," says Bauman, "the opposition between the terms modern and post-modern stands for differences in understanding the nature of the world, and the social world in particular, and in understanding the related nature, and purpose, of intellectual work."[14] The modern perspective sees the world as an orderly totality, open to intellectual discernment of its laws of motion and subject to control where there is adequate knowledge. Knowledge and control move from local to universal application. The role of the intellectual as a writer is thus one of legislator. The intellectual is best equipped, both analytically and dispositionally, to locate the fundamental laws of moral and social life and to propose directions for aligning errant (yet corrigible) human behavior more closely to the natural order. Objective morality, human nature, natural law, and social ethics are familiar conceptual tools of the modern scholar.

According to Bauman, the interpreter role is associated with the postmodern sensitivity, although one could argue the less dualistic proposition that the interpreter role, at least as Bauman describes it, also derives from the modern world view and coexists with it. The postmodern view of the world is radically pluralistic, recognizing the existence of multiple models of order with no privileged center for evaluating their moral or historical validity. There are no universal laws. Legitimacy of a moral or social claim, including that of modern science, is derived from the conventions of "local traditions." Thus, there are no universal criteria. The intellectual scribe is an "interpreter." Rather than being oriented toward "selecting the best social order, this strategy is aimed at facilitating communication between autonomous (sovereign) participants."[15] There is no objective moral order and no progressive agenda for creating one. Discourse, partial understanding, knowledge effects, and problematic are among the conceptual terms of postmodernism.

All seven of our chapters on the adulation of and attack on riches in Western culture examine legislative texts, that is, scriptures of wealth. Each of us examines a range of writings and narratives that set forth definite theses about the genesis and prospects, uses and abuses of wealth. But as writers about these legislative texts, we are distributed along the legislator-interpreter continuum, even though none of us strays too far from the center. By training and commitment, all of us know both roles, the boundaries between them, and the ultimate impossibility of separating the two.

To the extent that we are interpreters, we emphasize the deconstructive rather than constructive tasks of analysis. The deconstructive task is to excavate the symbols and practices of a text in an effort to reveal its normative discipline. To the extent that we are legislators, we seek to make a case for or against the historical understanding of wealth portrayed in the texts we choose to study. As Pierre Bourdieu puts it, we not only seek "to be understood but also to be believed, obeyed, respected, and distinguished."[16] As interpreters and legislators, however, we do not speak with one voice. While five of the chapters attend to the self-serving legitimations of wealth, two (those of Quinn and Schervish) spotlight the potentially positive morality of wealth. In each case, we eschew stale conventional thinking, offering instead an array of fresh perspectives.

David Gill's essay reviews three tableaux of the talk for wealth and against poverty in ancient Greece. Gill begins by citing M. I. Finley's view that the judgment of antiquity was that "wealth was necessary and it was good; it was an absolute requisite for the good life, and on the whole that was all there was to it." As for poverty, says Gill, a classics professor, the Greek view was that it was bad and that "on the whole, it was not possible to be both poor and a good person." The importance of this strand in Western thinking is that it is not influenced by Hebrew or Christian ideas and thus provides a contrast to the six other strands examined here. Indeed, says Gill, the remarkable fact is that "there were apparently no guilt feelings about wealth and not even much sign of pity or sympathy for the very poor, and practically no claim that they were in any way special in the eyes of the gods, or that one's treatment of them had anything to do with one's good standing with the deity or one's value as a human being." Wealth afforded the independence and leisure for true freedom. Given the zero-sum resources of the pre-industrial Greco-Roman world, there were no systematic philosophical or moral bases for challenging the uneven distribution of wealth. Still, there were political pressures on this closed dispensation, resulting in what Ste. Croix (1981) argues was a "sophisticated form of ideological class struggle" in which the superordinate classes sought to convince the oppressed to accept, and even "rejoice" in their exploitation. Along with Ste. Croix, Gill is personally critical of the "aggressive and unabashed" way "in which the wealthy, privileged minority justified its position over against the poor." In a word, the classical Greek period from 750 to 350 B.C. is replete with what Gill calls an antipopular rhetoric or aristocratic propaganda. To make his point, he examines one representative text from each of three periods: Homer's story of Thersites in the *Illiad* (750 B.C.), the poems of Theognis of Megara (550 B.C.), and Plato's *Republic* (350 B.C.). Throughout, Gill does his best to cull the faint voices of opposition contained in and around these texts. But ultimately, there is only a "rough theory" of the dangers of wealth. Greed, excessive wealth, ill-gotten wealth, or unjustly used wealth is reprehensible; but the uneven distribution of wealth and a closed mobility structure are never seriously indicted. The cultural scripture of the Greek rhetoric of wealth honored the privileges of birth, the distribution of virtue along class lines, the rule of the few, a hierarchical notion of justice, the ideological co-optation of the masses, and the dismissal of common labor.

If Gill sets out the historical setting at the dawn of the Christian era, Pheme Perkins, a New Testament scholar, explores the radical departure that marked the teachings of Jesus and the early Christian community concerning the meaning and responsibilities of wealth. What Perkins argues, however, is that the departure, while novel and bold, was not as religiously simple as many who turn to the Christian scriptures for a prophetic critique seem to believe. Without retreating a step to the "historical critical readings of the academy," Perkins explores the economic message of the New Testament precisely because this scripture remains an efficacious resource in the spiritual and political contests over why "all is not well with the acquisition, distribution, and cultural uses of wealth." Along with Gill, she acknowledges the minimal moral concern in Greco-Roman thought about the structural roots of wealth and poverty, attributing this in part to the static "limited goods" economy of the ancient world. Perkins also focuses on three sets of texts to forge her analysis: the sayings and parables of Jesus, the Pauline letters, and Luke's gospel and Acts of the Apostles. The religious problem of wealth is not its existence or how it is obtained, rather it is the egoism and excessive greed that deprives others of their subsistence, declines to assist those in need, and refuses the call for unreciprocated generosity toward the debtor and afflicted. Of the three models of justice—liberty, equality, and community—the Christian texts, concludes Perkins, "are fundamentally committed to community." There is a radical reproach of wealth but it is a relational rather than a structural one. The New Testament is not directly concerned with inequitable economic conditions and does not offer an historical-political agenda in which the existence of the poor becomes a moral problem. It is, however, preeminently concerned about the norm of "solidarity," that Christians "model their relationships to others on divine generosity."

The chapter that examines the lengthiest historical span and comes closest to a genealogical analysis of a single text is by Dayton Haskin. Haskin, a literary critic, documents twenty centuries of rereading—"remaking," in his terms—the parable of the talents. This parable is the gospel story of the man who, upon embarking on a journey, entrusts his goods in uneven numbers of "talents" to three servants. Upon his return, the protagonist rewards the first two servants for wisely investing the talents and punishes the third for failing to do so. Like Gill and Perkins, Haskin forthrightly expresses his reason for studying this text. It is not simply that the parable has "been and continues to be used in framing ethical questions." Its modern use he takes to be particularly questionable. Over the past four centuries, Haskin contends, the passage has been made "the great bourgeois parable" of capitalism, as it was meant to praise financial investment and capital accumulation and to criticize economic lethargy. This bourgeois reading derives in part from a conflation of the Greek meaning of talent as a very large (even burdensome) weight or sum of money and the notion of "mental endowment" or "natural ability." If the root sense is emphasized, the injunctions of the parable fall more heavily upon the wealthy or those in positions of responsibility, as in the patristic insistence on the duties of prelates to spread the Word. Even when applied to the common believer, the notion of talent as responsibility generates, via allegorical interpretations, a variety of religious obligations and lessons, including social responsibility. With the development of the modern sense, increasingly comes the tendency to render the parable "compatible with intense individualism and with the institution of private property." Sixteenth-century readings still focused on the duties of bringing salvation to others, and Calvin's emphasis was primarily on the duties of community building. Yet Calvin's reading ultimately opened the door to a this-worldly interpretation in which nothing the parable has to say "would interfere with ordinary business in the city." Once the parable could mean that one's natural abilities should be used to maximize one's personal potential, it could be joined to the economic model of the "invisible hand," consummating its bourgeois reading. When in the twentieth century, finally, the economic sense of "talent" is rediscovered, the parable has a renewed potential to become a full-bodied legitimation of wealth and capitalism. It enables the rich to espouse an obligation of stewardship while spurring others to dutiful work habits. For all this, the parable evinces a "dynamic concept of making 'meaning' "; and just as its residual prophetic power can be lost, it can also be regained.

Carol Morris Petillo continues the analysis by joining Gill, Perkins, and Haskin in choosing a subject that allows her to bring to the fore her own misgivings about wealth and privilege. She chooses as her texts the writings of three early-twentieth-century American women reformers. Her personal introduction makes it clear that she joins them and that her piece is, in effect, a fourth voice leveled against the notion that capitalism "not only effectively increased wealth, but also was the best available way to improve the lives of those working within it." As an American historian, Petillo suspected—before encountering Kevin Phillips's similar argument[17]—that the last three decades of the nineteenth century might in tenor and politics be instructive for understanding "concerns about wealth, poverty, reform, and philanthropy" at the end of the twentieth century. Drawing on her larger investigation of the lives and writings of eleven turn-of-the-century figures, Petillo focuses here on Jane Addams, Charlotte Perkins Gilman, and Elizabeth Gurley Flynn to "illustrate a different reaction to wealth and private philanthropy than is current here and now." Addams never viewed herself as a radical; nevertheless, she cuts a much more critical swath through the early twentieth century than the portrayal of her as the "angel of Hull House" suggests. An ardent and effective advocate of Progressivism, she combined her personal works of charity with an agenda for international reform, focusing (in part because of her inheritance) on the deformities of capitalism and the wiles of the wealthy in obstructing such reform and perpetuating what she called "the inequalities of the human lot." Gilman, in contrast to Addams, lived in poverty as a child, and into adult life she suffered emotionally. Combining a feminist vision with the notion that wealth is the product of the masses, Gilman took to writing and preaching about the harsh realities of capitalism, the promise of socialism, the need for economic independence for women, the rights of suffrage, and the urgency of pacifism. Civilization requires that people learn to serve each other and overcome the way capitalism "puts the immense force of sex-competition into the field of social economics." Flynn, born thirty years after Addams and Gilman, assumed the socialist outlook of her radical Irish immigrant parents. At seventeen, she was on the socialist lecture circuit, advocating economic democracy and the right to organize. "Everything she ever spoke or wrote responded to the questions about wealth and privilege," says Petillo. Permanently marked by her childhood impressions of poverty in New England textile towns, she became for Manchester, New Hampshire, what Frederick Engels was for Manchester, England: the chronicler of the "terror and violence against workers." She was proud to be, like Marx, "a mortal enemy of capitalism." "Capitalism and the philanthropy it spawned," concludes Petillo, did not, according to her three sources, "relieve the suffering of the majority upon whose efforts it was built." And adding her own voice, Petillo contends that circumstances "have not changed much since they spoke."

From the perspective of an economist, Joseph Quinn explains what makes capitalism a historically novel engine of wealth and so politically and morally compelling despite its numerous flaws. Without in the least defending the human and environmental toll of capitalism, he takes up the task of making the case for capitalism. He explains the philosophical and economic rationale for why "a capitalist economic structure does an excellent job of creating material wealth," a less good job at allocating it, and why modern capitalistic societies are willing to intervene in favor of more equitable allocation even at the cost of reduced output. Most important, however, is Quinn's exposition of the new historical and analytical headings that come about with the advent of capitalism. Prior to capitalism, the issues of economic morality focused, as we have seen, on the issues of distribution. With the rise of capitalism, the terrain of contest shifts from distribution to production, as in Haskin's account of what happened to the parable of the talents around the seventeenth century and in Petillo's three reports on anticapitalist sentiment. Quinn notes that philosophers of capitalism "were trying to do for social interactions what Isaac Newton had done a century earlier for the physical world—to explain a complex social order with some general 'laws of motion' based on simple underlying principles." Although there is much to criticize in capitalism, there are important political, ethical, and economic advantages to a market economy, which revolve around "the basic notion that individual preferences are the starting point of social analysis." There is also a case against an unregulated market economy. The regulative controls of competition often break down, societies pursue extra-economic goals, and "the attractiveness of an economy depends not only on the size of the pie, but also on its distribution." In regard to this last point, Quinn cites the persistence of dire poverty in the midst of plenty as the major challenge to capitalism. Still, on balance, he concludes that capitalism offers more potential benefit to humankind than any current alternative and "that changes within the system could alleviate" much of capitalism's distress.

What Quinn discusses in analytic terms, I address as a matter of culture and identity. I ask the question, to paraphrase Shama, "Just who, exactly, do the wealthy think they are?" As a sociologist, I respond that they are disciples of the American cultural scripture of wealth within which they frame their life stories as moral biographies. My chapter includes interviews with 130 millionaires in which they enunciate their autobiographies as accounts in which their financial and spiritual paths are intermeshed. By moral biography, I mean "the normative consciousness with which the wealthy define a virtuous identity in relation to money." Such a normative self-understanding grows out of and supports "a general cluster of shared sentiments about the use of wealth and the moral identity," that is, a cultural scripture of wealth. I examine two aspects of the moral biographies of millionaires with a view toward learning about the general meaning of wealth. The first is what I call the dialectic of fortune and virtue: the way the wealthy organize their discourse to "tell how they apply themselves to make more of their lives and of their circumstances by improving on what was given them by fate." The second aspect of their biographical account is "the way the wealthy fashion their stories into morality plays, equating stages of economic progress with stages of personal development." As dramatic narratives, these stories follow various literary conventions and embody motifs of initiation, healing, purgation, and learning. In depicting how the wealthy make sense of their lives, three issues of interpretation are important. To say that the biographies of the wealthy are moral does not mean they engage in "correct living," but that they experience and report their lives as subject to duty. Second, it is not only impossible but unnecessary to discern the "truth" of a personal narrative; what matters is to locate the "grammar" of morality by which the wealthy organize everything they say. Finally, in regard to the question of sampling, it is true that I generally interviewed people who have something "good" to say about themselves. But again, even when the wealthy have something "bad" to reveal, they confess it as something they are working to correct or have already changed. I conclude that "the major lesson to be learned about the cultural scripture of wealth from the biographies of the wealthy is that it is a moral scripture." Despite what we or others might say from the outside, the earned and inherited wealthy consistently view their lives as careers of moral agency. What needs be added is that for good or ill the singular "class trait" of the wealthy is that they are not just agents but hyper-agents. They are capable of actually creating the institutional and organizational world in which they live rather than simply finding the best place within it. Such hyper-agency, it must be emphasized, is experienced by the wealthy as a matter of duty as much as a matter of empowerment. If a critique of the wealthy is to be made, it must be aimed at their catalogue of responsibilities rather than their moral lassitude.

The final chapter, written by ethicist Lisa Sowle Cahill, addresses the relationship between scripture, morality, and social justice as it relates to the economic question of wealth and poverty in the contemporary world. This is, she says, the "problem of interpreting Scripture for ethics." Cahill argues that while "few biblical scholars or ethicists today view the Bible as a simple source of concrete directives for moral decision making," Scripture remains a privileged source of values for shaping ethical behavior. Instead of offering deductive rules, Scripture is "foundational." It offers a "defining source" of identity and community. It provides the basis for "critical consciousness" and a "community of moral discourse" when brought into dialogue with the concrete content of history. Yet some challenge this position for giving too much priority to faith while neglecting other defining forces such as philosophy, science, and culture. Cahill reviews this and other hermeneutical debates concerning the determination of "a normative function for the Bible today." Ultimately, Cahill identifies one contemporary approach as most promising. Exegetical research should consider New Testament communities to be historical "prototypes" for contemporary ethical action by examining the faith-inspired social strategies they pursued. "Moral norms," Cahill concludes, "are justified not as transcriptions of biblical rules, or even as references to key narrative themes, but as coherent social embodiments of a community formed by Scripture." In the end, the New Testament reflects a "community of discipleship," ethics emerges at the level of community formation, such community induces a solidarity that challenges unjust socioeconomic relations, and ethical claims receive verification through the praxis of overlapping communities. Cahill demonstrates these principles by analyzing the ethics that inform the Roman Catholic health care ministry, especially as it attempts to distribute the "wealth" of health care in light of scriptural and magisterial principles stipulating "the fundamental option for the poor." She concludes that a just society encourages "solidarity" with the marginalized and institutionalizes access to social and material capital for all its members, even when doing so is incompatible with the self-interest of the advantaged.

Today, as the discussion of wealth creation and distribution becomes framed less frequently under the rubrics of capitalism and socialism, it may be propitious to examine some of the numerous other pieces of the debate that come to us from our Western classical, biblical, literary, and ethical traditions. It turns out that the talk for and against wealth (and the wealthy) so well articulated by Smith and Marx is only one axis on which this important motif of Western culture turns. There are innumerable other texts to read and interpret. The chapters that follow read and interpret some of these other texts. They depict who various commentators think the wealthy are. They also disclose just who we think the wealthy are.

NOTES

1. See Michael Novak, "Wealth and Virtue: The Development of Christian Economic Thinking," in *The Capitalist Spirit: Toward a Religious Ethic of Wealth Creation*, ed. Peter L. Berger (San Francisco: Institute for Contemporary Studies, 1990).

2. Karl Marx, *Theories of Surplus Value*, vol. 31 of *Karl Marx and Frederick Engels, Collected Works* (London: Lawrence and Wishart, 1989), 197.

3. I am grateful to David Gill, the author of Chapter 2, for this phrase.

4. See Henry F. Myers, "His Statues Topple, His Shadow Persists: Marx Can't Be Ignored," *Wall Street Journal*, November 25, 1991, 1. The article foresees the continued relevance of Marx not for his predictions about a socialist future but for his analysis of the capitalist present.

5. Simon Shama, *The Embarrassment of Riches: An Interpretation of Dutch Culture in the Golden Age* (Berkeley: University of California Press, 1988), 51.

6. Ibid., 81.

7. Ibid., 97.

8. Harold Beaver, "Healthy, Wealthy and Worried Too," *New York Times Book Review*, July 5, 1987, 1.

9. It seems to me that Weber argued that wealth acted as a reassuring symptom and a "moral agitator." After all, it was Weber's central insight that the "spirit of capitalism" induced a "worldly asceticism."

10. Shama, 124.

11. Ibid., 124–25.

12. Thomas Carlyle, 1832, as quoted in Paul Davis, *The Lives and Times of Ebenezer Scrooge* (New Haven: Yale University Press, 1990), 51.

13. Zygmunt Bauman, *Legislators and Interpreters: On Modernity, Post-Modernity and Intellectuals* (Ithaca, N.Y.: Cornell University Press, 1987).

14. Ibid., 3.

15. Ibid., 5.

16. Pierre Bourdieu, "The Production of Belief: A Contribution to an Economy of Symbolic Goods," in *Media, Culture and Society: A Critical Reader*, ed. Richard Collins et.al, (Beverly Hills, Calif.: Sage Publications, 1988), 147.

17. Kevin Phillips, *The Politics of Rich and Poor: Wealth and the American Electorate in the Reagan Aftermath* (New York: Random House, 1990).

2

Antipopular Rhetoric in Ancient Greece

DAVID H. GILL, S.J.

The ancient Greek attitude toward wealth was quite simple.[1] As Moses Finley puts it, "Wealth was necessary and it was good; it was an absolute requisite for the good life, and on the whole that was all there was to it."[2] The opposite was also true, at least in the opinion of those who produced our literary evidence: poverty was bad, and on the whole it was not possible to be both poor and a good person. From time to time, as Finley notes, there were dissenting voices, mostly from philosophers asking about the private ethical aspects of wealth, whether and to what extent it was necessary for, or even compatible with, the virtuous life. "Fundamentally, however, 'Blessed are the poor' was not within the Graeco-Roman world of ideas, and its appearances in the Gospels ... points to another world and another set of values. That other world eventually achieved a paradoxical ideology, in which a fiercely acquisitive temper was accompanied by strains of asceticism and holy poverty, by feelings of unease and even guilt."[3]

In the context of the present volume, much of the interest in studying Greek attitudes toward wealth and poverty will, I hope, derive precisely from the fact that they are *not* influenced by Hebrew and Christian notions. Thus, the latter should appear in sharper focus when contrasted with the "foreignness" of a culture and a literature in which there were apparently no guilt feelings about wealth and not even much sign of pity or sympathy for the very poor, and practically no claim that they were in any way special in the eyes of the gods, or that one's treatment of them had anything to do with one's good standing with the deity or one's value as a human being.[4]

The point of view—one might want to call it a rationalization—behind Greco-Roman attitudes towards wealth and poverty, as formulated explicitly by the philosophers, was that without the independence and leisure that wealth afforded, a person could not be truly free. To depend on another economically was to be unfree, to be in some sense a slave, and hence to some degree less than fully human. The rich and truly free people, in fact, were the ones who did not have to work even for themselves. They could live from the labor of others, and preferably from agriculture (and not manufacturing or trade, especially not retail trade). These attitudes were the prevalent ones throughout antiquity.[5] They were rooted, no doubt, in the basic economic and social facts of a preindustrial, zero-sum society, in which the limited wealth and the accompanying privilege and political power were unevenly distributed, carefully guarded, and fiercely contested.[6]

This chapter is about some of the ways in which the wealthy, privileged minority justified its position over against the poor, less privileged majority in the period roughly from 750 to 350 B.C. in Greece. Superior force was one way, of course, but that was not always available; even in the earliest sources it was not felt to be an adequate justification all by itself. There was also persuasion, what Ste. Croix calls "a more sophisticated form of ideological class struggle . . . the attempt of the dominant classes to persuade those they exploited to accept their oppressed condition without protest, if possible even to rejoice in it."[7] What is most striking about the Greek defense of privilege is how aggressive and unabashed it was. It was really an offensive strategy. For the most part, the attack took the form of a flat denial that the masses had, or ever could acquire, the qualities that justified the privilege and power of the elite. But the denial is done with such gusto and such animus that it amounts to a regular put-down of the nonelite class, an antipopular rhetoric or aristocratic propaganda with its own terminology, images, and caricatures. Not only do the "better" people (as they called themselves) assert their own superiority; they ridicule and demean their "inferiors." This latter is what most jars the sensibilities of readers accustomed to the Judeo-Christian tradition. At the same time, it is quite typically Greek (and Roman).

To illustrate what I have called an antipopular rhetoric or aristocratic propaganda I have chosen to highlight one representative text from each of three periods: the episode of Thersites from *Iliad 2* (eighth century B.C.), the poems of Theognis of Megara (mostly mid-sixth century B.C.), and the main lines of the argument and some of the key images of Plato's *Republic* (mid-fourth century B.C.). Each of the texts comes from a quite distinct era of Greek history, and so in each case it will be necessary to take account of changing social and economic conditions, as well as of other parallel voices. In addition, there are in each period voices, mostly faint and at times distorted that speak in opposition to the prevailing aristocratic ideology.[8]

HOMER, HESIOD, AND THE INHERITED TRADITION

The Homeric epics are our principal literary evidence for the whole period from the beginning of Greek history in the Bronze Age (early second millennium B.C.) until the time when the poems became fixed in their present written form, probably in the middle of the eighth century B.C. In the other direction, looking forward, Homer was the single most important influence in the shaping of Greek ideas on just about everything until the end of antiquity. Though they became the common heritage of all Greeks, the *Iliad* and *Odyssey* were in origin aristocratic poems for an aristocratic society. The poet, like his character Demodocus in the *Odyssey*, may have been himself a servant of princes; he served, in part at least, by taking their point of view of how things were "back then."

The socioeconomic world of the poems is simple, agricultural, and hierarchically ordered. There are, broadly speaking, two classes of people, divided from one another by an unbridgeable chasm. On one side are the heroic nobles: rich, brave, and handsome warrior princes; on the other side are their subjects: a mixed array of foot soldiers, peasants, slaves, and retainers. Although the stories concern themselves primarily with the exploits and ideals of the heroic nobles, there are occasional glimpses of the situation and perspective of the lower class, the great majority of people who were neither rich nor—according to the "heroic" rhetoric—brave or even good-looking.[9]

There are two sides to the story as it is told by Homer and Hesiod. On the one hand, there is the claim that the nobles merit their wealth and privilege through divinely sanctioned hereditary right, through courage in battle—and because of the inferiority of the common people. On the other hand, there are also in Homer hints of the notion—more fully developed in Hesiod—that there are limits to the prince's power over his people. If he does not act justly, Zeus will punish the whole community. Might and right are never simply coextensive, much as individual princes might like to have it that way. Still, what justice there is flows downward from the top, from the princes down to the people. In other words, it has almost nothing in common with what we would call a "right."

Thersites: The Story

This is perhaps the earliest detailed account we have from anywhere in the world of an aristocratic/monarchical ideology and of what happens to a commoner or a rabble-rousing lesser noble (there is some dispute as to just which Thersites is supposed to represent) when he challenges the authority of his betters.[10] Several of the motifs in the story were destined for a long life, as we shall see.

As Book 2 of the *Iliad* opens, Zeus sends Agamemnon a false dream, in the shape of Nestor, promising that now at last he will take Troy (1–34). When he awakens, the king calls a council of his fellow princes and relates the dream. He then proposes to test the spirit and readiness of the army by suggesting that they give up the expedition and return home. The other "scepter-bearing kings" agree with the "shepherd of the people" and gather the host (35–100). Agamemnon rises to address them, scepter in hand (101–9). He pretends to regret the whole expedition and suggests giving it up as a lost cause (110–41). The men take him at his word and bolt for the ships (141–54); they might have gotten away, says Homer, had not Hera intervened and sent Athena to Odysseus to tell him to bring them back (155–81). Both gods and nobles want the war to continue, it seems. Odysseus goes to Agamemnon and gets his scepter, then he heads for the ships (182–87). When he meets some "king or man of status" he tries to persuade him with soft words, urging him to help restrain the troops and warning him of what Agamemnon might do to the Achaeans (188–97). With the common people (*dêmos*), Odysseus' approach is intimidation rather than persuasion. He strikes them with the scepter and lectures them (190–97):

Sir, sit still and listen to what others tell you. They are your betters; you are weak and no warrior. You are worthless both in fighting and in counsel. There is no way that all of us Achaeans can be king here. The rule of many is not a good thing. Let there be one ruler, one king, to whom the son of crooked-counseling Kronos gave the scepter and divine decrees, to decide for his people.

The troops return and quietly resume their places in the assembly, presumably to await further orders from their commanders (207–11).

Enter Thersites, to berate Agamemnon and in effect call for a strike by the army (212–42). Homer says that "he alone railed and was without measure in his speech." He could talk, but not with any order or decency, only things that he thought would get a laugh from the troops. He was the ugliest man to come to Troy: bow-legged, lame in one foot, with shoulders that curved together over his chest and a pointed head with just a tuft of hair (212–19). His greatest enemies were Achilles and Odysseus, whom he was always abusing. Now he attacks Agamemnon, and this angers all the Achaeans (220–23). He assails the king for taking a disproportionate and undeserved share of the war booty and for leading his subjects into danger (225–34). He then insults the rest of the Achaeans and calls on them to return home and show Agamemnon that he can do nothing without them. He closes with one final insult, blaming the quarrel with Achilles on Agamemnon (235–42).

Thersites makes some good points. Should not everyone share fairly in the spoils of war? Does not the commander have obligations to his troops? Was not Agamemnon clearly at fault in the incident with Achilles? All matters worthy of discussion—but not now, and clearly not with Thersites. Odysseus, echoing Homer's description, answers him with scorn and menace: You are a smooth talker, but you show no judgment and you are alone in making trouble for the princes. Furthermore, you are the worst man of all the Greeks at Troy and so you should keep your mouth shut. Any more of this foolishness and my name isn't Odysseus if I don't pull off your clothes and whip your arse all the way back to the ships (246–64). Next he beats Thersites on the back and shoulders with the royal scepter. The latter doubles up with pain and starts to weep as a bloody welt rises on his back. Then he goes back to his place helplessly, wiping away his tears (265–69), while the rest of the troops laugh at him and express their approval of Odysseus (270–77).

Thersites: Rhetoric and Ideology

The scene is masterfully designed to make its points. Like much of the material in the early books of the *Iliad*,[11] its purpose is not so much to carry the story forward as to fill in the general background of "how it was back then." By a series of flashbacks and typical scenes Homer provides an impression not only of the whole war but also of the society, culture, and values of those who fought it, of the "heroic world" as the aristocratic oral poetic tradition had chosen to remember it through the centuries of the Dark Ages that followed its collapse. There are two main aspects of the story: one a positive ideology to support the preeminent power and privilege of the nobles, the other a virulent antipopular rhetoric. These are expressed, typically of the epic, in both the actions and speeches of the characters, in the poet's own commentary on these, and in the frequent repetition of certain key symbols and concepts. Even the terminology betrays the ideology. The nobles are *agathoi*, the chief value term. The word has both moral and class overtones and it combines the senses of "good," "brave," "rich," and "handsome." Everyone else is *kakos*, "bad," "cowardly," "poor," and "ugly." The story, in the telling, makes Thersites into a type of the *kakos*.

The central symbol is the scepter. It is mentioned eight times in various contexts in the episode, and its meaning is clear. It originally comes from Zeus and has been passed on through Agamemnon's forefathers to the present monarch (101–9). Hence his position is based simply on his birth into the line of Pelops, and this arrangement is approved by Zeus. The implication of the present passage seems to be that this hereditary, divinely sanctioned authority entitles him to do pretty much as he pleases with the troops. The king leans on it when he addresses the army (109). Odysseus takes the "inherited immortal scepter" (186) when he goes to bring back the rebellious troops; he strikes them with it (198–99) as he reminds them that it comes from Zeus. Lastly, he uses the "golden scepter" to beat

Thersites into submission (265–69), and then holds it himself as he addresses the army (278–83).

Zeus' unwavering support for the king is also stressed. Odysseus appeals to it when he warns the other princes of Agamemnon's anger: "May he not in his wrath do any harm to the sons of the Achaeans. And great is the anger of Zeus-nurtured kings. And his prerogative [*timê*] is from Zeus. And wise Zeus is his friend and ally" (195–97).

The logic of the passage is a bit awkward because of the paratactic structure. In addition, kings are plural in one line (196) and singular in the next (197), indicating that Homer may have combined two traditional lines which did not originally go together. By further using these apparently traditional lines to comment on Agamemnon's anger, the poet achieves a very strong statement of royal prerogative: even if the king irrationally mistreats the army, Zeus will still support him (be his *philos*, be on his side). In other words, anything goes.

In the passage cited above (203–6) Odysseus tells the soldiers that along with the scepter Zeus gave the king "the divine decrees [*themistas*] to decide for them." This is the traditional claim that the king was custodian and interpreter for the people of the will of Zeus as it was passed down in the form of traditional and unwritten laws. In the same passage he also argues in effect that the rule of one man is more conducive to the common good: "The rule of many is not a good thing. Let there be one ruler, one king" (204–5).

The lesser nobles in the story, those who seem to rank between the top commanders and the troops, practice a kind of gentlemanly cooperation among themselves, and they stick together against the troops.

The role of the common soldier in this scheme is simply to do what he is told. He is needed for the fighting, to be sure, but he has no right to an opinion about how and when. His betters, we are told, are vastly superior to him in strength and courage as well as in giving counsel (200–3). The hero's ideal for himself was to excel as a "doer of deeds and a speaker of words." One way to put a commoner in his place was to tell him, as Odysseus does (202), that he is "worthless in fighting and counsel." This is, of course, at most only half true. The troops were useful and necessary in fighting, as the whole logic of the episode and most of the rest of the *Iliad* assume. Their worth in counsel was never tested, since they were not asked to give it, except in the form of a general yea or nay by acclamation. Again, the assumption of the story is that if they simply walk off the job en masse they can cause real problems.

Ridicule was another method, along with verbal and physical bullying, for handling popular discontent and resistance. Both Homer and Odysseus use it on Thersites. The poet gives him a significant name, "Rashman,"[12] and claims that he is a buffoon with nothing serious to say. He is also physically ugly, even grotesque: lame, hunchbacked, with a pointed head and nearly bald, the exact opposite of the handsome nobles. His two greatest enemies—surely not by accident—are the two paragons of the heroic ideal: Achilles, the mightiest doer of deeds (even though Thersites takes his side against Agamemnon), and Odysseus, the wiliest speaker of words. Thersites, therefore, is as far removed as possible from the ideal heroic type, the lowest of the low (212–19). This is exactly what Odysseus makes explicit when he calls him the most *kakos* (unheroic in general, including physically ugly) man at Troy (247–48), and then humiliates him with blows and insults and sends him back to the ranks in tears. Thersites is made to act out his cowardice for the rest of the troops.

There is one final, only slightly more subtle, bit of propaganda in the passage. It is the repeated and convenient claim that Thersites was an isolated individual and that the rest of the troops disapproved of him as much as their commanders did. When Thersites is first introduced (211–12), Homer says that the others were quiet, but "he alone still railed." As he starts to attack Agamemnon, the poet says that "the Achaeans were terribly angry and resentful at him" (222–23). Odysseus points out that he is alone in arguing with the kings (247). When Thersites was humiliated, the rest of the army "laughed sweetly at him" (270). This is Homer's bitterly ironic next-to-last twist for the man whom he had introduced as speaking only nonsense and "such things as he thought would raise a laugh among the Argives" (215–16). "To be laughed at by my enemies" was the ultimate dishonor for the heroes. Thersites must suffer it without being able to retaliate.

The last and perhaps most outrageously exaggerated stroke in an already overplayed scene is what Homer has the troops say about Odysseus' treatment of Thersites: "Bravo! Odysseus has done countless noble deeds in his life, both in proposing good counsels and in leading us in war. But this is by far his noblest deed . . . getting this loud-mouth out of the assembly" (272–75). The most heroic deed of one of the greatest heroes was to put the miserable agitator in his place! This clearly aims to underline the fact that the rank and file are in full accord with the nobles' view of things. They accept and rejoice in the aristocratic arrangement and its justification as altogether fitting and proper. That was how it was in the "good old days," at any rate.

To conclude, therefore, the nobles in the Thersites episode justify their position over against the commoners by appeals to birth, divine approval, the common good, and even descent from the gods, as well as by virtue of their own self-proclaimed superiority in war and counsel. They need the help of the masses to fight their wars, but they also have to keep them in line. This they do by a combination of sticking together among themselves, physical bullying, and outright ridicule. In addition, they co-opt the majority by getting them to believe that they are inferior in what really counts, namely war and counsel.

Two Variations on the Theme

The first variation occurs in Sarpedon's speech at *Iliad* 12.310–28. It is often cited as the classic statement of noblesse oblige—as well as of the so-called "heroic paradox"[13]—but for present purposes it is interesting mainly as evidence for what nobility does not "oblige."

As "godlike" Sarpedon, whom Homer calls Zeus' own son, and his fellow Lykian prince, Glaukos, are about to storm the Greek camp, the former pauses to reflect on the meaning of it all:

Glaukos, why is it that we are honored most of all in Lykia, with the front seats, the best wines, and the choicest cuts of meat? Why do they all look upon us as gods and assign us the best land by the banks of the Xanthos for our vines and wheat fields? [They do] and so now we must take our stand in the first ranks of the Lykians and share in the fierce fight. Then any one of our well-armed countrymen who sees us will say: "Not without renown are the kings who rule us in Lykia. They feed on fat flocks and drink choice sweet wine. But noble also is their strength, since they fight in the first ranks of the Lykians." But, my friend, what if we could escape this war and somehow be ageless and immortal? Then I would not fight in the first ranks myself, nor would I send you into glorious battle. But now as it is there are ten thousand fates of death standing near, and no mortal can flee or escape them. So let us go, to win glory or to yield it. (12.310–28)

The passage is rich and poignant, but looked at from a nonaristocratic point of view, what is most striking about it is the absence of any sense of what one might call social responsibility in connection with wealth and privilege. There is nothing, for example, along the lines of how the nobles' prowess works for the benefit of the people by protecting them or maintaining the peace or enriching them with booty or the like. Austin and Vidal-Naquet say that here "the king's excellence is martial and his 'economic' privileges are justified by his bravery in battle." And that is all there is to it.[14] Donlan sees in the passage "more than an implication . . . that should they fail in their duties [the nobles] would no longer merit the honors they received."[15] It is at most an implication. There is no explicit statement that the people can hold the nobles accountable if they fail in courage. It is as if the poet, because of his aristocratic perspective, simply did not consider the possibility. What the people do derive from their leaders' courage, he says, is the opportunity to admire them the more and to bask happily in the rightness of the established social and economic arrangement—and perhaps to hear their leaders' exploits celebrated in song. Sarpedon himself indicates how much he cares for public opinion when he says that, if it were not for his need of glory, he would not even have to fight.

The second variation is that just as the nobles both needed and despised the commoners in time of war, they partly admired and partly denigrated their work as artisans in peacetime—or rather they admired the work while belittling the worker.[16] In Homer, Hephaistos, the divine craftsman and patron of human craftsmen, is the heavenly reflection of this ambiguity about work and workers. His mythology is another piece of perhaps subconscious aristocratic propaganda, in this case projected—like other human social and political realities—into the court of Olympus.

On the one hand, Hephaistos performs marvelous feats of strength and skill: Agamemnon's scepter, Achilles' armor, the statues that guard the palace of King Alkinoos, and Pandora, the first woman. In the Homeric Hymn to Hephaistos he is regarded as a culture hero. His popularity among craftsmen, as an object of actual worship, is shown by the prominence of his cult in the more industrialized parts of Greece, in particular at Athens (the Hephaisteion), and by the frequency with which his positive exploits appear in vase paintings from the early sixth century B.C. onward.

The other side of Hephaistos betrays the prejudices of the aristocratic poetic tradition that created it. He is said in *Iliad* 18.397 to be lame (*chôlos*), like Thersites (same word); and he may have been bow-legged as well. In any case, he had an awkward limp which was a source of great amusement to the other gods in *Iliad* 1.595–600. He is cuckolded by Ares, whom he nonetheless outwits with his artistic skills, againt to the delight of the other Olympians in *Odyssey* 8.265–366. He is the son of Zeus and Hera (or Hera alone), and in one version his mother threw him out of heaven, "wishing to hide me because I was lame."[17]

Other Voices: The Demand for Justice in Homer and Hesiod

From the start, there were divinely sanctioned, though rather general, limits on the nobles' authority over their subjects. Briefly, here are three examples.[18]

(1) In *Iliad* 16.384–93, in a simile (hence probably late in the tradition), we are told that Zeus is angered when rulers "resort to violence and pass crooked decrees in the assembly and drive out fair judgment, failing to respect the will of the gods" (387–88). Zeus' reaction is a violent rainstorm which causes flooding and wipes out the fields of all the people. That is, if the king acts unjustly, the whole people will suffer. This doctrine does provide some sanction, but from the point of view of the people in general, it also implies a double unfairness. They suffer injustice at the hands of the king and then they get their fields wiped out to boot. The fact that Homer does not notice this aspect of the idea is just another instance of how top-down his view of the world was. The nobles are responsible for justice, but the people depend totally on them to provide it. And if they do not provide it, there is none and everyone will suffer together. The nobles *are* the community in some sense.

(2) The *Odyssey* seems to offer somewhat more. At the opening of Book 5 (7–12), Athena pleads with Zeus to help Odysseus to get home:

Zeus Father and you other blessed and immortal gods, let no scepter-bearing king ever again be kind or gentle or mild or virtuous. Rather let him be always harsh and cruel, since not one of the people that he ruled remembers godlike Odysseus, and how he was gentle as a father with them.

The argument is that the people—and Zeus—owe support to the king not merely because of his superior birth and strength in battle, but also because he treats them well in time of peace. Here there is at least the implication of more mutuality in the relationship between ruler and ruled. Good treatment should evoke loyalty, with the reverse implication that the king has to fulfill certain obligations if he expects the people—and Zeus—to help him against his enemies. He has to earn their loyalty by looking out for their welfare "like a father." The same argument, using the same traditional formula, is made by Mentor in 2.230–34.

In the rest of the *Odyssey* there is ample opportunity to experience the lives and views of servants, both good (Eumaios, Eurykleia) and bad (Melanthios, Iros, and the serving women), and of a wandering beggar (Odysseus in disguise). One recurring theme is the special obligation, apparently traditional and divinely enforced, to be kind to beggars and other needy strangers. (The suitors, of course, violate this rule grossly, as the plot and moral argument of the epic require.) There is also more on the theme of loyalty to the king. The good servants are very good and the bad ones are very bad indeed. The victorious Odysseus punishes the latter out of hand with lavish cruelty, including mutilation, and the story-teller clearly approves.

(3) Hesiod's *Works and Days* is roughly contemporary with Homer, and it is the first nonaristocratic voice we hear in Greece. Not that Hesiod was either poor or a revolutionary. He seems to have been a "reasonably well-to-do freehold farmer" who lived in a rural district, where a hereditary aristocracy held all the political power.[19] What he demands from the local princes is a fair trial (their traditional obligation) in the inheritance dispute with his brother, Perses, and the opportunity to better himself by means of hard work. His economic goal is the same as that of the princes, self-sufficiency and prosperity—but apparently with no demand for a share in political power. The means are new—discipline, frugality, hard work—as opposed to simply inheriting wealth. Hesiod is not against wealth and privilege, he simply wants fairness and a piece of the economic action.

He accuses the nobles of corruption, arbitrary behavior, and a disregard for justice. His reply to their attitude of "might makes right" is the utilitarian one that justice wins out over violence in the end (203–24). Where judgments are just, all the people enjoy a virtual Eden of peace and prosperity (225–37). Where there is violence and injustice, Zeus sends famine, plague, and devastation (238–47). This is the doctrine we have seen above in the *Iliad*, but Hesiod's perspective is different, and so he sees the problem of unfairness that seems to have eluded Homer, namely the fact that "often also a whole city suffers ill because of one bad man" (240). He repeats the complaint a few lines later when he tells how "the people [*dêmos*] pay for the outrages of their princes, who with evil intent pass crooked judgments" (260–62).

THEOGNIS AND THE ARCHAIC AGE

The eighth century B.C. was probably the high point of the political, social, and economic domination of the traditional aristocracy. But times were changing. The next two centuries saw a shift of resources and power in most Greek cities from the old hereditary elite to a new one that was based on money as well as property.[20] The old elite tried to adapt its self-image and rhetoric to the new realities. Donlan says: "The aristocratic class, its privilege lessened, had reacted by altering its frame of values in an attempt to prove its superiority and maintain its position of natural leadership. One way was to place greater emphasis on qualities that the lower class could not claim, such as noble birth, or to adopt a style of life that stressed external elegance and good breeding along with conspicuous display."[21] The rhetorical strategy, as in Homer, was to claim all the important virtues for your side and to attack the other side for having all the corresponding vices.

Theognis of Megara

The most famous spokesman for the losers in this shift in power arrangements—and for generations of dyspeptic aristocrats afterward, it seems—was Theognis, a disillusioned, class-conscious member of an old family, who apparently lost his property and was exiled from his native Megara. His short poems, written in the sixth century B.C. were preserved in aristocratic circles, added to (probably) in fifth century Athens, and quoted as moral proof texts by later writers. The resultant corpus of 1,389 verses survives in excellent condition. Its attitudes are varied and sometimes contradictory, but in general they reflect the values and interests of the "better people": good, old-fashioned morals; homoerotic love affairs; and very clear ideas about politics, money, and the superiority of their own social class.[22] In the line of pro-aristocratic, antipopular propaganda the Theognidean corpus holds a privileged position, since all by itself, as we shall see, it constitutes a nearly complete bridge between Homer and Plato. Most of the major themes are familiar from the epics; most will reappear in only slightly altered form in the *Republic*.[23]

Theognis's immediate target is not the lower classes (who are written off in a few lines) but the arriviste, new rich crowd who are displacing the older hereditary aristocrats at the top of society in Megara. To his mind, the gulf between old elite and new rich is as wide as that between nobles and commoners in Homer. And the moral/class terminology is the same: *agathoi* (or *esthloi*) for the former; *kakoi* (or *deiloi*) for the latter, though the content of the terms has changed somewhat with the changing times, as we shall see.

Any contact with the *kakoi* can lead to moral contamination. Hence the *agathoi* must avoid them and stick together against them. From the start, Theognis tells his young disciple, Kyrnos, not to "associate with the *kakoi*, but always stay with the *agathoi*. Eat and drink with them; sit with them and please them. They have great power. For from the *esthloi* you will learn *esthla* [good things]; but if you mix with the *kakoi*, you will lose even the mind you have."[24] The poems are sprinkled with admonitions to be careful in selecting friends and loyal in dealing with them. Treacherous friends are the greatest danger. Never trust anyone from the other side, even if you occasionally have to use him. Loyalty is a very important aristocratic virtue, especially in times of crisis.[25] This is a more elaborated version of what was acted out by the Homeric nobles in the Thersites episode.

Good birth is, of course, crucial. It defines the uncrossable boundary between the right and the wrong people: "Never by instruction will you make a bad man into a good one."[26] A "good" man who marries a "bad" woman for her money is equivalently guilty of miscegenation:

In the case of rams, donkeys, and horses we look for well-born ones and try to match them with good mates. But a good man does not hesitate to marry the bad daughter of a bad man if she gives him a lot of money. . . . Wealth dilutes the stock. So do not be surprised that the stock of the citizens is diminished, since good things are mixed with bad.[27]

In Homer, wealth and "virtue" (*aretê*) were closely linked. Now that the inferior people have become wealthy, the strategy is to claim that money is really not everything and to find fault with the new rich for thinking that it is. As Bernard Knox observes: "Theognis sees money as the destructive agent which has shattered the whole heroic mythic tradition, the sacred book of aristocratic ethics. This trenchant assessment is made in a poem which deliberately imitates the structure of Tyrtaeus' celebration of martial courage [the principal Homeric virtue] as the only form of excellence (*aretê*)."[28] In his imitation Theognis substitutes "wealth" for Tyrtaeus' "courage," thus ironically reminding his audience how different Sparta is from Megara, and how superior.

For the great mass of people there is only one standard of *aretê*: to be rich [not brave as in Tyrtaeus]. Nothing else is worth anything . . . [neither the wisdom of Rhadamanthys, nor the cunning of Sisyphus, nor the eloquence of Nestor, nor the speed of the winds]. . . . All must agree that wealth has the greatest power for everyone.[29]

On a somewhat inconsistent note, Theognis also complains a good deal about the demoralizing effect of poverty.[30] Greeks of all periods seem to have agreed on this point. Theognis makes the best of it, however, by insisting that the *agathoi*, because of their superior character, withstand its ill effects better than the *kakoi*.[31] On the other hand, wealth corrupts the *kakoi*, but not the *agathoi*.[32]

In general, like the commoners in Homer, the new rich lack all of the traditional virtues and practice all of the corresponding vices, though the content of virtue and vice has shifted somewhat: "*Agathoi* men have never ruined any city, Kyrnos. But whenever it pleases the *kakoi* to unleash their insolence [*hubrizein*], they corrupt the common people [*dêmos*] and hand down decisions that favor the unjust—and all this for the sake of power and private gain for themselves."[33] The *kakoi* disturb the peace and undermine the common good by stirring up the people, starting civil wars, and thus encouraging the rise of tyrants.[34] Unlike the *agathoi*, they know nothing of gratitude and reciprocal favors. They are insatiable and will quickly desert you.[35] They violate justice and have no regard for what people think of them. Their oaths are worthless.[36] "Shame has disappeared; shamelessness and insolence have prevailed over justice in all the land."[37] As the traditional language and the catalogue of vices indicate, Theognis is throwing (in Knox's phrase) "the sacred book of aristocratic ethics" at his enemies. He is also claiming for his side, and denying to the other, the traditional cooperative virtues. In Homer, when the aristocrats were on top and when martial virtues counted for something, these "softer" qualities were less prized. But now Theognis is eager to say that they are important and that they belong exclusively to his class.

Accordingly, he also lays upon his opponents the whole blame for the constant internal strife that plagues Megara. In an image that will reappear in the *Republic*, he compares the plight of the state to that of a ship that has lost its way because the crew has mutinied:

Now we have lost our white sails and are being carried from the Melian Sea through the dark night. They refuse to bail, even though the sea is coming in over the sides. They have removed the good and skillful helmsman. They are plundering the cargo. Order is lost. There is no more fairness. The crew is in command, and *kakoi* are in charge of *agathoi*. I fear that the ship will go down.[38]

Finally, Theognis has a fully stocked and fully traditional arsenal of venom and ridicule. These new rich *kakoi*, he says, "never knew anything about right and laws before. They used to wear old goatskins on their backs and graze outside the city like so many deer. And now *they* are the *agathoi*. . . . Who can bear to look at it?"[39] The reference to "right and law" is a verbal echo of Homer's description of the Cyclopses. If his enemies are as savage and uncivilized as Cyclopses—or even animals—Theognis can fantasize that he himself, in exile, is like the heroic Odysseus who wandered and endured until at last he returned home to avenge himself on the wicked suitors and be reunited with his dear son and faithful wife.[40] And in lines 541–42 he compares his antagonists to the Centaurs, "those devourers of raw flesh."

If the new rich are contemptible, the common people (*dêmos*) are beneath contempt, as this clear echo of the Thersites episode reveals: "Walk all over the empty-headed *dêmos*; lash them with a sharp goad; place a heavy yoke upon their necks. For you will not find anywhere on earth a *dêmos* that loves a master more than this one does."[41] And still further down the human scale is the slave who is physically deformed, with a bent head and crooked neck, and doomed to stay that way. "For no more does a rose or a hyacinth grow from a squill than a free child from a slave woman."[42] Poverty, like hard manual work, deforms both body and spirit.[43]

In conclusion, therefore, now that the traditional aristocrats at Megara are no longer in control militarily, financially, and politically, Theognis' strategy is to emphasize the central importance of good birth. This is one thing that the vulgar new rich do not have and can never get. The next step is to claim that birth is the indispensible presupposition for virtue. Thus, even without money and political power, the well-born ipso facto possess all of the other traditional virtues: loyalty, truthfulness, endurance, moderation, justice, intelligence, good sense, respect for the opinions of others, and physical beauty. The base-born, on the other hand, by definition lack all of these and can never acquire them. On the contrary, they are irremediably mired in all the corresponding vices.

Wealth can no longer be the principal measure of a person's worth, since the "best" people no longer have it all. In fact, wealth corrupts—but only when it gets into the wrong hands. Of course, poverty also corrupts and leads to vice. This was a persistent Greek notion, usually used against the poor. Still, the better people will be less debased by it than their inferiors.

Finally, with the rise of a more open and lively political discussion in the Greek city-states, the rules of the game now require that those who claim special privileges prove that they contribute more to the common good than the underprivileged can. Theognis' rather primitive version of this is to lay all of the blame for social tension and civil strife in Megara on the other party and simply to assert that this kind of thing would never have happened if he and his friends had remained in power.

Pindar: A More Cheerful Aristocratic Voice

Although he lived well into the fifth century, Pindar (518–438 B.C.) made his reputation by celebrating the glories of the old-fashioned hereditary aristocracy—and of more recent tyrants who liked to think of themselves in the old terms. This he did in the form of odes, usually commissioned by the victors, celebrating their triumphs in the various quadrennial pan-Hellenic games: Olympian, Pythian, Nemean, and Isthmian. Throughout Greek history these games, with their expensive chariot races and other contests, remained the international playground and showcase for wealthy aristocrats. Victory brought great glory to the home city and gave the victors the chance to claim that they were using their wealth in a socially productive way. Their fellow citizens seem to have agreed. At democratic Athens, for example, Olympic victors were awarded free dinners for life in the town hall.

Unlike Theognis, Pindar is almost wholly positive. In the celebratory odes his victors come out as gleaming Homeric-heroes-for-our-times. They are descended from the gods or divinized heroes, and their victories in the games are proof of inborn qualities of courage and skill as well as of the quieter virtues of justice, calm, and moderation.[44] They are the glory of their cities and their ancient families. With their power and wealth they will invariably do what is best for their fellow citizens, whose chief role seems to be to cheer on their splendid achievements—like the Lykians in *Iliad* 12.

There were places in Greece where aristocrats (or autocrats) still ruled the roost, and these were the places where Pindar found work and inspiration. The preservation of so much of his poetry is a sign of the elite nature of our sources, and it indicates that the point of view, like that of Theognis, found a sympathetic audience long after it had ceased to be a practical program in most cities.

Another Voice: Solon of Athens

The other great voice of Archaic Greece, that of Solon (about 640–about 560 B.C.), looks forward instead of back and forms a link to the Classical Period. He too came from an aristocratic family and shared its values, but "unlike Theognis, [Solon] realized that this same personal code of martial honour, elevated to the level of a political programme and blindly followed by the factions of the body politic, was a recipe for disaster."[45]

Briefly stated, in the early sixth century B.C. Athens was on the verge of civil war. The nobles were in control and the poor were in misery. Confiscations of land, debt slavery (offering one's own person as security), and the selling of debtors into actual slavery outside the country were threatening to tear Athenian society apart. Solon was appointed mediator—still a top-down approach, but an enlightened and fateful one by the ruling aristocrats. Solon steered a middle course between the extreme demands for no change at all and for the cancellation of debts and redistribution of land. His solution—cancellation of debts without redistribution, abolition of the institution of debt slavery, a new citizenship census based on wealth rather than birth, and the creation of constitutional limits on the power of the wealthy—pleased neither side wholly, but it made peace and ultimately helped pave the way for the full democracy at Athens in the following century.

Besides being the first politician in Greece to take the common people seriously as citizens and intervene effectively on their behalf, Solon was also the first to lecture the rich on the dangers of misusing their wealth. Riches are fine, he says in frag. 13 West, but they must be justly gotten and fairly used. Otherwise greed will lead to *hubris* (arrogant and abusive treatment of others) and ultimately to destruction. Zeus will eventually punish—if not the actual offender, then his innocent descendants. The root of Athens's problems is the greed of the rich.[46] The rulers should continue to rule (Solon was no revolutionary), but they should be fair about it, "for greed begets *hubris* when wealth gets into the hands of those who do not have the right attitude."[47] This complex of ideas comes ultimately from Hesiod. The formulation "greed leads to *hubris* leads to destruction" could be called the first rough theory of the dangers of wealth. It was taken over, with variations, in the next century by Aeschylus and Herodotus. In some cases, it is excessive wealth as such that is said to lead eventually to destruction. In others, it is only the wealth gotten or used unjustly.[48]

THE CLASSICAL PERIOD AND THE *REPUBLIC*

In this period (the fifth and fourth centuries B.C.), the central fact of Greek history, both in itself and for purposes of this discussion, was the Athenian democracy. There are several reasons for this. Not least important is the fact that the vast majority of our source material (perhaps 80 to 90 percent of the written evidence, for example) comes from Athens, which means that we get to see things almost exclusively through the eyes of Athenian citizens, though not all of them were by any means enthusiastic democrats. In addition, Athens was a powerful and successful democracy, politically and culturally dominant for much of the period. It was the center and symbol for democrats from all over the Greek world, just as Sparta was the city most admired by the aristocratically and oligarchically inclined.

In the fifth and fourth centuries B.C. much of the debate about privilege and the proper distribution of political power was framed in terms of democrats versus oligarchs, or as Aristotle put it, of poor majorities versus rich minorities.[49] According to Thucydides, the split between rich and poor ran through nearly every Greek city. It was the source of almost constant tension, and not infrequently long-festering resentments burst out into orgies of violence and recrimination like the one (described in lurid detail by Thucydides) at Corcyra in the 430s and 420s.[50] Plato realized that an oligarchy was in reality two cities, one of the rich and one of the poor, and that the two were more likely than not to be at war with one another. His chief preoccupation in designing an ideal republic was to overcome this class strife.[51]

Among the strengths of Athens was the fact that she managed, to a remarkable degree, to avoid open hostility between her rich and poor citizens. There were, to be sure, elites of birth, wealth, and talent at Athens as elsewhere, but the democracy kept them in the process and engaged their energies and financial resources in the common project. The wise mediation of Solon, an aristocrat, was a prelude. The actual establishment of a democratic constitution two generations later, in 510 B.C., was the conscious action of Cleisthenes, one of the city's most powerful aristocrats, apparently with the deliberate intention of breaking the political power of the old landed families and giving it to the majority. The shift was gradual, since in the fifth century, when the democracy was still new, members of the old families, by reason of their talent and notoriety, tended to get elected to positions of leadership (Miltiades, Kimon, Pericles, Alcibiades). Later, the Athenians worked out, more in practice than in theory, a series of socially effective compromises between privilege and equality.[52]

One of the most interesting and puzzling gaps in our record is the extreme paucity of democratic theory or ideology at Athens. Aside from the Funeral Oration attributed to Pericles by Thucydides, there is surprisingly little sustained theoretical defense of democratic government. Some scholars have argued that the Athenians never did develop such an ideology, that their ideas about themselves and what they were doing were always cast in terms of the older aristocratic ideals, and that democracy was conceptually nothing more than expanded oligarchy with privilege based not on money but on the facts of maleness and Athenian parentage on both sides. One justification of the empire was that the revenue it provided helped to maintain the so-called "people-king." There were brief oligarchic coups in 411 and 404 B.C., but they were quickly reversed. Writers like Thucydides and the Old Oligarch were critical, and Aristophanes poked fun. But the great majority of Athenians agreed in practice that they liked what they called their democracy, and they were confident enough of its strength to laugh at its foibles. Systematic criticism of democracy came in the fourth century with the philosophers, especially Plato. But before turning to him, let us consider briefly the most eloquent expression of the democratic ideal that we have from Athens.

Pericles' Funeral Oration

Thucydides says that Pericles delivered the speech in the winter of 430 B.C. at a ceremony for the Athenians who had lost their lives in battle during the first year of the war with Sparta. Ironically it is attributed to a democratic leader with impeccable upper-class credentials by an admirer with a clearly antidemocratic point of view.[53] A few short excerpts with commentary will show how it works—and how much it owes to traditional aristocratic ideas.

We have a form of government which does not emulate the laws of other states. Instead, we are a model for them rather than imitators. Our system is called "democracy" because the management of affairs is in the hands of the majority [*pleionas*] and not of the few [*oligous*]. With regard to private disputes the law provides equality for all. In choosing people for public service we judge not by what class [*meros*] a person comes from but by his ability [*aretê*] to serve the common good. Nor will anyone who has any service to offer be excluded because of his poverty.[54]

Not only passive equality, that is, fair treatment before the law, which was an ancient and acknowledged right under any form of government— though not always granted in practice, as the case of Hesiod shows—but active equality as well, in the sense that public office is open to all as long as they are capable. In fact, almost all offices were filled by allotment, so that every citizen was treated as ipso facto capable in practice. Distinctions of social class and wealth are not to be taken into account in reckoning suitability. Willingness and ability to serve the community are the sole criteria for judging the value of citizens. It is not who you are but what you can do that counts.

So much for the positive side—and even that is framed more in terms of reaction to aristocratic claims than as a positive ideology. Greek democrats were as little disposed as their elitist brethren to leave it at that. And so Pericles next indulges in a bit of gentle needling, which is apparently aimed as much at the ostentatious high living and cultural pretentiousness of certain local aristocrats as it is at the rough and tough (but notoriously uncultured) Spartan enemy. The point can be gotten, I think, by reading indicatives as simultaneously implying imperatives throughout:

We [ought to] love beauty without extravagance and we [ought to] love wisdom without softness. And we [ought to] use wealth more as an instrument for action than as something to boast about. As far as poverty is concerned, the shame is not in acknowledging it but in not taking steps to get out of it.[55]

Lastly, Pericles implies that, in fact, *all* Athenians are aristocrats and that the rest of Greece would do well to sit up and take notice:

In conclusion, then, I claim that our city as a whole is an education for the rest of Greece, and that our citizens, each and every one, in the most varied ways enjoys personal autonomy [*autarkeia*] with the greatest style and grace. [And the best proof of this claim is] the power which our city has acquired because of these very characteristics.[56]

In a sense, therefore, every Athenian citizen (by birth, be it noted) achieves the old aristocratic ideals of self-sufficiency and a distinctive elegance of style, along with power over others, none of which, it seems, could ever be fully enjoyed—or even validated in the extremely competitive, "shame culture" Greek environment—unless they were envied by the less fortunate. Even good feelings seem to have operated on a kind of emotional zero-sum principle: the worse you feel about my feeling good the better I feel about it.

Plato's *Republic*: Argument and Images

The *Republic* is the most brilliant and at the same time the most irritating piece of antipopular rhetoric that we have from ancient (or perhaps any other) times. Its brilliance lies in the grand and high-minded way in which Plato sweeps together most of what is good in prior aristocratic tradition and builds it into a structure that he hopes to convince the reader is firmly and simultaneously based on both human nature and the nature of political society. Neither wealth nor family background nor even gender will any longer be the basis for the privilege of ruling in the state. Only intellectual ability will count, along with years of the best education and, above all, total dedication to the common good of all the citizens. Ruling will, in fact, be less a privilege in any normal understanding of the term than a duty, perceived and carried out—even against their preference for pure philosophical speculation—by the philosopher kings. Full knowledge, which includes all the virtues, will make this self-denying service necessary and possible, if not pleasurable in any vulgar sense.

Beyond the elitist tone and conclusions, what most irritates all but the most devoted friends of Plato is the extremely harsh antipopular rhetoric of his argument. Plato is firmly within the Greek aristocratic tradition in this, and he is even better at it than his predecessors. If elevated tone, moral earnestness, and serious philosophizing are one part of the secret of the *Republic*, another is certainly the rollicking feast of wonderfully vivid antipopular images that it serves up. Plato simply cannot resist them, it seems. Many are purely gratuitous and hardly necessary for the flow of the argument, and his almost exclusively elite readership must have been delighted. Here are some of the most striking, in more or less the order in which they appear, along with some indication of their pedigrees where possible.

(1) *One man one task according to his nature.* This is basic and the definition of justice will rest on it. As in the *Iliad*, the city needs craftsmen of all kinds, and all citizens need one another. But not all are equal. Farmers, craftsmen, and traders—working people in general—are

servants [*diakonoi*] who in matters requiring intelligence are by no means worth associating with, but who have the bodily strength that is needed for hard work. And so they sell the use of their strength and they call the price that they get for it a "wage." Hence, I suppose, they are called "wage earners."[57]

(2) This class of necessary but inferior citizens is by far the largest in the state. There is a second, much smaller class, the warriors or helpers, who

are "by nature" outstanding for courage. On top is the smallest group of all, the guardians or rulers. For the sake of unity the founder of the state must convince the members of all classes that they are brothers, but not equals. *The noble lie* will accomplish this. It says that all are born from the same earth, but that each also contains elements of a different metal: gold, silver, iron, from top to bottom. The myth will teach the lower classes by story to acquiesce in what the philosophers know from reasoning, namely that birth is fundamental and that not all people are born equal. Still, for survival as well as for success, they all have to live together in harmony. And the only way to do this is as rulers and ruled, each part "doing its own thing" and not interfering in the thing of the others, as nature itself dictates. This is what justice in the state means.[58]

(3) *The lowest class of citizens is equivalent to the lowest part of the soul.* It is impossible to say which occurred to Plato first, the threefold division of the state or that of the individual soul. The idea of equating the lowest part of each, however, allows for almost unlimited antipopular cross-trumping. For example, the lowest part of the soul, the *epithumia*, is "that in the soul by which it loves [experiences *erôs*, blind lust], feels hunger and thirst and flies around the other desires, irrational and compulsive, companion to all sorts of replenishments and desires."[59] It corresponds more or less to what one could call the animal side of human nature. Given the equivalence, it becomes easy to assert all kinds of outrageous things about the majority of citizens in a seemingly calm and reasonable voice. They are fully irrational and so their principal function in the state is to obey their (fully rational) superiors. They are like children, women, slaves, or the "great and wretched mass of so-called free men."[60] They are also by far the most numerous class and hence can be dangerous, since the *epithumia* is

by nature most insatiable when it comes to money, and so it must be watched lest by getting its fill of the so-called pleasures of the body it become great and strong and stop attending to its own business and try to enslave and rule over those which because of its birth it should not and thus destroy the entire life of the whole.[61]

The theme of the vices of the lower classes is as old as Homer and Theognis. In the late fifth century it is taken up at Athens by the Old Oligarch, who attributes the "ignorance, disorder, and vice" of the mob to their poverty and lack of education—a quiet modern-sounding analysis, but without the corresponding suggestions for doing anything about it.[62] The theme occurs also in Herodotus' fictional debate about the best constitution, in which the speaker who proposes oligarchy argues that the masses are ignorant, irresponsible, and violent; they "have not a thought in their heads; all they can do is rush blindly into politics like a river in flood."[63] The other side of the picture, in all of the above and in the *Republic*, is the claim that:

(4) *Only the elite are virtuous*. And they possess *all* the virtues. In the last part of Book IV, Plato gives the old claim a new grounding. As we have seen, only the guardians rule the lower parts of their souls according to reason. Hence, they alone are just (by parallel with the just state). As such, they also possess all of the other traditional virtues (by mere assertion). They are honest, pious, loyal, trustworthy, faithful in marriage, good to their parents, and respecters of the gods.[64] The lower classes (by definition) can have none of these virtues in the proper sense. Their proper virtue is a kind of temperance, which amounts to acceptance of the appropriateness of the hierarchical arrangement of society.

(5) *Eugenics*. Plato's views on the subject are well enough known not to need much space here.[65] The parallels that he draws between human breeding and animal husbandry are reminiscent of Theognis. A difference is that while good birth is necessary for Plato, it is not sufficient in itself. Education, and lots of it, is also required for his rulers, and open only to them.

(6) *The defective constitutions*. The great problem of an oligarchy, which Plato thinks next best after the ideal of aristocracy, is "the fact that such a city is of necessity not one but two cities, one of the poor [*penêtes*] and one of the rich [*plousioi*], both occupying the same space and always plotting against one another." And the poor are reduced to beggary or crime.[66] Still, the oligarchic personality type, though divided, will be one in which the better desires prevail over the baser ones for the most part.[67]

Democracy evolves out of oligarchy when the oppression of the poor goes too far and the oligarchs themselves grow soft. The poor revolt and kill or banish the former rulers. The resulting society is one in which freedom turns to license; individualism is rife; civic responsibility is ignored; and low standards prevail.[68] The democratic personality is governed by the baser desires (food and sex) and has no guiding principle,

but he lives from day to day gratifying each passing desire: at one time drinking wine and playing the flute, at another taking only water and dieting; sometimes exercising, sometimes lying lazily about, and at other times seeming to busy himself with philosophy. Often too he participates in politics and jumps up and says and does whatever comes into his mind . . . and there is neither order nor discipline in his life, but he claims that he lives freely, pleasantly, and happily.[69]

Eventually, excessive love of liberty leads to chaos and social anarchy that extends even to the animals and in which "the father becomes accustomed to be like a child and to fear his sons . . . the teacher fears and flatters his students . . . and in general the young mistreat their elders . . . and the elders accommodate themselves to the young . . . and imitate them for fear of seeming unpleasant and despotic."[70] In the end, the politicians and the rich fight over money and the favor of the masses, who pick one man as their patron and protector. He attacks the rich and is either killed by them or triumphs over them and becomes a tyrant. Hence the outcome of too much freedom for all is slavery of all to one arbitrary ruler. If the *dêmos* gets political power, then all will eventually become slaves.[71]

(7) *Three strong images*. Plato does not rely solely on the device of the tripartite soul to make his points. Again borrowing from Theognis, he creates a vivid picture in the *Republic* (VI.488) of *the democratic state as a ship in mutiny* and lacking a qualified pilot. The sailors, who know nothing about navigation, fight among themselves for control of the helm, tie up the pilot, take command, and then proceed to devour the ship's stores in feasting. A bit further along (in VI.493), the *dêmos* is likened to *a great strong beast* (recall Theognis' figures of Cyclopses and Centaurs) which roars its approval or disapproval according to how skillfully the politicians learn to divine its moods and give it what it wants. Conversely, in *The Cave* in VII.514–15, the masses sit passively, absorbing at third hand what they in their supine ignorance take to be reality.

(8) *The image of the little bald blacksmith* shows Plato at his most effective. It also brings our discussion full circle in that it combines several themes and contains echoes of both the Thersites episode and certain passages in Theognis. Note too that Plato's butt is a blacksmith, like Hephaistos. What happens, asks Socrates, when philosophy is left "desolate and unwed" by the better natures? The answer is that:

Others, "little men," see that this place has been left unoccupied and that it is replete with fine names and posturings, and just like men who escape from bonds and take refuge in temples, they happily flee from their crafts to philosophy, those who happen to be most clever at their "little crafts" . . . men unfitted by nature, whose bodies have been corrupted by their crafts and trades, just as their souls have been twisted and broken by their manual labor. . . . Do they look any different to you than a little bald blacksmith who has managed to get rich—just out of bondage, freshly bathed, dressed up in a new suit like a bridegroom, and off to marry the daughter of his master who has fallen into poverty and hard times. . . . What are their children likely to be but worthless bastards?[72]

The passage is the more revealing for being the more gratuitous. It is almost as if Plato would like to blame what he sees as the low estate of philosophy on the working class: "little" people with "little" skills, inferior by birth and deformed by their manual work, in body and in soul, physically ugly, even comic in appearance, overly ambitious ex-convicts or slaves who are not in the habit of bathing.[73]

CONCLUSION

By way of summary, let us simply note once again some of the continuities that run through the ancient Greek rhetoric of privilege from start to finish.

(1) *The circumstance of birth* into the family of Pelops is what gave Agamemnon his divinely sanctioned authority to rule as he saw fit. Noble pedigrees routinely went back to a god or hero, and Zeus was thought to support the established order. In Theognis' day, when other more visible signs of superiority were no longer the sole prerogative of the hereditary nobles, the claim of a good bloodline became all the more urgent; it was one thing that the new rich could never buy. For Plato, "nature" endowed only the very few with the requisite mental and physical capability for the necessary education to be rulers. Even in democratic Athens, citizenship was treated as a male privilege based on Athenian parentage on both sides. Slaves, children, resident aliens, women, and foreigners were excluded. A later, even more radical, version of this was Aristotle's theory of natural slavery, in which the "natural slaves" were all non-Greeks.

(2) *Virtue and vice are distributed along class lines.* The most valued human qualities varied somewhat from period to period, but they were always claimed exclusively and in their entirety for the upper class. In Homer, physical courage and eloquence, along with wealth and beauty, counted as the *aretê* of the *agathoi*. They all, by definition, had all of these traits, and the commoners had none of them, as the case of Thersites is meant by its author to illustrate. For Theognis the "good" people, though less rich and powerful than before, are endowed with all the other traditional virtues, including now a sense of the common good of society. The *kakoi* are not only "base-born," but base in every other way. The class structure of Plato's just society is very like that of Homer, and "justice" means keeping it that way. The just individual, as defined in the early books of the *Republic*, will possess all of the other moral virtues. In the later books the rulers will be seen, by virtue of their philosophical training, to have both intellectual and moral virtue in their entirety. The equation of lower classes and the lower part of the soul, combined with the rule that mind must govern, gives a "philosophical" grounding to the old claim that the masses are wholly vicious and hence have no status except to follow their natural superiors.

(3) *The rule of the few is for the good of all.* Odysseus' version of this was the simple assertion that "the rule of many is not a good thing." It is the point of Theognis' blaming his opponents for the civil strife at Megara. It is what ultimately legitimates Plato's extreme measures, namely the argument that the very survival of the city depends on the kind of just order he describes in the *Republic* and *Laws*. Another way of stating the same thing is:

(4) *Justice comes from the top.* From the earliest times the king was the chief judge and Zeus demanded that he be fair; otherwise the whole community would suffer. Hesiod was apparently the first to point out that it was not fair for everyone to suffer because of one unjust man. In Athens all the citizens sat on juries. During the empire, many cases from the subject cities had to be heard at Athens, before the "people-king." A logical extension of

Plato's thinking is Aristotle's distinction in *Ethics* VI between "arithmetical" and "geometrical" justice. The former is one-for-one—for example, restitution in criminal or civil cases. The latter applies in the area of what we would call social justice. It requires that persons get power and privilege in society in geometrical proportion to their merit.

(5) *A kind of co-optation* seems to be at work in the pains that Homer gives himself to show that Thersites is an isolated individual and that the rest of the troops disapprove of him as much as the nobles do. A harsher version of the same is Theognis' claim that the *dêmos* loves a master and so the best way to handle them is with the goad and the yoke. Plato is gentler when he admits that the myth of the different metals in the makeup of the different classes is a "noble lie," and when he suggests that the masses do practice a kind of justice in accepting the rule of their betters, and a kind of temperance in liking it. Co-optation is a species of persuasion. Its reverse side is the characteristically Greek

(6) *Ridicule and put-down*. The continuity between the pictures of Thersites in the *Iliad* and the little blacksmith in the *Republic*—by way of Theognis' Cyclopses and Centaurs—is clear enough not to require further comment. Just a final reminder that this kind of nastiness had an Olympian sanction in the mythology of Hephaistos, the divine blacksmith, and a sort of philosophical grounding in the notion that manual work—necessary and admirable though its products may be—so deformed the worker in both body and spirit that he was useful for nothing else.[74]

NOTES

1. Some recent studies that I have found useful in the preparation of this essay are: Michel Austin and Pierre Vidal-Naquet, *Economic and Social History of Ancient Greece* (Berkeley and Los Angeles: University of California Press, 1977); Walter Donlan, *The Aristocratic Ideal in Ancient Greece* (Lawrence, Kans.: Coronado Press, 1980); Moses I. Finley, *The Ancient Economy*, 2d ed. (Berkeley and Los Angeles: University of California Press, 1985); Josiah Ober, *Mass and Elite in Democratic Athens* (Princeton, N.J.: Princeton University Press, 1989); G.M.E. Ste. Croix, *The Class Struggle in the Ancient Greek World* (Ithaca, N.Y.: Cornell University Press, 1981); and several articles in P. E. Easterling and Bernard M.W. Knox, eds., *The Cambridge History of Classical Literature, part 1, Greek Literature* (Cambridge and New York: Cambridge University Press, 1985). Translations from ancient authors are mine unless otherwise noted.

2. Finley, *Ancient Economy*, 35–36. Finley refers of course to the judgment of the writers of antiquity. We know almost nothing about the judgment of the poor and illiterate (the vast majority). It is difficult to imagine that they all thought of themselves as inferior or that they did not take pride in their work or admire their virtuous poor neighbors and friends. We just do not get this side of the picture in the evidence.

3. Ibid., 37–38.

4. This is the rule. There were some exceptions, for example the idea that beggars were sent by Zeus and so deserved kindly treatment (Homer, *Odyssey* 14.57–59). The contrast between Christian and pagan theory also raises the important and complex question of why practice in the areas of slavery, property, and treatment of the poor seems to have changed so little in late antiquity, after Christianity replaced paganism as the official religion of the Roman Empire. This is not the place to attempt an answer. Ste. Croix (*Class Struggle*, 440–41) discusses the question at some length and offers the challenge:

At the present time there is a debate going on among Christians whether (to use the language I have employed) it may not be absolutely necessary to reform the relations between men and men—in particular the relations between States and between classes within States—in order that the relations between man and man may not be forever distorted and damaged. Among other relations between man and man, I would suggest that a central role is played by property relations, including in particular ownership of property and the way in which production is organized. Those of us who watch the debate within the churches from the outside may feel that careful study of what actually happened in the early Christian centuries, both in the field of ideas and in actual social life, might shed some light on current problems and controversies, and as a result might have a powerful influence on the future of man.

5. Finley, *Ancient Economy*, 40–61; and Austin and Vidal-Naquet, *Economic and Social History*, 11–18. The latter (8–11) also has a good discussion of the key concept of the "embedded economy," the phenomenon of societies like those of classical antiquity in which "The Economy" does not have the kind of quasi-autonomous character that it does in modern industrial society.

Greek vocabulary in the matter of wealth and poverty is informative. It distinguishes among the *plousios*, the "rich" person who does not need to work at all; the *penês*, the "poor" person who might have a farm of his own and even some slaves, but who has to work for a living; and the *ptôchos*, the "beggar" who has neither land nor steady work.

6. This situation is the background of the constant strife within (*stasis*) and between (*polemos*) the Greek city-states. It also lies behind the famous—and sometimes overly romanticized—Greek "competitiveness." For a fuller discussion of the parallel situation in the New Testament world and some of its implications for moral attitudes toward wealth and poverty, see Chapter 3 in this volume. Consider too almost any Central American country even now.

7. *Class Struggle*, 411 and all of Chapter 7.

8. Almost all extant Greek literature and philosophy is written from an elite perspective. There is no opposition voice in any real sense. When we do hear one, as in Hesiod and Pericles' Funeral Oration, it seems to echo the standard line.

Athenian drama is not taken up here for reasons of space and time. It was popular in that it was part of a civic festival and attracted large audiences. A common theme of the tragedies was the fall of the mighty, and that may have been part of their attraction. Euripides explicitly introduces nonaristocratic characters and points of view. Aristophanes mocks him for this. He also mocks Cleon, the tradesman, and pokes fun at other aspects of democracy, for example the popular courts in *Wasps*.

9. The epic tradition is complex. It began with the Trojan War (about 1200 B.C.) or before and was transmitted orally and with constant variation and refinement by illiterate poet-singers through a long Dark Age (about 1100–800 B.C.).

With the introduction of the alphabet in the eighth century (Archaic Age, about 750–500 B.C.), our *Iliad* and *Odyssey* were written down; the texts became more or less fixed, and the oral tradition effectively ended.

The poems presumably contain cultural elements from every historical stage of the tradition. Sorting these out is an extremely tricky business. M. I. Finley's *World of Odysseus* 2d ed. (London: Chatto and Windus, 1977) is generally thought to be the best effort. The picture of classes and their relations is fairly consistent throughout the poems. What precise historical period they correspond to (Finley concludes the tenth century B.C. for the *Odyssey*) is not of crucial importance for the argument here.

For a recent concise statement on most questions Homeric, see G. S. Kirk in *Cambridge History*, 42–91 and 721–24. See too the serially appearing (starting in 1985) *The Iliad: A Commentary*, edited by Kirk and published by the Cambridge University Press.

10. Donlan, who in general argues for a more egalitarian view of Homeric society than most scholars, stresses that this is the only example in Homer of open tension between princes and commoners (*Aristocratic Ideal*, 19–23). Against Donlan I would urge the following considerations: (1) Like much in the early books of the *Iliad*, the scene is probably intended to be typical, to fill in the general background of what kinds of things happened in the nine-plus years of the war not covered in the poem; (2) its position very close to the opening of the story gives it more weight than it might otherwise have had; (3) the good comradeship between leaders and led may itself be part of the aristocratic propaganda of the poems ("This is the way it was in the good old days"); (4) Dayton Haskin points out that it is indicative of the general aristocratic perspective of the epics that the common soldier's voice can be heard at all only in such a clearly "staged" way; and (5) the *Odyssey's* view is not so egalitarian.

For recent commentary and earlier literature on the episode see G. S. Kirk, *Commentary*, 138–45; H. D. Rankin, "Thersites the Malcontent, A Discussion," *Symbolae Osloenses* 47 (1972): 36–60; and W. G. Thalmann, "Thersites: Comedy, Scapegoats, and Heroic Ideology in the *Iliad*," *Transactions of the American Philological Association* 118 (1988): 1–28. Thalmann suggests that the ideology may not be as straightforward as earlier scholars have thought. In the whole context of deception, poor leadership, and abuse of authority, the nobles do not look very good either.

11. For example, the Catalogue of Ships (Book 2), the Viewing from the Wall (Book 3), and the meeting of Hector and Andromache (Book 6).

12. Kirk, *Commentary*, 138: "Thersites is a 'speaking' name formed from *thersos*, the Aeolic form of Ionic *tharsos*, implying either boldness or rashness—in his case, obviously the latter."

13. The paradox, which is alluded to in the second part of the passage, can be summarized as follows: Mortals cannot physically live forever. To a degree they can overcome death by glory, by living on in the memory of their great deeds, but the only really great deeds are those of heroic combat, and by engaging in that you will eventually get yourself killed.

14. *Economic and Social History*, 195.

15. *Aristocratic Ideal*, 20.

16. This prejudice against manual labor and those who did it lasted throughout antiquity; it extended even to what we (though not the Greeks) elevate to the

separate category of "creative" arts. Compare the famous remark of Plutarch (about A.D. 50–120): "We [right-thinking people] take pleasure in perfumes and purple garments, but we regard dyers and perfumers as men unworthy to be free and as mean artisans. . . . No young man of good birth having seen the [statues of] Zeus of Pisa [Olympia] or the Hera of Argos desired to become Pheidias or Polycleitus [the sculptors], nor Anacreon, Philemon or Archilochus [poets] for having been delighted with their poems" (*Pericles*, I.4–II.1=Austin and Vidal-Naquet, no. 11; their translation).

17. *Iliad* 18.396–97. Similar ambiguities occur in the myth of Prometheus: great inventor of the arts and benefactor of the human race on the one hand, trickster and bitter enemy of Zeus on the other. He too was worshipped by craftsmen. Hermes, the patron of traders, was also the patron of thieves. Athena, another deity of arts and crafts, managed to escape any bad reputation, possibly because her arts were originally those of women (spinning and weaving), and the tradition had no problem with women doing manual labor.

18. For a fuller discussion, see my paper "Aspects of Religious Morality in Early Greek Epic," *Harvard Theological Review* 73 (1980): 373–418. A more recent statement on the whole matter is that of J. P. Barron and P. E. Easterling in *Cambridge History*, 98–99: "Hesiod's preoccupation with ethics and with the justice of Zeus is a whole world away from the old aristocratic view of the divine right of kings, which is unquestioned in the *Iliad* and still largely prevails in the Odyssey. . . . In particular, it is noteworthy that in Hesiod's view injustice leads ultimately to war as the worst of evils. War, of course, is the sport of princes, and in this passage above all Hesiod turns his back on Homer and the heroic tradition."

19. Ste. Croix, *Class Struggle*, 278.

20. The social and economic changes in the period were far-reaching and complex. They included population growth, a change in military tactics, colonization, new contacts with the non-Greek world, and the introduction of coinage.

21. *Aristocratic Ideal*, 75.

22. Of Archaic Greek lyric poetry only Pindar's—a bit later and also aristocratic—is as well preserved as that of Theognis. The good preservation of the latter—along with its continual editing and augmenting and its later use as a sort of moral florilegium—is one of our proofs that, in some circles at least, the old ideas lived on in the changed conditions of the classical period and beyond, even in democratic Athens.

23. For an authoritative recent essay on Theognis, see B.M.W. Knox in *Cambridge History*, 136–46.

24. 31–36. All references are to the standard line numbers of the elegies of Theognis.

25. For these attitudes, see also 27–38, 61–68, 87–92, 101–4.

26. 437–38.

27. 183–92. Plato too will go in for eugenics; and the little blacksmith who gets rich and marries his master's daughter will win his choicest scorn. The blacksmith seems to be a combination of the Thersites passage and this one.

28. In *Cambridge History*, 143. Tyrtaeus, be it noted, was the national poet of Sparta, the most brutally aristocratic—and for many later philosophers and non-Spartan aristocrats the most admired—city-state in Greece. He also wrote elegies on the Spartan repression of Messenia.

29. 699–718. Elsewhere (867–68) Theognis explicitly equates *aretê* with courage, and in another place (147–48) with justice (*dikaiosunê*). This latter has surprised commentators, since it is by far the earliest claim that justice and virtue are coextensive (Plato's project in the *Republic*). On the other hand, it is consistent with Theognis' desire to claim all virtues, including the "cooperative," for his side.

30. 173–82, 320–22, 621–22.

31. 320–22, 383–92, 1025–30.

32. See also especially 151–54, and 523, 693, 747–52.

33. 43–46. Note how this complaint echoes that of Hesiod against the "bribe-devouring" nobles of his day.

34. 42–52. This looks forward to Plato's version of the deterioration of constitutions.

35. 105–12.

36. 279–88.

37. 291–92.

38. 671–80. Note here also the variation on the theme that the *kakoi* care only for private gain and nothing at all for the common good.

39. 53–58. The imagery here is reminiscent of Anacreon's (slightly earlier in date) ridicule of a certain Artemon, a new-rich acquaintance who failed to bring it off with style (Donlan, *Aristocratic Ideal*, 63–64). Artemon once wore an ox hide and associated with bread sellers and whores. Often he was beaten for his crimes. Now he wears golden earrings and rides in a carriage.

40. 1123–28.

41. 847–50.

42. 541–42.

43. 649–51.

44. Charles Segal in *Cambridge History*, 231. Both Xenophanes (frag. 2 West) and Socrates (*Apology*, 36d–e) made fun of the idea of the nobles' social usefulness. They claimed that intellectuals like themselves rendered a far greater service to the city.

45. Knox in *Cambridge History*, 149.

46. Frag. 4 West.

47. Frag. 6 West.

48. Another of Solon's measures, according to Plutarch, was to promote craftsmanship in order to create work for land-poor farmers. "But Solon, who adapted the laws to reality rather than reality to the laws, and who saw that the poverty of the soil barely afforded a living to farmers and could not sustain a large and idle crowd, brought the various trades into credit, and ordered the Council of the Areiopagus to examine how every man got his living and to punish the idle" (*Solon*, frag. 22 West). The aristocratically minded Plutarch grudgingly approves, but elsewhere (*Solon*, frag. 3 West) he judges that Solon must have been a "tradesman" because his poetry is so vulgar. The judgment was no doubt based more on the antiaristocratic content of parts of the poems than on their style. See Austin and Vidal-Naquet, no. 37 (their translation used here).

49. For a discussion of Aristotle's views and of the extent to which one can speak of "class struggle" in Greek cities, see Austin and Vidal-Naquet, *Economic and Social History*, 22–26; and Ste. Croix, *Class Struggle*, 69–80.

50. *Peloponnesian War*, III.69–85 and IV.46–50.

51. *Republic*, VIII.550c–552d. See also Ste. Croix, *Class Struggle*, 69–71.

52. Most recently studied by Ober in *Mass and Elite* using the evidence of speeches by elite speakers at trials before popular law courts in the 4th century. For most of the 5th century the income from the empire was a real factor for social peace, since it provided massive public employment and reduced the need for taxing the rich.

53. Thucydides came from a wealthy old family and admired Pericles as a leader precisely because the latter did not let the people run away with him. In the view of Thucydides, Athens prospered under Pericles because it was a "democracy in name, but in fact it was the rule of the first citizen." Thucydides thought that the oligarchic constitution of 411 B.C. was the best he had seen at Athens. After Pericles—his version goes—new leaders arose, the demagogues, who pandered to the mob and eventually lost the war to Sparta. The favorite whipping boy is Cleon, a nonaristocratic demagogue and son of a wealthy tanner. The connection with trade, especially such a smelly one, was probably enough in itself to discredit him in the eyes of the well-born.

54. II.37.1.

55. II.40.1. Poverty here refers to the *penia* of the worker, not the state of the destitute *ptôchos*. Pericles is in the tradition of Hesiod and Solon in pushing hard work as a way out of this kind of poverty. Wealth—and not having to work for it—is still the ideal.

56. II.41.1–2.

57. II.371e. A closer English equivalent to the flavor of what Plato is saying might be something like: We "employ" (make use of) working people, hence they are called "employees."

58. III.414b–415c. It has been pointed out more than once that Plato's division of society (a small minority of rulers and fighters who have all the authority) and his definition of justice (staying in the place assigned you in the "natural" order of things) do not differ essentially from those of the Homeric poems.

59. IV.439d.

60. IV.431a–c.

61. IV.442a–b. The passage is itself a good example of how easily Plato goes back and forth between *epithumia* and the lowest class. Here he starts off talking about the soul, but by the end of the sentence, he has slid into language that seems more appropriate to the state.

62. The "Old Oligarch" is a modern pseudonym for the unknown author of the *Constitution of Athens*, a cynically clever oligarchical tract written probably about 430 B.C. at Athens and falsely attributed to Xenophon. It poses as an explanation for an outsider of why the Athenian democracy works so well. The secret, argues the author with tongue in cheek, is that it is a perfectly coherent system for guaranteeing that power stays firmly in the hands of the worst elements in society, namely the majority.

63. *Histories*, III.80–83, is the oldest example (probably mid-fifth century) of the debate about ideal constitutions which was common in fourth-century philosophy.

64. V.443. Later in the *Republic* it will become clear that the philosopher kings also (and exclusively) possess all of the "intellectual" virtues.

65. V.459–69.

66. VIII.551d–552d.

67. VIII.554d–e.

68. VIII.557a–558c.

69. VIII.561c–d.

70. VIII.562e–563b.

71. VIII.562–67. A further extension of the argument that democracy leads to tyranny is found in Xenophon's *Memorabilia*, I.2.40–46. There the argument is that democracy *is* tyranny, in the sense that when the majority enact a decree that is not to the liking of the wealthy minority they are in effect tyrannizing them. Ste. Croix (*Class Struggle*, 414–16) calls this "one of the best anti-democratic arguments produced in antiquity—better, anyway, than anything in Plato."

72. VI.495b–496a.

73. Thersites, or rather his soul, appears in person in the *Republic*, X.620c, where he is about to be reincarnated as an ape. Plato refers to him in Homeric terms as *gelôtopoios*, one who provokes laughter. Ironically, Plato's hero Socrates was a craftsman, a sculptor; he was also poor and ugly in appearance. In his case, however, these are made out to be attractive qualities. Many of his examples are taken from the crafts; his poverty is adduced in the *Apology* as proof of his devotion to philosophy; he is sexually attractive to Alcibiades in the *Symposium*. On the other hand, his pupils are almost all from the upper class, and his ideas about politics are far from democratic.

74. Earlier in this essay I raised the issue of the relation between pagan and early Christian attitudes toward slaves, workers, and the poor. As a postscript let me cite a biblical passage (noted also by Ste. Croix, *Class Struggle*, 413) that seems to show the influence of Greek attitudes toward craftsmen on a Jewish writer. It is from the Deuterocanonical book of *Ecclesiasticus*, 38:14–39. The author, Jesus Ben Sirach, was a learned Jew from Palestine who wrote in Hebrew in the early second century B.C. The surviving version is a Greek translation made by his grandson in 132 B.C. The general thesis of Chapters 38 and 39 is that only the scribe can attain true wisdom. Some excerpts, in the *Jerusalem Bible* translation, give the flavor.

Leisure is what gives the scribe the opportunity to acquire wisdom. . . . How can the plowman become wise . . . his conversation is of nothing but cattle. . . . So it is with every workman and craftsman, toiling day and night . . . the blacksmith . . . the breath of fire scorches his skin. . . . So too the potter. . . . All these put their trust in their hands. . . . A town could not be built without them . . . but they are not required at the council, they do not sit on the judicial bench. . . . They are not remarkable for culture or sound judgment. . . . But they give solidity to the created world, while their prayer is concerned with what pertains to their trade.

3

Does the New Testament Have an Economic Message?

PHEME PERKINS

RAISING THE ECONOMIC QUESTION

The economic and political crises of our time have fostered popular images of the economy as an independent, reified entity which plays a leading role in shaping societal structures, international relationships, communal behaviors, personal relationships, and even individual self-image. The contrast between our society and traditional agrarian societies like that of the New Testament has led some interpreters to insist that economic analysis cannot be applied to the ancient world. There the economy does not stand as an independent entity. Economic behavior is embedded in the larger social structures—political, religious, social, and familial—that determine what we call economic behavior.[1]

Scholars are increasingly wary of the assumptions about wealth, consumption, class, and domination that provide the basis for much historical reconstruction of New Testament times.[2] Whereas Gibbon declared the Roman Empire of the mid-second century the happiest and most prosperous in human history,[3] scholars since the 1930s have emphasized the disastrous consequences of the Roman imperial consolidation of power. If the dispute were merely a matter of how to assess fragmentary, conflicting, and incomplete reports in ancient authors,[4] the problem of appropriate models might be left to the academics. However, a conceptual "myth" of the evil consumer city-state which colonializes and destroys the rural peasant populace has played a significant role in Marxist development theory as applied to the Third World in recent decades.[5]

This perspective has found its expression in Christian circles in liberation theology, which understands the biblical stories of the creation of a new people through the exodus of Hebrew slaves from Egypt; the prophetic critique of oppression by Israel's kings, aristocracy, and cultic priesthood; and the suffering of Jesus on the Cross, as testimony to a God who always takes the side of the poor and oppressed. Anyone who claims to be a disciple of Jesus must take up the struggle for personal and social transformation that liberates the oppressed:

The scandal of the cross is the scandal of God identified with all the victims of history in the passion of Christ. That identification was not a passive acceptance of suffering but an empowering transformation whereby the forces of death and evil were overcome through the resurrection. This empowering transformation was not an isolated, individual event cut off from the rest of human history. It was an event the meaning of which challenges those who believe to engage in a discipleship of faith, hope, and love. The discipleship is a life lived in a dying identification with the victims. Prophecy is constituted by an agapic life or praxis whereby the cries of victims are articulated into a voice protesting the victimization of humans by other humans.[6]

With its emphasis on interpretation that demands socioeconomic transformation, liberation theology has challenged the claims of historical critical interpretation of the Bible. The alleged objective reconstruction of what biblical texts meant in their own period has been castigated by liberation theologians because it refuses to engage in the historical struggle for liberation from which the biblical tradition is born. Instead, its method of describing what the Bible means transforms the living message—an unrelenting call for justice—into a chaff of historically conditioned particularities around the small kernel of abstract, timeless truths about persons and their relationship to the transcendent.[7] Liberation theology insists that the authority of the Bible does not lie in the historical critical readings of the academy but in the understanding of the message that emerges when the Bible is read and appropriated by communities of persons engaged in the concrete struggle for liberation.[8] Critics of this liberationist hermeneutical principle decry its often naive universalizing of the message of what is historically conditioned text. At the same time, the debate fueled by liberation theology highlights the complex relationship between the Bible and the community of faith that exists in every act of interpretation. To whom does the Bible belong? The university scholars? The socially and materially established churches of North America? The poor of Latin America?[9]

If we ask the question about the economic message of the New Testament today, we do so because there is a strong social sense that all is not well with the acquisition, distribution, and cultural uses of wealth. We do so because whatever one's view of the claims of liberation theology or materialist exegesis may be, we recognize that the biblical tradition has played a leading role in determining the moral uses of wealth in Christian societies. As Paul Veyne points out, the Greco-Roman society Christianity inherited knew how to deal with the poor through its own system of civic benefactions and personal ties that bound client to patron often over several generations. But this system does not render the existence of the poor a moral problem for society. It does not require that religious institutions care for the poor or make charity toward the unfortunate an index of the individual's standing with God:

"The wise man," writes Seneca, "will give a coin to a beggar without dropping it in a contemptuous manner, as do those who wish to be charitable only for the sake of appearances." The coin given to the beggar was thus a feature of everyday reality, but this reality did not include welfare institutions, which the Christians invented. . . . Philanthropy was noble only if it relieved elevated misfortunes. Almsgiving was an everyday action but not a duty of state or an act of high morality, and philosophers scarcely mention it.

All this changed with the coming of Christianity, in which almsgiving resulted from the new ethical religiosity. Now that it had become a highly significant form of behavior, charity was worthy to rank as a state duty of the upper class, for whom it took the place of munificence. By its material importance, its spiritual implications and the institutions it engendered, charity became the new historical virtue.[10]

Whether a St. Anthony gives all he has to the poor in order to save his soul by ascetic retirement to the desert or wealthy Christians assure their salvation through almsgiving, the gift remains in the power of the giver:

There will therefore be an easy transition from asceticism to a "class morality" in which almsgiving is a merit for the rich man, who shows himself obedient to God's commandment, but not a right for the poor. God has called on the rich to give, but has not willed that the poor be poor no longer. Furthermore, it remains understood that the rich man gives *if* he wants to and *what* he wants to.[11]

Liberation theology has departed from this traditional perspective by insisting upon the right of the poor to demand support in their struggle for liberation. The social analysis employed by liberation theologians challenges the assumptions many Christians have inherited about charity. Not all charity counts as evidence of the gospel of freedom which the Exodus story, the prophets, and Jesus brought to the poor and oppressed. Almsgiving and philanthropy that permit the socioeconomic structures that create poverty and oppression to continue unchecked are just as reprehensible today, it is argued, as were the elaborate religious ceremonies in which wealthy Israelites claimed to honor God with riches they had gained through a system of exploitation.[12]

RICH AND POOR IN THE SOCIAL WORLD OF THE NEW TESTAMENT

Is the New Testament engaged in criticism of the structures of society that generate classes of wealthy and poor persons? Or is almsgiving merely the response of a heightened compassion for the poor as fellow members of the Christian community? Both readings of the New Testament can be found in today's churches. In order to understand what statements about the rich and wealth in the New Testament might mean, we must ask what can be known about the rich and poor in a first-century cultural context.

Most historians assume that for the 80 percent of the population that lived at subsistence level, economic activity meant struggling to obtain the necessities of daily survival.[13] A surplus that would make possible ostentatious consumption, especially to exhibit social status, was the prerogative of the rich. However, the impoverished peasant model of the first-century society may not be an appropriate description of the economic situation. Donald Engels's study of Roman Corinth concludes that tenant proprietors must have had more disposable surplus than is commonly presumed. The city provided for an extensive outlay of wealth in the form of religious temples, festival games, educational and judicial opportunities, as well as the temporary lodgings and other services required by visitors to its games and temples. The more extensive the market in a particular city, the more extensive the other services also provided in the area.[14]

At least by the end of the first century, the urban Christian churches reflected in the Pastoral Epistles (1, 2, Tim.; Tit.) and James were dominated by well-off benefactors who were evidently part of the local elite.[15] Prospective leaders of the church are warned against excessive greed and love of money (1 Tim. 3:3, 8; Tit. 1:7). Wealth, itself, is not condemned, nor are the social structures by which it is either inherited or gained. But *philarguria* (love of money) is the root of evils (1 Tim. 6:9–10). Arrogance and false confidence might lead the wealthy away from the good works that are the basis of their future reward and place in the community (1 Tim. 6:17–19).[16]

In the first century, greed was commonly understood to be wealth used for oneself rather than returned to the community, as were the benefactions of a wealthy patron. This attitude is clearly reflected in the rich man of Luke's parable: "There was a rich man, who was clothed in purple and fine linen and who feasted sumptuously every day. And at his gate lay a poor man named Lazarus, full of sores who desired to be fed with what fell from the rich man's table" (16:19f).[17] The Lucan parable echoes, with less venom, the condemnations of the rich found in 1 Enoch (c. second century B.C.), a writing highly critical of existing social divisions between an exploitative, wicked class of rich persons and the poor and righteous:

Woe unto you, O rich people! For you have put your trust in your wealth. You shall ooze out of your riches, for you do not remember the Most High. In the days of your affluence you committed oppression . . . (94, 8–9)

Woe unto you, you sinners! For your money makes you appear like the righteous, but your hearts do reprimand you like real sinners, this very matter shall be a witness against you, as a record of your evil deeds. Woe unto you who eat the best bread! And drink wine in large bowls, trampling upon the weak people with your might! Woe unto you who have water available to you all the time, for soon you shall be consumed and wither away, for you have forsaken the fountain of life . . . (96, 4–6)

For you men shall put on more jewelry than women, and more multicolored garments than a virgin. In sovereignty, in grandeur, and in authority, [in] silver, in gold, in clothing, in honor, and in edibles—they shall be poured out like water . . . (98, 2)[18]

These passages describe the tensions created by wealth in Greco-Roman Palestine. Accumulations of silver and gold are only part of what it means for a person to be wealthy. More striking is the easy access to and conspicuous consumption of those basic elements of life: food, clothing, shelter, and water. In order to understand the moral condemnation of the piling up of such resources by the rich, it is necessary to distinguish between surplus in a modern economy and excess wealth in the ancient economy. Surplus wealth produced in a modern, capitalist economy is perceived as available to participants at various levels of individual wealth, social status, and power or influence. As such it encourages individuals to expect changes in their wealth, status, and influence as a consequence of the general prosperity of the socioeconomic system.[19] In the ancient world, which must be described as a limited-goods economy, all of these elements—power, honor, material goods, and even personal freedom—are in a fixed and limited supply.[20] Consequently, if one person increases his or her share of such goods, someone else loses.

Local social groups like the village or the extended household of family members, slaves, and other dependents devote their energies to preserving the goods that belong to the group as a whole. They tend to be traditionalist and suspicious of outsiders. Even a person of means like a discharged Roman soldier has to be formally introduced if he expects to settle in a village. In the following letter, a man is asking his brother to assist a veteran to whom he expects to rent his property:

Receive with my recommendation the bearer of this letter, Terentianus, an honorably discharged soldier, and acquaint him with our villagers' ways, so he isn't insulted. Since he is a man of means and desirous of residing there, I have urged upon him that he rent my house for this year and the next for sixty drachmas, and that he take a lease of my field for sixty drachmas, and I'd like you to use the one hundred and twenty drachmas to buy for me from our friend the linen-merchant by the temple in the city . . . [21]

Luke makes sure that the centurion who wants Jesus to heal his slave presents his request through leaders of the Jewish community, who are indebted to him because the centurion was the benefactor of their synagogue:

Now a centurion had a slave who was dear to him, who was sick and at the point of death. When he heard of Jesus, he sent to him elders of the Jews asking him to come and heal his slave. And when they came to Jesus, they besought him earnestly, saying, "he is worthy to have you do this for him for he loves our nation, and he built us our synagogue."(7:2–5)

As this example illustrates, the limited-goods society is organized in terms of personal relationships which bind persons together as family, as friends, and as patron and client. Both friendship and patronage relationships can be inherited. Patterns of exchange, whether economic or in some other form of assistance or nonmaterial goods like honor, are determined by the nature of the relationship between the persons involved. Since the entire Roman system of government depends upon complex patterns of patron and client, no one was free of the possibility that a patron might demand some form of service in return for prior benefits bestowed. Such relationships are an asymmetrical form of exchange in which it is very difficult to measure the relative value of the services performed by a patron—often mediating access to some higher official or personage—and the return made by the client. Within a relatively stable population, neither the benefactor nor the client is free to terminate the relationship. Those who move from one community to another have to initiate such relationships by drawing upon the "goodwill" of others, as in the cases above. Patron-client exchanges presume status inequality between the parties as well as inequality in what is actually exchanged. "Friendship," which implies some measure of equality, also carries its obligations to mutual aid, as in Jesus' description of the friend who comes at midnight to demand bread so that he can show hospitality to a sudden visitor (Luke 11:5–8).[22]

Patron-client and friendship relationships even govern the administration of justice. Roman law was not a system of principles before which individuals stood as neutral parties. Each community and each governor administered affairs as they chose so long as public order was maintained, taxes and other dues were paid, and the like. The administration of the empire was determined by social and personal relationships. Persons were either one's friends or they were benefactors and authorities with the power to command obedience to their desires.[23]

Under this system, those with enough power to seize the property of others may even expand their holdings through violence. In Jesus' parable of the wicked tenants (Mark 12:1–9), the tenants attempted to control the vineyard by beating those sent to collect the rent and then murdering the owner's son. Jesus' tale is only slightly more violent than cases attested in legal papyri:

To Apollonios, *strategos* of the Arsinoite *nome*, from Thouonis son of Skousilaos of Ares' Village in the Polemon division. [Yesterday] as I was settling accounts with Bentetis son of Bentetis, a herdsman of [the village of] Oxyrhyncha of the said division, regarding pay and rations that he owes me, he then, wishing not to pay me but to cheat me, treated me and my wife Tanouris daughter of Heronas with contempt, right there in our aforesaid Ares' Village. And not only that but he also mercilessly rained on my wife Tanouris many blows on whatever part of her body he could reach, even though she was pregnant, with the result that she miscarried and was untimely delivered of a dead fetus and she herself is bedridden and in danger of her life. I therefore ask that you write to the elders of Oxyrhyncha to send the accused to you for the due consequences. [24 November A.D. 47. Signature][24]

Judging by similar cases, this man will only get redress if he succeeds in wearing the *strategos* out with repeated appeals like the window in Luke's example of the Unjust Judge (18:2–5). The petitioner apparently cannot appeal to any persons known to the *strategos* in order to compel him to punish the offender, since they would otherwise be mentioned in his request. Nor does he have the support within his own village to force Bentetis to pay him what is owed. Even if punishment were forthcoming, it would in no way compensate for the loss of the child and possibly of the wife—which were economic as well as personal hardships in such a society.

GENEROSITY, DEBT REMISSION AND RELIGIOUS STATUS IN THE NEW TESTAMENT

The Mosaic law and a heritage of prophetic condemnation of the leaders of society who exploit its weaker members for personal gain provided Jewish communities with religious sanctions against exploitative use of wealth. That tradition sought to moderate the ability of individuals to accumulate wealth, honor, and power so that the majority of the population would not become enslaved to the aristocracy. Legal provisions for debt relief and reapportionment of land might prevent the permanent enslavement and impoverishment of small, peasant farmers. Sayings of Jesus such as the petitions in the Lord's Prayer, which commend "forgiving" others their debts (Matt. 6:12), and the parable of the unforgiving servant (Matt. 18:23–35) show that an ethos of such unreciprocated remission of debt as a way of securing one's religious status before God was still recognized among Jews in the first century.[25] Jesus insists that willingness to forgive the imprisoning debts of others is one of the conditions for entering the Kingdom of God.[26] The objection that "material" remission of debt and divine forgiveness of sins should not be equated because the two "goods" are radically different does not hold for Jesus' world. In the patron-client model of social relationships the exchange of benefits is always asymmetrical. Contemporary historians often find it difficult to specify exactly what it is that the clients of powerful patrons or the populace of a city really give back in return for the material benefits they receive.[27] The teaching of Jesus is consistently clear: human generosity which tends to be grudging and partial should be modeled on a divine generosity which gives to all without consideration of their merit, social status, or even their religious behavior (e.g., Matt. 5:38–48). The reward for such behavior lies in one's status as a participant in God's Kingdom, not in some form of human reciprocity. Luise Schottroff captures this facet of Jesus' teaching in her analysis of the parable of the vineyard workers (Matt. 20:1–15): "The parable intends to speak of the generosity *of God* (See espec. v. 15) and of the *behavior of human beings toward one another* as contrasted with the goodness of God (e.g. the envy and grumbling of the long-shift workers)."[28]

Despite these ideals, many scholars think that economic behavior in Jewish communities was essentially the same as in the surrounding culture. The problems of debt were a dominant factor in the tensions between the owner/creditors and the populace, as Oakman notes:

The problem of debt exacerbated the quality of relations between the owning class of first-century Palestine and those who were forced for one reason or another into tenancy or wage labor. Debt was one of the major mechanisms whereby the rich kept getting richer and the poor, poorer. Through debt, ownership of patrimonial land of the peasantry could be, and was, wrested from them. The "rights" of the creditor were another manifestation of the insensitive egoism of the empire's elites that demanded security and securities to the detriment of many disprivileged.[29]

The problem with the rich throughout the New Testament does not appear to be grounded in the unequal distribution of wealth. That is taken for granted. Further, if members of the local community are to act as effective benefactors and mediators over against the Roman authorities, they would have to have the wealth, education, and leisure that elevated them above the general populace.

Rather, the religious problem with the rich is an egoism and excessive greed that piles up wealth in a way that deprives others of the resources needed for subsistence. The mechanisms by which such wealth is filtered downward in society—the gift of debt relief to a poor client/tenant, or the provision for public facilities and public entertainment in the form of banquets and festivals—were frequently being neglected in favor of private consumption of the fruits of wealth by the rich and their friends. This is the pattern of greed condemned in the introduction to the parable of the rich man and Lazarus. Tensions generated by this situation may also be responsible for the assumption that the "unjust steward's" use of his master's money to cancel some of the debts owed would in fact win him support when he is fired (Luke 16:1–8). Oakman notes:

The political astuteness of the move is, from an agrarian perspective, self-evident. Through the mechanism of releasing debtors from their obligations, the steward creates some positive alternatives for himself. Yet it cannot be overlooked that there is, from the viewpoint of the dominant culture, αδικια ["injustice"] involved. Why does Jesus then praise the man? Is he siding with the oppressed peasantry against the rich? To do so would not change the dominant ethos of self-sufficiency. No, the story would seem to be aimed at the rich themselves (as Luke has well understood).

What is laudable about the steward's behavior is his generosity (with other's goods!)—a generosity certainly motivated by self-interest, but with particularly salutary effects.[30]

The value of certain forms of economic exchange, especially in cases where generosity is not immediately reciprocated, depends upon its effect in the overall context of personal and social relationships. Greed figures predominately in the moral condemnations of the wealthy because its manifestation can destroy the social and religious fabric of life by putting the whole community at risk.[31] Greed may cause some persons to deprive others of the means of survival. Luke's criticism of the Pharisees draws on the prophetic tradition. They claim to uphold purity laws out of a concern to maintain the boundaries and holiness of the community, while their greed makes them impure in God's eyes (11:29, 34, 37–44). The Old Testament prophets castigated those who would maintain the cultic purity of the land while ignoring the nation's injustice. The Pharisees serve as Luke's model of unscrupulous rich persons, who establish their status by external means, in this case religious purity. He insists that they should be recognized as the most defiled of all because of their behavior:

To Luke the real and grave impurity was that which consisted in plunder and greed. This was an uncleanness that was a result of negative social relations to others. . . . Luke sees a direct link between their [=the Pharisees] concern for purity laws and their exploitation of people. The very Pharisees who are most eager to be ritually pure and to make society clean through the observance of purity laws are themselves unclean because they are greedy, plunderous, and wicked. Consequently, their claim to leadership is illegitimate. In terms of M. Sählin's classification system, this is "negative reciprocity," "the antisocial extreme"; it is taking from a client without giving anything in return. This is an accusation that is frequently voiced against leaders from common people.[32]

This criticism of the rich points to a second failure: refusal to act as benefactor toward those who seek assistance. Such refusal cuts social ties between the wealthy and the rest of the community. Purity laws could play into that pattern of behavior by legitimating withdrawal from relations with impure persons, a category into which the poor would almost inevitably fall.

We should not take the prevalence of such criticism in the New Testament and elsewhere as evidence that the economy of the Roman Empire was in any sense stagnant or declining. Such archaeological evidence as the volume of shipwrecks, the expansion of population, the extensive building projects, and the employment of even larger numbers in trades that took them away from the land all point to a flourishing economy. Some analysts even think that traditional models of the Roman economy should be modified to include genuine economic expansion during this period.[33] The artisan class to which Jesus as carpenter and Paul as tent maker belonged included individuals of substantial means. Consequently, Jesus may have been in the position to mediate between the subsistence level villagers and local wealthy patrons. His trade would have brought him into economic relationships with the latter. As a "holy man" and charismatic healer, He also functioned as mediator between the outcast and sick persons and their divine patron, God.[34] Though Jesus' call for unreciprocated generosity toward the debtor, afflicted, and poor and His challenge to the selfish blindness and preoccupation with individual security of the rich may appeal predominately to a peasantry that is already economically and socially marginalized as liberation theologians customarily hold,[35] that setting is not an appropriate description of the socioeconomic context from which Jesus and those followers about whom we have information emerge. Jesus' appeals for new forms of generosity make sense only if they are addressed to persons of some means and social standing.

This lengthy exploration of the socioeconomic context in which the New Testament emerged makes it evident that principles cannot simply be abstracted from their ancient setting and injected into a modern economic, legal, and social system. This fact is sometimes used to justify the claim that the New Testament has no economic message at all. Is it, then, the case that the Christian will support charitable ventures as an expression of his or her assent to the kind of generosity called for in the gospels purely as a matter of private piety? If so, then some would argue that Christianity has nothing to say in the public debate about the distribution of society's resources.

This view neglects the social concerns of the biblical tradition. The New Testament authors are acutely aware of the socioeconomic situation of their own time, and they do presume that persons ought to challenge some of the accepted patterns of socioeconomic exchange. The reasons behind their critique are not predominately economic, since New Testament writers assumed that both the economic system itself and the social hierarchy that distributes its benefits will remain in place until God's judgment ends the power relations of this world. Rather, the economic teaching of the New Testament, if I may call it that, is concerned with the social, communal, and personal relationships expressed by the various examples of economic exchange. Attempts to serve God and mammon such as those attributed to the Pharisees and the religious elite that controlled the Jerusalem temple rupture patterns of generosity and communal obligation. This division threatens the survival of persons whom society has pushed to its margins. In the name of God, Jesus takes up the cause of such "little ones":

For Matthew, the "little ones" are those who are "low" on the social scale—that is, both in regard to social prestige and in regard to economic status: they are in need of active mercy. . . . In 25:31–46 the "least" are not presented as coming solely from among Christians, for if they were, their benefactors would not be so astonished at the final judgment.[36]

SOCIAL ETHICS, ECONOMIC THEORY, AND SCRIPTURE

The New Testament criticism of greed-driven, egocentric acquisition by the wealthy raises the question of the value accorded to various modes of human activity. In order to ensure that economic resources are not hoarded in ways that ultimately destroy the community as a whole, the biblical writers invoke religious law and other forms of exemplary discourse to encourage the wealthy to return some of what they have gained to the community. Those in the conquered Roman provinces were acutely aware of the fact that Roman taxation took wealth from the community and thus impoverished it. Jewish, pagan, and Christian oracles all castigate Rome for depriving the eastern provinces of their wealth in order to feed the appetites of the distant capital. The following Jewish example is typical:

However much wealth Rome received from tribute bearing Asia, Asia will receive three times that much again from Rome and will repay her deadly arrogance to her. Whatever number from Asia served the house of Italians [= as slaves], twenty times that number of Italians will be serfs in Asia, in poverty and they will be liable to pay ten-thousandfold. O luxurious golden offspring of Latium, Rome, virgin, often drunken with your weddings with many suitors, as a slave you will be wed without decorum.[37]

Christians are familiar with polemic against bloodthirsty, prostitute, wealthy Rome, which takes very similar form in Revelation (e.g., Chapters 17 and 18).

In order to move from such descriptive analyses to evaluation of the modern situation, some scholars presume that the problem is bigness as such. Superpowers are now in the position of Rome vis à vis the economies of Third World countries, which are hostage to the greed of wealthy nations.[38] Such arguments depend upon observed similarities between the ancient and modern accounts that bypass the profound differences between our world and that of the Bible in conceptualization, knowledge, communication, and the sphere of human action. In the New Testament, the most an individual could anticipate was local reordering of personal, social, and economic relationships as a way to foster the well-being of local communities. Perceptions of justice and the "fit" between human actions and the values of a religious system were likewise locally managed. Most human needs, whether for food, shelter, companionship, education, or sex, were attached to the private sphere of the household. Now they are predominately the concern of the public realm, where they are often discussed not in terms of how best to provide for the human development, social interaction, and even religious expression of members of the community but in economic terms. What does it cost to deliver a certain level of service or security from risk in such areas? What is the cost if certain needs are not met either in programs of public welfare or in educational projects to warn people about risks such as AIDS?[39]

Warren Copeland identifies three competing definitions of justice in the writings of economists who would prescribe an economic policy to address contemporary woes: liberty, equality, and community. The biblical writings are fundamentally committed to community, though a strong doctrine of human sinfulness like that of St. Augustine or Calvin can lead Christian theologians to be suspicious of the values and requirements of community as well as the natural tendencies of individuals.[40] Copeland suggests that the social ethicist should introduce questions of value, especially those concerning the human need for creative action which provides for self-transcendence, into any vision of appropriate economic policy. There is no a priori reason to presume one economic system more capable of fostering a religious understanding of the relationships among persons, communities, and God than another. Copeland observes that the U.S. Roman Catholic bishops' pastoral letter on "Economic Justice for All" (1986) expresses principles that depend upon accepting the biblical priority given to community over liberty and equality. Its authors define solidarity as another name for "the social friendship and civic commitment that make human moral and economic life possible" (sec. 66).[41] But the letter's radical adherence to principles that imply a socialist, communitarian vision and adoption of economic policies appropriate to that structure disappears when the bishops turn to more conventional proposals for reform. There the dominant ethos is an essentially capitalist system of moderate individualism. The logical flaw in the argument lies in both the inability of the bishops to see the historical conditioning of the principles of communal solidarity taken from the biblical world and their willingness to recognize that calling for an organic society rather than one committed to pluralism and individualism is to express a social theory, not an abstract religious absolute.[42]

What the New Testament communities did for their time is possible in ours only if religious and symbolic commitments which were shaped by the ancient situation can be translated into patterns of behavior and value suited to shaping individual, social, and religious interactions in the context of modern communities as they actually exist, not as they are imagined to operate. The New Testament forged its socioeconomic vision from the perspectives of three different groups in society: the urban elite, which identified with the Roman order; the emergent artisan class, which valued the economic prosperity of the successful artisan;[43] and the peasant villager, who was a traditionalist and sought to hold onto what he had against outsiders. The New Testament does not in fact privilege any one of these perspectives, though Christianity's greatest success was among the artisan and trader class of the urban centers.[44] They responded to the call to create new forms of community, since they could not participate in the polis as citizens. Nor did they have the inherited communal structures of the village.

SOLIDARITY AS A RELIGIOUS IDEAL IN THE NEW TESTAMENT

The New Testament contribution to understanding the obligations of persons to one another in community, which is often described as solidarity in modern literature, developed among the gentile converts in the urban areas of the empire. Our best firsthand evidence for the views of these Christians comes from St. Paul's epistles. However, the authors of the gospels also address churches belonging to the Greek-speaking city areas. Consequently, the sayings and parables of Jesus, which originally addressed Galilean villagers, farmers, fishermen, and craftsmen, are viewed through the lens of the urban community.

Diaspora Jewish communities were the first source of converts to the new movement. Gentiles with an interest in Judaism, who had not became full proselytes, are prominent converts to Christianity. Jews in the diaspora had learned to create their own communal structures, to preserve their distinctive identity as a people. In its turn, first-century Christianity made socioeconomic demands on its members that were more characteristic of the diaspora Jewish communities than would have been the case in the other religious cults to which individuals might turn. However, refusal to participate in civic religious cults ensured that Jews and Christians would remain outsiders to the ruling elites in local cities, even if foreign origins had not excluded many from citizenship. Veyne finds a sectarian solidarity in Christian radicalism, which was made possible by the fact that early Christians were not responsible for the larger social order.

This was an "irresponsible" ethic . . . for the good reason that it was *by* a man and *for* men who bore no share of responsibility. All they had to do was to persuade each other to mitigate, for their mutual advantage, an order and laws of which they were not the authors and which they had never agreed to. . . . To turn the other cheek, instead of claiming one's right to retaliate against a brother in poverty: for one ought not to insist on getting one's due absolutely—even when justified, one should concede something to an opponent, and besides what good would it do for a poor man to plead before those in power? . . . Finally, there is one duty which is incumbent on all Jews and which serves as an emblem of all the rest—almsgiving. He who gives alms mitigates the harsh law of the economic order and puts himself in the place of the poor, feeling solidarity with them.[45]

Demands on the wealthy to act as benefactors to the poor members of the community can become strained when the normal patterns of reciprocal relationships and increased personal authority over the recipients are cut off by the egalitarian ethos of the community.[46] The wealthy must be content with the promise of a divine reward for those who renounce possessions in following Christ (Mark 10:23–31). Christianity also expands the boundaries for charity among members from concern about local, face-to-face communities, which is the basis of most benefactor relationships, to concern for distant churches. Christians insist on material assistance even for churches that have no personal links with their benefactors, as in St. Paul's collection for the church at Jerusalem.[47]

St. Paul also turned the artisan ethos of self-sufficient independence into a communal ethic of charity for members of the group which freed it from dependence upon outsiders (1 Thess. 4:11–12). This ethic had to be reaffirmed against some members who apparently abused communal resources supported by the religious claim that the "new age" had already arrived (2 Thess. 3:6–13). Paul's own example of laboring to provide for himself so that he could preach the gospel without burdening others (e.g., 1 Cor. 9)[48] implies that such labor enables Christians to "do good" to others (2 Thess. 3:13; cf. Acts 20:33–35). Paul also uses this ethos as evidence that he is not motivated by the greed and covetousness often charged against philosophical preachers who sought support from rich patrons. His churches are to be assured that he has their welfare at heart, not personal gain (e.g., 1 Thess. 2:3–12).[49] Exhorting his communities to live quietly, labor, and be dependent on no one may also have been a way of moderating the suspicions of outsiders.[50]

All of Paul's particular statements about desirable economic transactions between Christians—and those outsiders to whom they would also "do good" (cf., Gal. 6:10)—use the norms of charity and self-sufficiency to dismantle social benefactor-client relationships and the associated realities of inequality and the benefactor's authority over the lives of clients. By insisting upon the needs of the "weaker" Christians at Corinth, even when the "strong" uphold views that Paul supports (1 Cor. 10:23–11:1), Paul opposes the normal claims of the wealthy, educated elite to determine the lives and opinions of others in the church.[51] When Paul rejected the Corinthian suspicion that his refusal to demand communal support implied that he was somehow inferior to other preachers, he admitted that his behavior is contrary to the saying of Jesus, which told wandering missionaries to depend upon those to whom they preached for support (1 Cor. 9:14; cf. Matt. 10:8a–11).[52] Paul interprets the Jesus tradition as exemplifying a "right" he freely gives up.

This countercultural emphasis on generosity, which does not carry the obligations of benefactor-client relationships and hence preserves the equality of all members of the Christian community before God, reappears in the Lucan writings. Luke preserves sayings from the Jesus tradition that describe disciples who renounce possessions, home, and family in order to follow Jesus (e.g., 5:2–11, 27–28). Though Peter and the sons of Zebedee abandon family and trade (in which they were prosperous enough to own the boats) and Levi, a tax collector who is prosperous but socially stigmatized,[53] are willing to leave all to follow Jesus, the rich ruler cannot part with his possessions in order to do so (Luke 18:18–23). This episode evokes comments on the difficulty that the rich have in entering the Kingdom (verses 24–27). The danger that wealth poses for the follower of Jesus has also been expressed in the allegorical interpretation of the parable of the sower. The rich are the seed among thorns for whom the "cares and riches and pleasures of life" keep the seed from maturing and bearing fruit (Luke 8:14). The utopian portrait of the earliest Jerusalem community in the beginning of Acts (e.g., 2:44–47) describes a communal life of prayer and joyous sharing of meals in which no one is in need because those with wealth sell their possessions in order to provide for others.[54]

The tradition of shared possessions and meals which break down the barriers of socioeconomic status, in imitation of Jesus' meals with "sinners and tax collectors" (Luke 15:1–2), points to the significance of a solidarity that breaks with the norms of Greco-Roman society. Luke's teaching about possessions is directed toward the well-off, not the poor. The rich are to break with the usual benefactor-client relationships by giving to those who cannot repay. From the prosperous, Luke demands unreciprocated generosity: invite those who cannot repay to eat (14:13f.), keep giving to those who ask (6:30), lend to those who you know cannot repay (6:32–35).[55] Almsgiving (11:41; 12:23) is apparently Luke's understanding of how persons can "make friends from the mammon of unrighteousness" (16:9).[56]

Modern readers tend to find the shift between giving up all things to follow Jesus and almsgiving, which indirectly fulfills Jesus' promise that salvation has come for the poor,[57] disconcerting. They often perceive the former as radical and the latter as a moderating adaptation to the churches of prosperous Christians in the cities of the Pauline mission.[58] This perception is not sufficiently attentive to the way in which economic exchanges encode social relationships and make statements about the relative value of different groups of people before God. For the communities to which Luke speaks, sharing meals with the "despised" and extending unreciprocated generosity strain the conventions of fellowship and "close relations" well beyond the normal bounds of obligation. As Moxnes notes, even the simplest form of reciprocity, "gratitude" (praise, honor), is omitted:

It is rather the socioeconomic aspects of the relationship that is stressed. He is concerned with the type of relationship that this invitation will establish between the Pharisee and his guests: "invite . . . because they do not have that with which to repay you" (14:14). Jesus urges a social system without reciprocity. How could that be, and what kind of system is this? This is called vertical generalized reciprocity, that is, giving from the top downwards. In Sählin's terms, it is chiefly redistribution. Through this hospitality, the "poor, the maimed, the lame and the blind" are made members of the group, like the beggars at the house of Odysseus. Compared to Homeric society, however, the characteristic element in this exhortation is that there is no expectation of reciprocity; not even gratitude or praise is mentioned.[59]

Which is more radical? To abandon possessions in order to adopt the posture of a wandering, itinerant philosopher—a type with its own social mores that Paul must partially correct[60]—or to remain among one's associates and friends but restructure one's customary patterns of social and economic exchange in the ways that Luke proposes? In the gospel, the Pharisees criticize Jesus for the latter. Their complaints may also reflect the experience of Lucan Christians, maligned for their hospitality to those who do not belong to the class of respectable associates.

Where Jesus had contested rules of purity and honor with the Pharisees, Luke sees a system of redistribution in which patrons meet the needs of the poor in the community while renouncing the power that such benefaction would normally have given them. The norm for this new system is God: "With this change in systems, Luke brings in God as the source of redistribution and as the great benefactor. Luke does not say something new about God, but he brings a common, accepted belief in God to bear on this particular situation."[61] In attacking the conventional benefactor-client pattern, Luke negates the claims that any people might make to superiority over others. Luke is just as adamant as other New Testament writers that one's religious status is at stake in the reordering of socioeconomic relationships.

The Pauline letters and the gospels depict a Christianity that operates within the socioeconomic relationships of the ancient city. Its members, much like their Jewish counterparts, formed a cohesive group which focused on mutual assistance and face-to-face relationships that broke down social barriers within the group. However, Revelation, also addressed to churches in a number of prosperous cities of Asia Minor, finds such accommodations unacceptable. In order to avoid corruption by the evils of the Roman Imperial cult, a sharper break with society is required.

The prophet of Revelation castigates the prosperous community of Laodicea in Asia Minor for permitting its wealth to mask lukewarm discipleship (3:14–22). Christian economic activity is also limited by the seer's conviction that use of coins that carry the "mark of the beast"—that is, the imperial insignia—represents idolatry (Rev. 13:17).[62] Condemnations of Rome for the violence and economic appropriation of the wealth of her provinces form part of the author's vision of the coming divine judgment (Rev. 17:4; 18:11–13). Revelation clearly presumes that there is a tension, if not complete incompatibility, between wealth and discipleship. Attaining wealth in the expanding commercial world of Asia Minor's cities requires that disciples accommodate their Christian allegiance to "veneration of Caesar."[63] Consequently, the only social strategy available to the persecuted

Christian community is withdrawal from commercial exchange into a semi-isolation like that of the Essenes.

Those Christians at Laodicea who participated in the economic prosperity of the city at the end of the first century might well have appealed to inherited Pauline tradition (cf. Col. 4:13–17) to justify their activities. The Roman *imperium* bears a more benign visage in Rom. 13:1–7 and 1 Pet. 2:13–14 than in Revelation. Both Paul and 1 Peter presume that Christians will suffer persecution for their belief but do not advocate the type of sectarian withdrawal from engagement with the larger society that we find in Revelation and in some Jewish apocalyptic writings like 1 Enoch. More recent examples of sectarian withdrawal and partial economic isolation from a larger society which is seen to be corrupted with evil can be found in Christian communities from the Anabaptist tradition like the Amish and Mennonites or in communities of Hasidic Jews. In all of these examples, members sacrifice economic and personal independence to intense involvement with communal activities which are religious, social, and economic. In various ways the economic needs and activities of individuals and families are subordinate to religious and communal goals. An individual's economic choices may even be decided by those who are the religious leaders in the community. These contemporary examples indicate that the socioeconomic posture of Revelation is not inherently impossible today, however bizarre it may seem to mainstream Christians and Jews. Nor does it have to be sustained by the apocalyptic sense of living in the "last days"—a conviction which the Essenes maintained for the two-hundred-year history of their sect.

CONCLUSION

We have examined three facets of the New Testament picture of economic activity: the way in which sayings and parables of Jesus challenge the socioeconomic relationships of first-century Palestine; the modification of the artisan ethic in the Pauline letters; and the radical restructuring of generosity in communal relationships found in Luke-Acts. Each example adheres to the biblical perception that one's religious status is a function of how the exchanges of such limited goods as wealth and honor are distributed in the community. Its patterns of distribution must be different from those typical of the "evil age" in which believers find themselves living. Modern readers find this claim difficult to assess. Since we are constantly encouraged to identify ourselves in terms of material possessions rather than inherited personal or social relationships to others, loss of things may feel equivalent to loss of self-identity. It is this modern privileging of the economic category as a measure of personal independence and self-expression that makes it appear more radical to leave all things to follow Jesus than to enter into the new community of relationships that the Lucan images of economic exchange advocate.

Clearly, the socioeconomic messages of the New Testament are not modifications of a single set of simple principles. Though all of our examples agree that Christianity demands restructuring of communal, social, and religious behavior in ways that also demand changes in both the type and significance of an individual's economic exchanges with others, they cannot be said to support a single policy or even a single vision of Christian community. They all agree that Christians must distance themselves from relationships that are characteristic of the powerful people in their world. Relationships between Christians challenge the social divisions that support such power. However, the consequences of these general conclusions are by no means clear even within individual New Testament churches. Claims by liberation theologians and others to derive a single ideology or economic policy from New Testament evidence requires ignoring substantial evidence for real diversity within the New Testament itself.

There is a fundamental suspicion of wealth throughout the New Testament insofar as it gains a hold on persons so that they are no longer servants of the Lord (e.g., Matt. 6:19–21, 24). The power and apparent self-sufficiency that accompany wealth commonly isolated individuals from their communal obligations to less fortunate fellows for whom they should be benefactors (e.g., Luke 16:19–31). But these divisive attitudes are not limited to the rich in the New Testament. The unforgiving servant contrasts the generosity of the king with the servant's tenacious determination to extract the amount owed from a fellow servant (Matt. 18:23–35). The sayings against the all-consuming anxiety over subsistence (e.g., Matt. 6:11, 25–34) speak to the situation of the majority of the populace. Other negative examples of socioeconomic behavior by those at the lower end of society include the tenants who kill the owner's son (Mark 12:1–10) and the servants who resent the owner's gift of a day's wage to workers who had been left without employment until the last hour (Matt. 20:1–15). Solidarity requires that all members of the community, whatever their socioeconomic status, model their relationships to others on divine generosity. The New Testament is not concerned with economic conditions for their own sake. The questions it raises concern the social and religious attitudes expressed in the economic exchanges that occur between persons. This concern embraces both the tradition of almsgiving and the demand that socioeconomic relationships of domination and oppression be resisted.

NOTES

1. For a brief description of "embedded" economy as represented in the New Testament, see H. Moxnes, *The Economy of the Kingdom: Social Conflict and Economic Relations in Luke's Gospel* (Philadelphia: Fortress, 1988), 28–32.

2. See Paul Veyne, *Bread and Circuses. Historical Sociology and Political Plural- ism*, abridged with an introduction by Oswyn Murray, translated by Brian Pearce (London: Penguin/Allen Lane, 1990); Donald Engels, *Roman Corinth. An Alterna- tive Model for the Classical City* (Chicago: University of Chicago Press, 1990); and Reggie M. Kidd, *Wealth and Beneficence in the Pastoral Epistles* (Atlanta: Scholars Press, 1990).

3. Edward Gibbon, *The History of the Decline and Fall of the Roman Empire*, ed. H. H. Milman (Philadelphia: Porter and Coutes, 1845), I:95–96.

4. Justo L. Gonzalez, *Faith and Wealth. A History of Early Christian Ideas on the Origin, Significance and Use of Money* (San Francisco: Harper and Row, 1990), though admitting that his interest in the question stems from the questions raised by liberation theology, limits himself to just such a catalogue of opinions.

5. See Engels, *Roman Corinth*, 134–42.

6. Matthew Lamb, *Solidarity with Victims. Toward a Theology of Social Transfor- mation* (New York: Crossroad, 1982), 1.

7. See Kuno Füssel, "Materialist Readings of the Bible: Report on an Alterna- tive Approach to Biblical Texts," in *God of the Lowly. Socio-Historical Interpretations of the Bible*, ed. Luise Schottroff and W. Stegemann (Maryknoll, N.Y.: Orbis, 1984), 13–25; Dorothy Sölle, "Between Matter and Spirit: Why and in What Sense Must Theology Be Materialist?", in *God of the Lowly*, 86–102.

8. For examples of such reading, see Robert M. Brown, *The Bible through Third World Eyes* (Philadelphia: Westminster, 1986).

9. James M. Dawsey, "The Biblical Authority of the Poor," *Expository Times* 101–10 (July 1990): 295–98.

10. Veyne, *Bread and Circuses*, 31.

11. Ibid., 33.

12. See the discussion of Amos in Willy Schottroff, "The Prophet Amos: A Socio-Historical Assessment of His Ministry," in *God of the Lowly*, 27–46.

13. For an attempt to calculate the likelihood that the Galilean peasant had enough to subsist after taxes, religious tithes, rent, and grain needed for the next planting, see D. Oakman, *Jesus and the Economic Questions of His Day* (Lewiston, N.Y.: Edwin Mellen, 1986), 49–80.

14. *Roman Corinth*, 121–30.

15. Kidd, *Wealth and Beneficence*, 61–95.

16. See ibid., 93–98. Kidd points out that Plutarch decries those wealthy people whose "love of money" leads them to purchase a communal honor, which they do not deserve, or to overspend on benefactions, such as the games and shows demanded by the populace, which are not really to the benefit of the city.

17. Cf. Moxnes, *Economy*, 92, who notes other examples such as Luke 7:25, in which the life-style of the powerful, Herod's court, is compared unfavorably with that of the Baptist, and the mockery of Jesus before Herod by dressing the power- less victim in "royal apparel" (Luke 23:11).

18. Translation from J. H. Charlesworth, ed., *The Old Testament Pseudepigrapha*, (Garden City, N.Y.: Doubleday, 1983), vol. 1, 5–89. For a discussion of the parallels in the portrayal of wealth and the evil rich in the parables of Luke and 1 Enoch, see G. W. Nickelsburg, "Riches, the Rich and God's Judgment in 1 Enoch 92–105 and Luke's Gospel," *New Testament Studies* 25 (1978–79): 324–44.

19. This is apparently the case even though economic efficiency and equality are in conflict with each other. See the treatment of poverty in Paul A. Samuelson and William D. Nordhaus, *Economics*, 12th ed. (New York: McGraw Hill, 1985), 744–56.

20. Moxnes, *Economy*, 76–79.

21. N. Lewis, *Life in Egypt under Roman Rule* (Oxford: Clarendon, 1983), 22.

22. Moxnes (*Economy*, 62) notes that while helping a friend in need was expected, there was also the assumption that persons would not make excessive demands of friends.

23. See P. Veyne, *A History of Private Life 1: From Pagan Rome to Byzantium* (Cambridge: Harvard University Press, 1987), 175f. Rome was a state in which people did not obey laws but the orders of the governing class. Everything depended upon the relative strength of the parties in contention.

24. Lewis, *Life*, 79.

25. S. Ringe, *Jesus, Liberation and the Biblical Jubilee* (Philadelphia: Fortress, 1985).

26. See Pheme Perkins, *Jesus as Teacher* (New York: Cambridge University Press, 1990), 86–93.

27. Veyne (*Bread and Circuses*, 260–61) points out that in the Roman system, the powerful did not in fact need the support of the populace to gain or hold their offices. He concludes that the system of benefactions must fulfill a more general human desire to be well thought of in the community.

28. "Human Solidarity and the Goodness of God: The Parable of the Workers in the Vineyard," in *God of the Lowly*, 135.

29. Oakman, *Economic Questions*, 149.

30. Ibid., 151.

31. Moxnes, *Economy*, 4–9, 93–94.

32. Ibid., 112.

33. K. Greene, *The Archaeology of the Roman Economy* (Berkeley: University of California Press, 1986).

34. Oakman, *Economic Questions*, 196.

35. Cf. L. Schottroff and W. Stegemann, *Jesus and the Hope of the Poor* (Maryknoll, N.Y.: Orbis, 1986), 1–37.

36. Schottroff, "Human Solidarity," 144.

37. Sibylline Oracles iii, 350–58; Charlesworth *Old Testament*, 1:370.

38. Cf. R. A. Horsley's treatment of the infancy narratives as a political condemnation of the superpowers' policies in Latin America in *The Liberation of Christmas: The Infancy Narratives in Social Context* (New York: Crossroad, 1989).

39. W. Copeland, *Economic Justice. The Social Ethics of U.S. Economic Policy* (Nashville: Abingdon, 1988), 114, notes Hannah Arendt's protest that these concerns have largely crowded genuine politics in the classical sense off the agenda.

40. Ibid., 112.

41. Ibid., 129. The purpose of social institutions is to guarantee that all persons can participate actively in a society's economic, cultural, and political life (sec. 77).

42. Ibid., 138–41.

43. Veyne (*Private Life*, 176) thinks this ethos derived from the self-understanding of Athenian artisans. Praise of this version of self-sufficient craftsmanship is often attributed to Socrates in the early Platonic dialogues and represents a

certain suspicion of the traditional "wisdom" of the aristocracy and its claim to guide society.

44. This is the group most responsible for the spread of new religious movements throughout this period, as the development and diffusion of Manichaeism from the third century and Islam from the seventh demonstrate.

45. Veyne, *Bread and Circuses*, 22–23.

46. The strain between rich Christians, who sought to have a meal worthy of their friends, and the poor, who should have been content with the little they were given, corrupted Christian meal celebrations (1 Cor. 11:17–34). W. Meeks, *First Urban Christians* (New Haven: Yale University Press, 1983) 78f., notes that Christian benefactors even had to do without the elaborate titles of honor that their counterparts in pagan mystery cults (and to a lesser degree in Jewish synagogues) received.

47. Apparently a disaster in the short run, since the Jewish Christian community in Jerusalem was not certain that it would accept money from Paul's gentile churches in public fashion—perhaps because such an identification with non-Jews would have led to persecution from fellow Jews in Jerusalem. However, Paul's commitment to this collection among the gentile churches did establish a new communal principle that permitted "outsiders" to make a claim on the resources of a distant community (cf. Meeks, *Urban Christians*, 110).

48. A point of great contention between Paul and the Corinthians, who would have preferred that their apostle-founder demonstrate the "aristocratic leisure" of the philosopher supported by his wealthy patron "friends."

49. Cf. A. Malherbe, *Paul and the Thessalonians* (Philadelphia: Fortress, 1987), 15–20, 55f.

50. Ibid., 46f., 65.

51. Kidd finds the same phenomenon at work in the pastoral epistles. The parallel between ecclesial and social power is broken by warning the churches not to ordain those who are recent converts. Rich women patrons are excluded from any position in which their opinions might shape those of the community (*Wealth and Beneficence*, 84–86, 98–106).

52. The Jesus tradition prohibits the preachers from taking gold and silver with them, so they are not personally enriched by any hospitality that is received from the local community.

53. Schottroff and Stegemann (*Jesus*, 6–13) attempt to distinguish the attitude toward tax collectors by socioeconomic rank. The educated scorned and looked down on them, the tradesmen—who had the majority of the dealings with them—quarrelled with them, while the destitute poor had nothing to do with them. They argue that Luke's critique of the arrogant Pharisee (18:9–14) is really directed at "respectable" Christians who despise tax collectors and other poorly paid trades. However, the tax collector disciple in Luke's account is always a person of significant means. He is able to throw a large banquet in Jesus' honor (5:29; 19:2,6). The ambiguity in the narrative is that this gesture of commensalism is accepted by Jesus and the source of criticism by others who think that the hospitality of such persons should not be accepted. Moxnes's treatment of the significance of the meal in the pattern of economic exchanges in Luke (*Economy*, 87–90) does not address the socio-religious tension evoked when the meal in question is provided by a person considered marginal or an outsider. Luke underlines the tension by pre-

suming that the other guests at such occasions are "tax collectors and sinners," whose company Jesus is criticized for joining. The impoverished members of the community would have little occasion to worry about the status implications of accepting food from anyone who offered it (cf. the parable of the Great Banquet: Matt. 22:9–10; Luke 14:21–23). (Schottroff and Stegemann [*Jesus*, 16f.] have misread the evidence for the economic conditions in Palestine of this period.) Though liberation theologians characteristically place Jesus and His disciples among the destitute poor, the gospel traditions all presume that Jesus has sufficient resources and status to choose His company.

54. This description recalls the admiration expressed by Philo for the Essenes in which communal property, restricted economic activity (not hoarding gold and silver; not participating in any crafts that manufacture goods for armies), and the abolition of slavery have provided a setting in which the basic evils of human life in this world are already transcended: poverty, war, and slavery. Philo, *Quod Omnis Probus Liber sit*, 75–80.

55. This type of lending is classed as an example of "love of enemies."

56. R. Tannehill, *The Narrative Unity of Luke-Acts*. (Philadelphia: Fortress, 1986), 1:127–30.

57. Ibid., 129.

58. E.g., J. Fitzmyer's classification of the two traditions on wealth in Luke as "radical" and "moderate" in *The Gospel According to Luke I–IX* (AncBi 28; Garden City, N.Y.:Doubleday, 1981), 247–51. Fitzmyer emphasizes the eschatological element in Lucan teaching. Reversing some patterns of human behavior now anticipates the eventual reversal of the human condition (p. 250). New Testament writers are working out the implications of an eschatological vision, not seeking to reform the existing social structure.

59. Moxnes, *Economy*, 132.

60. E.g., Malherbe (*Paul*, 19) notes that Lucian's attack on the Cynics includes the charge that tradesmen abandoned their occupations in order to adopt that life-style.

61. Moxnes, *Economy*, 137.

62. Cf. A. Y. Collins, "Revelation," in *New Jerome Biblical Commentary*, ed. R. Brown, J. Fitzmyer, and R. Murphy (Englewood Cliffs, N.J.: Prentice Hall, 1990), 1003, 1009.

63. Ibid., 1013.

4

Tracing a Genealogy of "Talent": The Descent of Matthew 25: 14–30 into Contemporary Philanthropical Discourse

DAYTON HASKIN

This chapter takes as its starting point a telling feature of the autobiographies of wealthy Americans studied in Chapter 7 of this book by Paul Schervish. A number of people interviewed in his study of wealth and philanthropy enlist the concept of stewardship and in particular use the word "talent" to express a sense that they are accountable for how they use their wealth.[1] "The Bible teaches invest," says Patrick Lockwood. "Jesus gave these three guys talents. One He gave more to than the others, and one went and invested it and came back, and one guy was slothful and he buried it." Lockwood abstracts a general moral from this story, expressing it in language borrowed from what the Book of Genesis (1:28) reports as God's original command to humankind: "So I believe," he says, "we ought to be fruitful and multiply what we have. You're responsible for what God gives you."

Patrick Lockwood is representative rather than unusual in voicing a sense of accountability. Drawing on extensive interviews, Schervish has concluded that the idea that their wealth is held in trust is "one of the most significant forces that shapes the consciousness" of those who have inherited it. By this metaphor, wealthy persons express a "perception" that they live under "a strong ethical imperative of obligation and responsibility" to put their money to "productive uses." While those who have inherited their wealth seem likeliest to compare themselves to stewards, transcripts of the interviews show that those who have acquired it by other means are equally insistent that they feel socially accountable for the disposition of their resources. Wealthy people from both groups express a consciousness of obligation by invoking the idea that they have been given many gifts, and they urge that they feel duty-bound to use their "talents." To these conclusions drawn by Schervish, I would add that by expressing such a perception in terms that are ultimately derived from the Christian Bible, the wealthy are also attempting to legitimate their holdings.

The so-called parable of the talents in Matthew 25:14–30 is the text from which the modern concept of "talent" has descended. Schervish's studies make it clear that many wealthy people find this parable useful for articulating a sense of their position in the world. Here, I will trace the history of how this parable has been interpreted and applied through the centuries, with a view to understanding the apparent utility of the concepts of talent and stewardship in these recent attempts to legitimate the holding of wealth. In other words, I mean to explore some ways in which the biblical parable has been and continues to be used in framing ethical questions. The guiding assumptions, which I share with the other contributors to this volume, are that the consciousness in which ethical questions are framed and pursued is a worthy object of scrutiny and that developing a critique of consciousness has become, at our moment in history, a crucial operation in any quest to promote socially just behavior.

If the study of wealth and philanthropy provides my starting point, the decidedly historical perspective I want to offer has also been inspired by Pheme Perkins's chapter in this book, "Does the New Testament Have an Economic Message?" Perkins describes some substantial differences between economic structures in the ancient world and the modern. She concludes her description of the socioeconomic context in which the New Testament was created by insisting "that principles cannot simply be abstracted from their ancient setting and injected into a modern economic, legal, and social system." This does not mean, she contends, that the New Testament has no economic message. In the latter part of her essay, she shows that in the New Testament there is an extensive, perhaps even pervasive, suspicion of wealth insofar as the pursuit of it proves a threat to Godlike generosity and human solidarity. Moreover, she proposes that because economic categories now exert a privileged role in interpreting human experience and because personal independence and self-expression are considered values of the first order, modern readers are likely to overlook or misconstrue what may be the most challenging implications of the New Testament's diverse teaching on wealth and possessions. That teaching, she maintains, involves a varied but fairly constant insistence that "Christians must distance themselves from relationships that are characteristic of the powerful people in this world."[2] In light of her findings, we may ask to what extent contemporary interpretations of the biblical parable of the talents (especially as these appear in philanthropical discourse) may be deemed responsible and legitimate.

A third influence on the shaping of my questions was Simon Schama's study in *The Embarrassment of Riches* of the unprecedented prosperity experienced by the Dutch in the seventeenth century.[3] This work has helped to raise the question, "In a period of especially intense Bible-reading, what economic message was the Bible thought to have?" Schama has shown how extensively the Dutch used the Bible as "a sourcebook of analogies for their own contemporary history." The Book of Exodus, for example, served to legitimate an historic rupture by which they were cut off from the past and looked hopefully to a providential future. What Shama has referred to as the Dutch "patriotic scripture," that is, their appropriation of ancient biblical materials for new political purposes, he shows to have been richly complex and to have served diverse purposes, many of them contradictory. By accommodating their experience persistently and yet variously to biblical precedents, the Dutch were able to create for themselves a sufficiently large imaginative space within which to negotiate their "embarrassment." In this respect, the Dutch experience, far from constituting further evidence for the popular theory whereby wealth is said to have functioned in early modern Europe as a sign of election, shows that Protestants could be profoundly agitated by their material success. Repeatedly, they ruminated on *overvloed*, "a drowning surfeit" (p. 124). They were as likely to interpret their success as a temptation as to see in it a godly reward. Their Bible was not a stable source of meaning ready to be appropriated for capitalist purposes. They found in it rival interpretations of their experience and varying perspectives with which they could criticize new economic relations. In short, Schama's study helps us to frame questions about what others living in different times, places, and circumstances, have made out of biblical materials, especially materials that explicitly concern the ethical uses of wealth. My study of how the parable of the talents has been interpreted in earlier eras is meant to provide a counterpoint to recent appropriations of it by persons who seem to assume that its meaning is timeless and transparent.

In dwelling at length upon the early modern period, I will emphasize that the parable can be made to mean many different and often contradictory things, but I do not mean to imply that modern readers ought to return to an "authentic" interpretation that was in place in a lost golden age. My survey shows that in various epochs of history readers bring different concerns and questions, even radically different assumptions, to the processes by which they derive meaning from the parable. This means that both opportunities and temptations change over time, especially with changes in economic conditions and human consciousness. In our time people have an opportunity to find in the parable inspiration for productive philanthropy, as evidenced in a number of cases in Schervish's study; the corresponding temptation is to find in the parable grounds for an essentially private cultivation of self. Similarly, those with a well-developed historical consciousness can discern analogies across time that make the parable, even among persons who do not regard the Bible as normative for their own lives, prove challenging to whatever is unjust in the status quo. At the same time we should acknowledge that those who would relegate the Bible to a past that is deemed no longer pertinent in our radically changed circumstances and those who assume that this literature has already been rendered compatible with existing power relations thereby seek to neutralize the enduring challenges to be found in the complex economic message of the New Testament.

In choosing a time frame for this chapter, I have taken a longer historical view than Schervish, Perkins, and Schama. Inevitably, then, it is a more narrowly focused view. I have not settled on the parable of the talents at random. It is a biblical text that, as we will see, literally concerns the use of money and as such offers a perspective, at any particular period in the history of its interpretation, on the relations of money and religion in the consciousness of its interpreters. We will also see that the economic implications of the parable were mostly suppressed in early Christian history and throughout the period of European feudalism. Since the seventeenth century, however, with the emergence of a capitalist economy in the West, the parable has proved extraordinarily serviceable in some ways that were unprecedented. This serviceability now seems well established, as the frequent references to the parable by wealthy "stewards" in the study on wealth and philanthropy reveals.

Without doubt, in the past three or four centuries this parable has often served to encourage the idea that amassing wealth provides evidence of election and assurance of salvation. On the face of it, this would seem to be the great bourgeois parable and the scriptural confirmation par excellence of the Protestant work ethic. It emphasizes the importance of accumulating capital, it promises a large return on investments, and it provides a vivid example of punishing laziness. In a memorable structural pattern of repetition and contrast, it presents, in terms of fiscal growth and stagnation, the norms by which individual persons are to be judged. The judge is himself a wealthy businessman, who entrusts large but unequal sums of money to three employees. He returns later to receive their financial reports. The most highly endowed trustee has by then doubled his funds, and he receives congratulations and a promotion. Likewise, the next most well endowed. The man with the single talent, however, is castigated for having failed to provide a return on the investment. The businessman takes all his money away from him and gives it to the one who made the largest return; and he makes a public scene of firing the sluggard and kicking him out.

Or so the parable will seem to say when paraphrased in a modern idiom. Whether and to what extent this interpretation may be deemed legitimate is a question I will attempt to pose only later, after having surveyed the history of how the parable has been interpreted and put to use in other eras. My working assumption is that taking into account alternative interpretations helps to defamiliarize the currently dominant understandings of the parable and helps as well to unsettle a number of assumptions about the nature and applicability of biblical materials that many persons are likely to import into their attempt to answer this question.

This study proposes that the meaning and implications of the parable are not transparent and that the current sense of the world "talent" obscures more than it reveals about early Christian interpretations of the biblical text from which it is derived. I do not mean to imply that it is my goal to provide either a normative definition of the word "talent" or a definitive interpretation of the parable.[4] The current senses of the word "talent" are not assumed here to be lineal descendants of some original discourse to which the present owes allegiance. They are seen as the fossil record of successive upheavals in Western history. This assertion implies that my goals here may be understood to be on the model of an anthropological concept of genealogy. This is a process that Michel Foucault has usefully described as "the violent or surreptitious appropriation of a system of rules . . . in order to impose a new direction, to bend it to a new will, to force its participation in a new game."[5] Such an appropriation or bending may have, I assume, both positive and negative outcomes. Those outcomes may be inextricably linked with one another. The sedimentation that we will be examining is what has made it possible in our time to inflect the world "talent" with various and often contradictory implications.

A TEXT OF THE PARABLE AND A BRIEF HISTORY OF THE WORLD "TALENT"

At this point it will be useful to have the entire text of the parable before us. Before including it, however, a few other assumptions should be made clear. Modern biblical scholarship points out that it is likely that, whatever story Jesus may have told in Aramaic, the parable that we have in Matthew's gospel, which was written in Greek, bears unmistakable signs of a redactor's alterations and adaptations. There is, after all, a similar parable in Luke's gospel, where the monetary denomination (often rendered as pounds in English Bibles) is much slighter, the number of servants entrusted with money greater, and the amounts of money are distributed equally to all. Luke includes his version of the parable just after telling the story of Zaccheus, a rich tax collector who repents and makes restitution to those whom he has cheated. For his part, Matthew places the parable in what he represents as Jesus' last discourse before His Passion, between the parable of the ten virgins and the vision of the final judgment. In other words, Matthew's version of the parable, although it exaggerates the amounts of money involved, at the same time downplays the ostensible injunction to accumulate wealth; and, by following the talents with the story of the separation of the sheep and goats, Matthew provides a climactic insistence upon socially responsible conduct toward the hungry, naked, and imprisoned. (There are various other differences between the parables in Matthew and Luke that might be noted; for our purposes here, these will suffice.)

Given a disposition not to accord normative status to any particular interpretation of the parable, there is a question of what version to cite here. Few readers will be able to follow Matthew's "original" Greek, and clearly some translation into English is in order. (It may be observed, by the way, that the issue is not the rendering of the Greek *talanton*; virtually all English translations of every period seem to enlist the world "talent.") I have chosen the Authorized or King James Version on two (seemingly contradictory) grounds: the breadth of its dissemination and the relative foreignness of its language. The King James Version has been, historically, the most widely influential of all translations into English. Yet, to an untrained twentieth-century ear, it sounds antiquated and may for that very reason serve to suggest something of the ancient and foreign quality of a parable first told many hundreds of years ago in a culture very unlike that of modern America.

[14]For *the kingdom of heaven* is as a man traveling into a far country, *who* called his own servants, and delivered unto them his goods. [15]And unto one he gave five talents, to another two, and to another one; to every man according to his several ability; and straightway took his journey. [16]Then he that had received the five talents went and traded with the same, and made *them* other five talents. [17]And likewise he that *had received* two, he also gained other two. [18]But he that had received one went and digged in the earth, and hid his lord's money. [19]After a long time the lord of those servants cometh, and reckoneth with them. [20]And so he that had received five talents came and brought other five talents, saying, Lord, thou deliveredst unto me five talents: behold, I have gained beside them five talents more. [21]His lord said unto him, Well done, *thou* good and faithful servant: thou hast been faithful over a few things, I will make thee ruler over many things; enter thou into the joy of thy lord. [22]He also that had received two talents came and said, Lord, thou deliveredst unto me two talents: behold, I have gained two other talents beside them. [23]His lord said unto him, Well done, good and faithful servant; thou has been faithful over a few things, I will make thee ruler over many things: enter thou into the joy of thy lord. [24]Then he which had received the one talent came and said, Lord, I knew thee that thou art a hard man, reaping where thou hast not sown, and gathering where thou hast not strewed: [25]And I was afraid, and went and hid thy talent in the earth: lo, *there* thou hast *that is* thine. [26]His lord answered and said unto him, *Thou* wicked and slothful servant, thou knewest that I reap where I sowed not, and gather where I have not strewed: [27]Thou oughtest therefore to have put my money to the exchangers, and *then* at my coming I should have received mine own with usury. [28]Take therefore the talent from him, and give *it* unto him which hath ten talents. [29]For unto every one that hath shall be given, and he shall have abundance: but from him that hath not shall be taken away even that which he hath. [30]And cast ye the unprofitable servant into outer darkness: there shall be weeping and gnashing of teeth.

For understanding the history of the parable, the single most important observation to be made is that in the Koine Greek of the first-century Mediterranean world the word *talanton* did not denote natural abilities. The word, which seems to derive from the Greek root *tla-* (meaning "to bear"), referred in the first instance to a unit of weight, and a heavy weight at that. In time it came also to denominate a unit of money (cf. the English word "pound"). In fact, it was the largest unit of all, so that a talent (whatever its equivalent in modern currency might be, if it were possible to propose an exchange rate across time and between radically different economic systems) was a very large amount of money. Clearly, all three servants in Matthew's parable, even the one with only a single talent, were entrusted with such large sums that, if the money had been their own, they would all be considered wealthy.

The sense of the English word designating a "mental endowment" or "natural ability" seems ultimately to be derived from the parable in Matthew 25.[6] The *Oxford English Dictionary* records as the earliest instance of this sense of the word a passage from an early fifteenth-century poem. Over the course of centuries, a certain allegorical interpretation of the parable had become so widely disseminated and deeply entrenched that, not only in English but in most of the languages of Western Europe,[7] the word "talent" came to be used with increasing frequency to refer to natural abilities. Two observations on this development are in order. First, the creation of the modern sense of "talent" differing from the one designating weight or money is somewhat remarkable in that, in verse 15, the parable explicitly distinguishes between money and abilities when it says that the lord gave talents "to every man according to his several ability." Secondly, the degree to which the more recent sense has almost completely displaced the ancient sense in twentieth-century usage entails a suppression of the economic inflection of the term. This suppression dates back into the patristic period of church history, when the parable was (as we shall see in the section that follows) commonly applied to the situation of the clergy. Nonetheless, there has always been a certain consciousness on the part of some, especially the more learned, that "talent" referred in the ancient world to a unit of money.

INTERPRETATION OF THE PARABLE IN ERAS PRIOR TO THE RISE OF CAPITALISM

In the New Testament

The parable in Matthew's gospel is not utterly unique in the New Testament. Its relation to the parallel in Luke's gospel (19:11–27) has long been debated; and there is no mistaking the fact that details unique to one have often been intruded, sometimes silently, into the interpretation of the other. The focus here falls on Matthew because only his gospel enlists the term "talent," and so my concern is to notice how details from Luke have influenced the interpretation of Matthew. This is not to deny that influence has also worked in the other direction, frequently resulting in a confluence. Probably the most telling detail from Luke that has been used in interpreting Matthew's parable is the instruction recorded in verse 13, which makes the lord's expectation explicit: "And he . . . said unto them, Occupy till I come" (in the Vulgate, *negotiamini dum venio*). Probably the most common confusion in remembering Matthew's version has been a substitution of the image of hiding money in a napkin (Luke 19:20) for that of burying the single talent.

From the point of view of modern biblical scholarship, it seems just to remark that both parables may represent adaptations of a single original told by Jesus, that they may be based on different parables, or even that one or both may have been composed by the evangelists or other early disciples on the model of parables that their teacher had told. It is a presupposition of such scholarship that a literary unit such as this parable is decidedly not something like a transcript of Jesus' (Aramaic) words and actions. After Jesus' earthly career, the gospels developed through a period of oral transmission. The canonical gospels as we now have them in Koine Greek represent the results of considerable adaptation of the materials through the course of a generation or two. When we consider the gospels of Matthew and Luke as wholes, some of the differences between the two versions of the parable can be seen to be congruent with consistent patterns. Matthew tends to place his materials in urban settings, for instance, to tell stories that involve large sums of money, and to be especially concerned with the motif of judgment.

It has been a principal concern of biblical scholarship since the nineteenth century to attempt to reconstruct, so far as this is possible, the history of the process of transmission. Scholars have found helpful a hypothesis that underlies the description I have given in the preceding paragraph, namely, that the life of Jesus, the period of oral transmission, and the period in which the oral materials were transcribed constitute more or less separable periods, and that it is to some extent possible to reconstruct what happened in each. This hypothesis helps readers to see that, from the first century onward, Jesus' parables were already being adapted and applied analogously in altered situations. Whereas Jesus likely spoke a parable addressed to peasants, who were slow to take the risk of following His teaching, later generations of His followers, having preserved a memory of the parable, read it allegorically as an injunction to spread the Word and to make converts to a new religion. If we assume that the sums of money in Luke's gospel are closer to the "original" parable and that Matthew raised the sums to "talents," then this suggests he was redirecting the message of the parable to the situations of persons who could imagine themselves, like the stewards in the parable, as having unusually large responsibilities. Such adaptations show that aspects of Jesus' teaching that may have been tailored to one set of concrete circumstances were early on thought to be susceptible to reinterpretations to fit altered circumstances. Adaptations were accomplished by assuming that the teaching could be made to answer general questions that spanned historical, geographical, and ethnic changes. For instance, it might be assumed that the parable of the talents is meant to answer a question such as, "How do I as an individual insert myself into the public world?" Or, "How do I do what is right and get rewarded?"

Since there is an enormous body of scholarly commentary on the gospels in general, and on the parable of the talents in particular, it would be impossible to summarize it and presumptuous to attempt to select from this astonishing mass a single line of interpretation that might be presented as normative. What requires emphasis here, as I decline to provide a lengthy section setting out the "original" meaning of the parable, is that were I to attempt it, it would be precisely a work of reconstruction. Much of what I would have to say, even if it were entirely true and brilliantly perceptive, would have been entirely unknown to the vast majority of people who have read the parable through history, from the second century to the twentieth. This is not to denigrate the valuable work performed by modern biblical scholars, but only to insist that this work is itself historically conditioned. The idea of recovering the way things "actually" happened, *wie es eigentlich gewesen*, reached a climax in the massive historical projects undertaken in the nineteenth century. In our century, with good reason, new grounds of skepticism about how accurately and objectively the past can be reconstructed have dampened the enthusiasm that marked nineteenth-century projects. Still, there has remained in biblical scholarship a significant residue of the older historians' agenda, motivated to some extent by habits tied to the classic Protestant commitment to "the Bible only," apart from human traditions. Twentieth-century biblical scholarship represents an approach to the text that befits an era with a well-developed historical consciousness and with tools for reconstruction (archeological excavations, knowledge of little known ancient languages, sophisticated theories of historiography) not available earlier.

My concern in this and the next major section is to characterize the principal ways in which the parable of the talents was understood in the patristic, medieval, and Renaissance periods. Much of what I have to report will be strikingly different from what those who think that the Bible teaches timeless truths might expect, and to them in particular much of this matter may seem tiresome and irrelevant. Yet it is precisely the seemingly intractable difference and irrelevance that makes these materials valuable for raising the questions that need ultimately to be explored.

In the Writings of the Church Fathers

There is no sharp line distinguishing patristic from medieval interpretations of the parable. Many of the views put forward by the church fathers were repeated for about a millennium, and some remain prevalent today. Still, because the first four or five hundred years of Christian history were formative, I should like to separate them out for consideration.

There is already a good deal of evidence in the canonical gospels that by the end of the first century Jesus' parables were being read allegorically. The lengthy explanation of the parable of the sower (Matt. 13) is a case in point. In the patristic period the parables were subjected to a variety of allegorical activities, and by the end of the period Augustine had formulated a theory that encouraged a multiplicity of interpretations. From the large body of commentary on the parable produced by this allegorical activity, certain broad lines of interpretation became well established. It was widely agreed, for instance, that the man going away at the start of the parable represents Christ, that his departure takes place after the Crucifixion, and that his return figures the Second Coming. Beyond this, it was commonly thought that the reward given to the faithful servants signifies the blessings of salvation, and the punishment meted out to the unfaithful servant refers to damnation.

There was a much greater variety of interpretation, however, when it came to other details. What did the "talents" signify? What did it mean to "multiply" talents or to "bury" a talent? What was the significance of the differences between Matthew's parable and the similar one in Luke? Who (what group or class of persons) was represented by the three servants, and to whom did the parable apply? What, to be even more specific, was to be made of the fact that in Matthew 25:29 the lord commands that the single talent be taken from the man who had not invested it and given to the man who already had ten talents?

A coherent tradition of answering these questions seems already to have been taking shape by the third century. The parable was frequently supposed to apply conspicuously to the situation of bishops and other prelates, whose positions of power and influence made them analogous to persons who had been entrusted with considerable sums of money.[8] Origen (c. 185–c. 254), in a homily on Exodus 35, when he came to expounding a particularly difficult passage, enlisted the parable of the talents in a long digression, explaining to his auditors that this parable teaches the duty that each person has to do something with God's Word. "Interest on the word of God," he explained, accrues when we put into deeds the words that we have heard. "If, then, when you hear the word, you use it and act according to those words which you hear and live according to these words, you are preparing interest for the Lord. Each of you can make ten talents from 'five talents' and hear from the Lord, 'Well done.' "[9] Similarly, Clement of Alexandria (fl. c. 200), in introducing his miscellanies, presented the activities of preaching and writing about the Word as a fulfillment of this parable.[10] Already there was a tendency to define burying the talent in ways that suppressed its monetary sense: "burying" was read as a failure to take the Word seriously, whether out of a desire to enjoy earthly wealth and glory or out of mere slothful neglect.

Several church fathers appealed to the parable to urge that the preeminent responsibility of bishops is communicating the Word. St. Athanasius, in a letter written in the mid-fourth century, invoked it to chide a bishop who had been negligent in this matter. St. Augustine proposed a similar interpretation in a similar situation, claiming that one of the ways in which those entrusted with the Word are to fulfill the parable is by "answer[ing] murmurers." He went on to castigate bishops who fail to attend to their charges and heads of households who show little concern for the spiritual welfare of their families. In a sermon preached at the consecration of a bishop, St. Caesarius of Arles (d. 543) connected reading the Scriptures and preaching and teaching out of them with multiplying talents.[11] In short, the dominant line of interpretation in the period read the "talent" as the Word of God, or as doctrine, and proposed that talents are "multiplied" by interpreting the Word and putting it into action. This was taken to be preeminently the responsibility of those in holy orders, although some preachers were at pains to apply lessons from the parable, proportionately, to the situation of all Christians. Among these, John Chrysostom (c. 345–407) stands in the first rank. "What Christ showed by the parable was this," Chrysostom explained:

After hearing a sermon (for this is depositing the money), those who have received the instruction must make it produce interest. The interest from the teaching is nothing other than proving through deeds what you have been taught through words. Since I have deposited my money in your ears, you must now pay your teacher back interest, that is, you must save your brothers.[12]

Chrysostom referred to the parable frequently, sometimes acknowledging that fulfilling it was burdensome and likely to cost energy, money, or even bodily pain. In his view, the talents "are each person's ability, whether in the way of protection, or in money, or in teaching, or in what thing soever of the kind." Preeminently, they are the human power of speech. He paraphrases the Lord's observation that the one-talent man should have invested the money, urging that one ought "to have spoken, to have admonished, to have advised." As he insisted that the parable teaches the necessity of good works and an obligation to bring one's neighbor to salvation, he proposed that the human power of speech requires to be diligently cultivated and ever used "for the common advantage."[13] While others seem often to have cited the parable in threatening tones, Chrysostom sometimes proposed more generous interpretations of its implications. He once began a homily by insisting that one's "spiritual wealth" is increased when one gives it to others, that a spiritual treasure is multiplied for both those who hear the Word and those who speak it: "he who shares with others increases the wealth he has on hand, while the one who conceals his wealth diminishes his whole profit."[14]

Among the more remarkable uses to which the parable was put among the fathers, however, is the construction placed on it almost incidentally in the preface to Augustine's *De Doctrina Christiana*. While setting out what amounts to the most sophisticated account of the interpretive rules for reading that has survived from the period, Augustine quotes the condemnation the lord pronounces on the slothful servant, deploying it as a threat to readers who, whether through sloth or because of extraordinary pride, excuse themselves from the obligation to consult other reliable interpreters. Those who suppose that they can directly extract an understanding of the Scriptures without the help of others he compares to the man who buried his talent—and deserved the condemnation he got:

Every one who boasts that he, through divine illumination, understands the obscurities of Scripture, though not instructed in any rules of interpretation, at the same time believes, and rightly believes, that this power is not his own, in the sense of originating with himself, but is the gift of God. . . . But reading and understanding, as he does, without the aid of any human interpreter, why does he himself undertake to interpret for others? Why does he not rather send them direct to God . . . ? The truth is, he fears to incur the reproach: "Thou wicked and slothful servant, thou oughtest to have put my money to the exchangers." Seeing, then, that these men teach others, either through speech or writing, what they understand, surely they cannot blame me if I likewise teach not only what they understand, but also the rules of interpretation they follow. For no one ought to consider anything as his own, except perhaps what is false. . . . For what have we that we did not receive?[15]

In the paragraph that follows, without any more direct allusion to the parable, Augustine offers an especially powerful interpretation of what it means to "multiply" talents: it is far better, he proposes, to teach people how to interpret than it is to teach them the (right) interpretation of any particular passage. This perspective bore a variety of fruits.

Further Allegorical Interpretations in the Medieval Period

If in the patristic period there was a decided tendency to interpret the parable with reference to powerful officials and authorized interpreters within the ecclesiastical hierarchy, in the medieval period the parable was more often considered to have wider applicability. By the late Middle Ages, as the emergence of the transferred sense of "talent" meaning natural aptitude or ability attests, the parable was well known, having been disseminated both in popular artwork and in the liturgy, where it was regularly read on feast days commemorating a confessor pope.[16] Most people in Western Europe seem to have been familiar with the parable through preaching. Since sermons typically involved allegoresis, allegorical interpretations multiplied, as if in fulfillment of the patristic allegory whereby the story was read as an injunction to spread the meaning of the Word. Various and divergent interpretations were not only accepted but encouraged, as long as they could be considered compatible, as Augustine had framed the rule, with the general tenor of the gospel and the dictates of charity.[17]

The interpretations that have survived are likely the more pious and charitable ones. There is some evidence, however, and it dates back to the period of the early church, that the parable was sometimes interpreted in racial terms.[18] In its nastier form, this line of interpretation assimilated the unfaithful servant, who hid his talent, to the Jews, who were said to have failed in fidelity to the Torah when they rejected Christ. A less overtly anti-Semitic interpretation saw in the first servant (there were, after all, five books of Torah) the conversion of the Jews and in the second servant the conversion of the gentiles. The slothful servant was at some times taken as a figure for unconverted Jews and at others (as we have seen) as a negligent Christian clergyman. In any event, such interpretations were a two-edged sword, since they could be readily invoked to justify forceful conversions as if in fulfillment of Christ's teaching. As more and more Europeans were baptized at birth, what had been an early emphasis among the fathers, the idea that the parable enjoined the making of converts to Christianity, was altered to accommodate a more usual situation.

It was Gregory the Great (c. 540–604) who gave definitive formulation to the idea that the parable teaches the obligation of converting nominal Christians to morally upstanding ones.[19] This was a work which, although it might especially befit clergymen, could be practiced by everyone. In fact, one change in the interpretive tradition during this period was that the enormity of the sums seems to have been forgotten, or deemed irrelevant. This made it possible to apply the lessons of the parable more broadly to persons of every rank and station, even to those who were not literate.

Another interpretive allegory, one that will (as I promised earlier) likely seem implausible and irrelevant to twentieth-century readers, was often repeated. Already in the patristic period St. Jerome had proposed that the five talents suggest the five (carnal) senses, the two talents understanding and action, and the one talent reason. This interpretation was reiterated by Gregory the Great and by many others, sometimes with various nuances, for hundreds of years. "The five talents," said Gregory, "represent the gift of the five senses, that is, knowledge of externals; the two talents signify theory and practice; the one talent signifies theory alone."[20] What is striking about this line of interpretation is that it sees the second servant as the most privileged and makes the first servant, despite his greater number of talents, relatively needy. (One advantage of this was that it helped to explain why the lord, when he takes the single talent away from the slothful servant, gives it to the man who already has ten.) This allegory is not without considerable significance in the history we are tracing, for it marks a certain keenness of attention to the fact that the servants in Matthew's parable (unlike those in Luke's) have differing and unequal capacities, and it attempts to make some sense of this by emphasizing that in telling the parable Jesus must have been referring to differing spiritual gifts. This sort of interpretation helped to establish the idea that the story might have different applications for different persons, and suggested that its requirements are tailored to the particular situations of individuals. Gregory's proposal that because their talents were of different orders "the one who received two had more than the one who received five" prompted attention to differences that might prove either beneficial, by promoting respect, or detrimental, by providing grounds for unjust discrimination. As in every era, an interpretive breakthrough ushered in new possibilities and new dangers for applying the message of the parable.

The most important development during the patristic and medieval periods was a growing emphasis on the idea that the parable teaches lessons of social responsibility. There is nothing in the parable per se that spells out the idea that multiplying talents means anything more than amassing a larger sum of money. Yet Matthew followed the parable with the vision of the Last Judgment, in which a king will judge each person according to the ways in which he has dealt with the "least brethren." This sequence often served to delimit the possible range of meanings for the idea of multiplying talents, even to suggest a content for what it means to multiply them. Chrysostom's sermon on Matthew 25:1–30 (the ten virgins and the talents) emphasized that the parable is meant as a threat to those who "neither in money, nor in word, nor in protection, nor in any other things whatever, are willing to assist their neighbors, but withhold all." Chrysostom went on to insist that "nothing is so pleasing to God, as to live for the common advantage."[21] The assumption that the parable teaches lessons of socially responsive and responsible conduct became established early and seems to have remained firmly in place throughout the entire medieval period. In the early modern period, there is abundant evidence that preachers, exegetes, commentators, and ordinary Christians came to feel this feature of the traditional interpretation to be particularly threatened.

INTERPRETING AND APPLYING THE PARABLE IN THE EARLY MODERN ERA

In Early Protestantism

In this section I will concentrate, somewhat arbitrarily, on interpretations that have been at one time or another available within the English-speaking world. The sixteenth century marks not only the time when, belatedly, the Renaissance reached England, it also marks, throughout Europe, the birth of Protestantism. With the sense of urgency for getting the Bible into the vernacular languages and into the hands of ordinary people facilitated by the development of printing, it is not surprising that a massive amount of evidence about how people were reading the parable has survived from this period. In my own field, literary studies, there has been in recent years a decided emphasis on the distinctively Protestant ethos of writing from the English Renaissance.[22] Scholars have charted a "Protestant poetics" that grew out of sixteenth-century biblical commentary, meditation manuals, emblem books, and *ars praedicandi* materials. Vigorous attention to the Protestant ethos in which Donne and Herbert and Milton wrote religious poetry has given a proper acknowledgment to the biblical pretexts with which Renaissance writers often worked. It has also underlined the importance of understanding how people were reading their Bibles. This critical approach has often, however, obscured the degree to which biblical interpretation was, even in the era of the Council of Trent and the Synod of Dort, carried out across denominational lines as well as across national boundaries. In many instances Protestant and Catholic interpreters worked together in the quest to find the meaning of the Scriptures for contemporary life, and this is particularly true of interpretations of the parable of the talents. Despite the fact that the parable looks as if it calls for action, Catholics were not dragging out this text to prove the insufficiency of "faith alone," and Protestants were not much troubled by the implication in the parable that Christ was teaching the necessity of "good works." Many interpreters judged that the real threat to Jesus' message lay in the possibility of taking the parable as a license for regarding "talents" as personal property to be developed for one's own benefit. Catholics and Protestants alike maintained, against a strict literal reading of a text that treats each of the three cases as a discrete matter between the individual servant and his master, that the parable teaches a concern for the needs of others.

The recent emphasis on Protestantism in the study of Renaissance literature has drawn silent support from the theory that Protestant theology was closely tied to a spirit of emerging capitalism. Max Weber's theory and R. H. Tawney's amplification of it were both illustrated, however, chiefly from seventeenth-century writers. The availability of "the Protestant ethic" to sixteenth-century thinkers and writers ought not to be assumed a priori. To discover whether and to what extent interpretations of Scripture reinforced the rising middle classes in a concern for diligent hard work and prudent thrift is a desirable goal for which to aim; to assume that the middle classes necessarily heard biblical texts in ways that encouraged mercantile enterprise is a poor base from which to begin. The terms "Protestant ethic" and "capitalist spirit," unless tested against specific data, too easily conceal unexamined presuppositions about the nature of Western society in the early modern era. The discussion moves to too high a plane of generalization too quickly.

In the half-century since Tawney published *Religion and the Rise of Capitalism*, there has been a good deal of debate about the precise connection between Protestantism and capitalism. Tawney himself treated mainly the later phases of Puritanism, and he drew especially on the writings of Richard Baxter to illustrate that puritans abandoned the traditional Christian suspicion of economic motives. Others, however, have sought to project the Protestant ethic into pre-Restoration Calvinism and in particular to find it in the works of William Perkins, since he was the principal spokesman for the doctrine of the calling.[23] Literary critics have claimed, more casually than convincingly, that in the works of sixteenth-century writers, including Dekker, Deloney, Heywood, and John Browne, a bourgeois work ethic is to be found. But a good deal of recent scholarship on religious and social history has demonstrated that, from the sixteenth to the seventeenth century, there was considerably less continuity in the development of English Protestant piety than Weber and Tawney assumed.[24] In the first sustained study of Elizabethan writing about merchants and craftsmen, Laura Caroline Stevenson showed that there was no particular class consciousness in Elizabethan writers who recommended diligent hard work and thrift. These were in fact traditional virtues that had at least as much appeal to the aristocracy as they did to the middle classes.[25] In a recent study of Milton, moreover, Keith Stavely has argued persuasively that this writer, far from having been an uncritical spokesman for capitalist values, sometimes dissented sharply from the emerging alliance of Protestantism and capitalism.[26] My research on the interpretation of the parable of the talents offers further grounds for skepticism about facile projections of Weber's thesis onto the experience of sixteenth- and seventeenth-century English Protestants. It suggests that divines and biblical scholars in the era of Shakespeare and Milton were often heroic in their resistance to the appropriation of the biblical tradition by self-serving forces within emerging capitalism.

It is not my purpose to review the whole controversy about the relations between Protestantism and capitalism to which the works of Weber, Tawney, and others have given rise.[27] In the remainder of this section my principal goal is to answer the question, "How were people interpreting the parable of the talents in the sixteenth and seventeenth centuries, notably in England?" Some materials that I will consider had been written and first published on the Continent (by Erasmus and Calvin, for instance). The focus will fall chiefly, however, on materials that were published in England (some in Latin, more of them in English; some by Continental writers, more by Englishmen).

A Parable of Social Responsibility

Given the leading sense of the word "talent" in modern English, it is not surprising that current readers of the parable generally think that it teaches that each person has a responsibility to develop his or her natural abilities. This line of interpretation renders Jesus' teaching compatible with intense individualism and with the institution of private property. But in the era when capitalism was only beginning to emerge, most interpreters and exegetes, likely sensing a potential in the parable to be interpreted in ways that would encourage the accumulation of private wealth and the pursuit of what we now think of as personal fulfillment, sought to interpret the parable as an injunction to socially responsible conduct. Nor is there much evidence from the sixteenth and seventeenth centuries that these interpreters simply assumed that what was best for a particular individual was also best for society. They did not invoke the parable to encourage "healthy competition." (It should be noted that when it is taken as a separable unit, the parable says nothing about whether exercising talents is to be done in solidarity with others or in competition. Each of the three cases is handled as a discrete matter.) Rather, they tended to think that the parable demands sacrifice of one's own interests for the sake of others, on the model of Christ's death. The popular preacher John Preston was typical rather than exceptional when, in a sermon on the exercise of callings and the use of talents for "the profit of others," he proclaimed that "God hath commanded vs to *deny our selues* in our profit, in our credit, and our pleasures."[28]

There is little evidence that, in the sixteenth century, the parable of the talents was read along the lines that are prevalent in the twentieth century. For one thing, many readers still recognized that "talents" referred to a sum of money. The marginal comment in the Geneva Bible took this for granted when it sought to provide a contemporary monetary equivalent. Early compilers of English world lists, from Sir Thomas Elyot (1538) through Thomas Cooper (1565) and John Marbeck (1581) to John Bullokar (1616) and even Edward Leigh (1650) and Edward Phillips (1658), glossed "talent" only in its monetary sense.[29] Less learned people did not have a very good idea of the worth of a talent. In *Timon of Athens*, where uniquely among Shakespeare's plays the talent is the principal monetary denomination, there are striking confusions about its worth.[30] It is likely that only readers of scholarly commentaries knew that in the ancient world a talent was the highest unit of value, equivalent to several years' wages for a worker.[31]

By the sixteenth century the newer sense of talent as a mental endowment or natural ability, to which popular allegorical interpretations of the parable had given rise, had also become current in the languages of most of Western Europe. This sense of the word seems to have come into English, and later into German, from the French. (In Germany, the process of "naturalizing" the talents was retarded somewhat, by virtue of the fact that Luther's Bible employed *Zentner*, rather than *Talent*, to render Matthew's word *talanton*. *Zentner* suggests a heavy burden, *Zentnerlast*, rather than natural abilities.) By the end of the seventeenth century, in England, among ordinary people the newer sense had largely displaced the older one. This is attested by the differences between two commentaries associated with Matthew Poole. While the Latin *Synopsis Criticorum* (1669–76) prints an array of scholarship on the history of the word and provides something like conversion tables for ascertaining the relative worth of a talent in different times and places, the English *Annotations upon the Holy Bible* (1683–85) evinces a new willingness to allow as how talents can be thought of as "*Natural Parts*" and "indowments," as opposed to graces that "flow from Christ as *Mediator*."[32] With the translation of the Bible into the vernacular and the growth of a reading public that did not know Latin, much less Greek, it had become increasingly possible—and likely— that readers of the parable would suppose that the text is literally about the duty to use one's natural abilities. Beyond this, they could suppose that it implies that attaining salvation is compatible with personal ambition. From this perspective, readers were likely also to overlook the implication in Matthew's parable that having talents is something of a burden.

The parable had such a potential for encouraging those whom we would now call upwardly mobile, and for striking terror into the hearts of those with fewer privileges and opportunities, that exegetes and pastors interpreted the talents in ways that emphasized social duty rather than personal property. Erasmus, in the tradition of the church fathers, equated the talents with "the doctrine and giftes" that Jesus gave his disciples.[33] Other writers and preachers routinely interpreted talents as "graces" rather than as natural endowments.[34] Richard Baxter included "the Word" among the talents God gives his people and suggested that the figure with only a single talent is like people who have available to them only "the Light of Nature."[35] Calvin, who with Luther insisted on the importance of the literal sense of Scripture, interpreted talents not as personal abilities but as opportunities to participate in the work of bringing others to salvation.[36] William Perkins, in his popular advice book on callings, *A Treatise of the Vocations*, capped his whole argument with a lengthy discussion of the final account that every person will have to make before the divine judge. He drew heavily upon this text, insisting that each person was to be held finally accountable for his "talents," namely, "knowledge, faith, hope, love, and repentance."[37] Others, like Isaac Barrow (d. 1677) and Ezekiel Hopkins (d. 1690) in his treatise on the Last Judgment sought to define using one's talents in terms that precluded the idea of competition or advancing at another's expense.[38]

To observe that allegorical interpretations of the talents persisted into the seventeenth century is not to deny that Calvin gave new prominence to the literal sense. Rejecting the traditional readings that equated the talents with fixed qualities, and seeking to read the parable in dynamic and functional terms as a story about historical process, Calvin held that multiplying the talents referred to the building up of the community. He thus provided a this-worldly perspective from which to see that Christians were expected to participate in the mutual exchange entailed in the social and economic life of society.[39] In this sense Calvin introduced the possibility of making the parable the watchword for the rising middle classes. By the end of the seventeenth century, the dean of St. Paul's was explaining to his congregation that the parable says nothing that would interfere with ordinary business in the city.[40] Nonetheless, early Protestant interpretations of the parable were not doggedly literal, and Calvin's interpretation, which bears a family resemblance to interpretations by Catholics of the same period, did not effect an immediate fusion of Protestantism and capitalism. Despite what we might expect by virtue of the explicit message of the parable, in the sixteenth and early seventeenth centuries the case for reversing the medieval prohibition of usury seems not to have enlisted this promising text in any substantial way.[41]

While spiritual writers of the sixteenth and seventeenth centuries commonly understood that the parable might offer consolation to those who sought their own private ease, the evidence does not show that they singled out the middle classes for praise of their active use of God's gifts. Both the Geneva Bible and Calvin's commentary on the synoptic gospels disseminated the idea that the parable provides a warning against sloth or self-indulgence. Hiding talents was said to be "consulting [one's] own ease and gratifications" and "avoid[ing] all duties of charity."[42] But exegetes, preachers, and ordinary Christians exercised a good deal of ingenuity trying to counter the prospect that the self-righteous (whatever their class background) would find in the parable a warrant for self-interested behavior. They insisted that Jesus told the parable to stir his disciples, as Erasmus put it, to use their talents "thorough their diligence and carefulnes . . . to the profit of their neyghboure."[43]

For over a hundred years this remained the dominant line of interpretation. In the Latin variorum Bible commentary compiled by deprived clergy after the Restoration of 1660, the first comment on the parable was a remark by Sebastian Munster (1489–1552) that the Savior was seeking to encourage service of one's neighbor. This commentary, which printed Catholic and Protestant interpretations together, also cited the Franciscan scholar Zegerus (d. 1559), who urged that all God's gifts, whether material or spiritual, are to be used with zeal and vigilance for the good of one's neighbor. Restoration preachers offered similar interpretations. In a sermon on the industrious conduct expected of Christians, Isaac Barrow drew upon the parable to create a picture of the "world as a family," in which each person is God's servant, concerned, according to his station and capacity, to make "provision for the maintenance of himself and of his fellow-servants." Baxter, who took occasion to remark that the parable condemns "all

Usury . . . that is against *Justice* or *Charity*," likewise observed that the multiplication of talents means a concern with "the good of others."[44] Against a growing tendency to assume that talents were natural abilities to be used to achieve one's maximum personal potential, preachers and devotional writers, intent on showing that the parable actually calls for socially responsible behavior, looked to the work of scholars.

In Learned Commentaries

Various questions addressed by learned commentators proved relevant to the practical application of the parable. In the variorum commentaries, the glosses on the parable raised three principal issues: (1) the relationship of Matthew's parable to Luke's; (2) the reason for an unequal distribution of talents—five, two, and one—in Matthew's version; and (3) the meaning of the remark that the talents were "delivered . . . to every man according to his several ability." Scholars generally handled all these questions in ways that may be thought to promote socially responsible behavior.

The question of the relation between the parallel passages in Matthew and Luke divided critical opinion. Some commentators felt that for all the differences the general sense of both parables was the same.[45] On the other hand, it was clear that the evangelists had placed the parable in quite different contexts and the fact that in Luke's version all participants received an equal share called attention to the differentiation made among the three in Matthew's and suggested that the parables carried different meanings. One way of explaining that difference was to see Luke's parable, in which all receive the same initial sum, as a parable of salvation and damnation proper. Each person receives the general calling of the Christian, but not everyone responds to it. By contrast, Matthew's parable is more elaborate, and as Grotius suggested, it concerns the uses of one's peculiar gifts, the sorts of charisms in which Paul took an interest on several occasions—for instance, in the twelfth chapter of First Corinthians, where he differentiates among the varying functions of the parts of the body only to insist on the need for their coordination. Perkins saw Matthew's parable as a story about particular callings and as an adjunct therefore to Luke's parable about the general calling of the Christian. In the final accounting on the Day of Judgment, said Perkins, all people will be held responsible for the use they have made of the peculiar gifts that come with their calling, "which are the talents of the Lord."[46] In this view, the criterion for judgment is not merely whether one accepts the general offer of salvation but also what use one makes of particular opportunities to be of service to others.

The unequal distribution of talents remained a crux, especially in view of the master's instruction at the end that the single talent be given to the man who already had ten. To explain this, the Italian Benedictine Isidore Clarius (1495–1555), proposed that the phrase *unicuique secundum propriam virtutem* was to be interpreted in a manner that made *virtus*, or "ability," a metaphor for faith. But granting that faith is a free gift of God, this did not fully answer the question why some persons have more than others, or why (as Clarius himself observed) it was the man with only one, and not the man with five or the man with two, who hid his talent.[47] Some commentators proposed that the enumeration of figures with different abilities insured that the parable applied to everyone, from magistrate to ordinary Christian, so that even those with few personal resources or little faith could not excuse themselves from social duties.[48]

When there was any controversy between Catholics and Protestants in interpreting the parable, it generally centered on the implications of the details whereby the talents were apportioned "to every man according to his several ability" (verse 15). Although Clarius interpreted *virtutem* as "faith," Protestants sometimes claimed that other papists sought to make this verse prove that God allots His graces in proportion to human merit. Edward Leigh gave the standard answer to this when he took occasion to insist that human "dispositions . . . also were the gift of God, and bestowed on us freely."[49] The principal strategy for conferring on the parable a socially edifying significance was to urge the principle that Scripture is the best interpreter of itself and to appeal to considerations of context. In the twenty-fifth chapter of Matthew, the sequence makes of the parable of the talents a bridge between an injunction to maintain vigilance and an injunction to do good works on behalf of the hungry, thirsty, naked, and imprisoned.[50]

Hearing a Threat in the Parable

So far this report on the interpretation of the parable in the early modern period has shown that it was commonly said to teach a doctrine of social responsibility. Most religious writers and preachers, knowing the background of the pivotal word, interpreted talents not as natural abilities, but as gifts or graces, even as the special opportunities that God gives all persons in their particular callings. In view of this prevailing line of interpretation, it seems fair to say that, whatever its potential for consoling the self-righteous, the parable was important in seventeenth-century England also because it threatened with damnation those whose aim in life was their own personal profit.

That an individual Christian might find in the parable a threat rather than a promise is well illustrated in the personal narrative of a woman identified only as "M. K." Her story appears in a collection of conversion narratives from the early 1650s.[51] In the course of this autobiographical work, M. K. tells of having married a minister's son and of taking a house with him in Westminster, where they rejected their religious upbringing, found a new set of friends, and spent almost all their means. Unlike her husband, M. K. resolved to change her new situation. Her husband refused to quit the company of heavy drinkers, and she decided to kill him. Having thus run away from her true "Captain," Christ, she nonetheless remembered God's previous favors to her and did not execute her bloody plan. But she was haunted by a particular text. She was obsessed, she reports, with the idea that God was coming "to see what use *I had* made of the talent that he had given me." She feared that God would find that it had been "not only wrapt up in a napkin, but exceedingly abused" (170–71). From here she went on to describe, in the conventional terms of puritan conversion narratives, what God would find in her heart: "a sinke of sinne, a Cage of uncleane Birds, a Den of Theeves, a place for Dragons." The result, she explains, was that Satan then tempted her to believe that *"thou shalt never be called to an account for any thing"* (173), so that she should take her fill of sinning. As we might expect, however, from the fact that her story was included in this volume, M. K. was at last assured of God's love for her. She even ends her testimony with a prayer that her divine master *"come quickly."*

The story of M. K. suggests that, for some readers in the English Calvinist tradition, the urgency of the parable of the talents lay not so much in the possibility that the text could be made to turn up a safe way to salvation. It was more a function of the fact that the stakes were high and the parable warned against a sure path to hell. The reason that it seemed particularly useful as a deterrent against sinful behavior was well summed by Jeremy Taylor when, in his treatment of cases of conscience, he explained the relevance of biblical passages that contained both promises and threats: "a threatening in all laws," he proposed, "is of more force and efficacy then a promise; and therefore when under a threatening more is requir'd, . . . [since] one thing is enough to destroy us, but one thing is not enough to preserve us."[52] This principle provides relevant background as well to the use that Milton makes of the parable in the best-known reference to it in seventeenth-century literature, the sonnet in which the speaker "consider[s] how [his] light is spent" and confesses his inclination to interpret his loss of light as the equivalent of the punishment, being cast into "utter darkness," meted out to the man who hid his talent.

It is commonly said that the parable of the talents was Milton's favorite. He alluded to it in especially personal ways in a letter of 1633 and in the long autobiographical excursus in *The Reason of Church Government* (1642). If we listen to his allusions—"that command in the gospell set out by the terrible seasing of him that hid his talent," "remembering . . . that God even to a strictness requires the improvement of . . . his entrusted gifts," "that one Talent which is death to hide"—it seems more as if this was Milton's least favorite parable, almost as if the dreadful, threatening voice that damned the man who buried his talent was his personal equivalent of a sentence of damnation.[53]

In the light of seventeenth-century commentary, it is clear that thinking about the parable in this way was not unique to Milton and M. K. Most commentators, fearing its being taken as a license for self-serving behavior, found in it afflictions to be unleashed upon the comfortable, and tended to pass over its capacity for consoling the industrious. Within the spiritual life of puritans in particular the greatest importance of the parable lay in the fact that it carried a threat of damnation, to chasten the conscience and thus to prepare the "bruised reed" to hear a really consoling text, a gospel promise. This is the use to which Milton put the parable in his sonnet, where for a time, before the speaker's memory of the threat gives way to a counsel of patience, he seems intensely anxious about his lack of productivity:

> When I consider how my light is spent,
>   E're half my days, in this dark world and wide,
>   And that one Talent which is death to hide,
>   Lodg'd with me useless, though my Soul more bent
> To serve therewith my Maker, and present
>   My true account, least he returning chide,
>   Doth God exact day-labour, light deny'd,
>   I fondly ask; But patience to prevent
> That murmur, soon replies, God doth not need
>   Either man's work or his own gifts, who best
>   Bear his milde yoak, they serve him best, his State
> Is Kingly. Thousands at his bidding speed
>   And post o're Land and Ocean without rest:
>   They also serve who only stand and waite.[54]

The latter part of Milton's sonnet constitutes a powerful correction of the tendency to fix on the case of the third figure as a threat. The poet couches his allusion to the parable within a larger network of allusions to a whole range of biblical passages, including the ones that immediately precede and follow the parable of the talents in Matthew 25: the parable of the wise and foolish virgins, who need oil for their lamps when the bridegroom comes, and the picture of the last judgment, when the heavenly King will separate the sheep from the goats on the basis of their treatment of the "least brethren." With its highly charged final declaration, "they also serve who only stand and waite," Milton's poem challenges a facile understanding of all these passages. It asks readers to apply biblical texts to their lives with responsible intelligence—and with belief in a God who does not measure productivity in the terms of what is now routinely denominated "the Protestant ethic."

Some Conclusions Referable to the Early Modern Period

Acknowledging that there had been a dominant emphasis on asceticism in medieval European Christianity, many people have noticed the more positive valuation of material goods to be found in post-Reformation

Christianity and, with Molière and other satirical writers, have been fascinated with the self-deception, and outright hypocrisy, of people who cloak their worldliness in religious garb. From this perspective the parable of the talents might be thought the proof of Christianity's essential worldliness, whether "talent" is interpreted as a sum of money or a natural endowment. For in either case the parable—which (as we have seen) carries no obvious sense of requiring socially responsible conduct, so that interpreters have often felt obliged to produce one—can be interpreted as teaching the opposite to the idea of self-sacrifice. "Let a man be perswaded that *God* takes care of him," John Preston proposed; "it is [God] that giues the reward, the wages belongs to him, the care of the worke onely to vs." We should deny ourselves, he taught, and "vse those talents that God hath given" to do business "not for our owne good, but for the good of others."[55] This may well be the single most striking feature of sixteenth- and seventeenth-century commentary: the frequency and urgency with which interpreters stressed that fulfilling the injunctions of the parable required the sort of trust in God that looks to others' welfare and exacts personal costs. The fact that interpreters regularly tried to produce lessons of social responsibility from the parable suggests at least two things: (1) that they felt there was danger that the parable would be taken out of context and made to mean things compatible with merely self-serving ends; and (2) that they were using an overriding criterion such as the "analogy of faith," or Augustine's rule of charity, to control the meaning of the parable and to facilitate or promote a certain sort of application of it.

READING AND INVOKING THE PARABLE IN TWENTIETH-CENTURY AMERICA

Implications of the Current Sense of "Talent"

With the emergence of an expanding economy in which one person's financial gain does not necessarily entail financial losses for others, the ways in which the parable of the talents is likely to be understood have been quite thoroughly transformed. Some aspects of it have come to seem quite irrelevant to what people think it means: that it envisages, for instance, a world of master/slave relations and that it sets up a distinction between "talents" and natural abilities. Moreover, few readers in our time are likely to be as fascinated with the third figure's anxiety about holding the master's money and his fear of being accountable as people were in the period of early Calvinism, when readers searched the Scriptures for promises and threats that would help to predict whether they were ultimately to be saved or damned. What we can glean from having surveyed the long history of interpreting the parable is that, as new economic conditions have emerged, readers have inevitably asked new questions of the parable, sometimes in an attempt to find guidance from an authorized religious guide, sometimes in an attempt to legitimate views that they might wish to hold in any event. Each new economic era ushers in new problems and new opportunities. Changes in interpretation of the parable can provide one index of these. Returning then to Paul Schervish's findings in his study on wealth and philanthropy, we can reconsider some recent uses of the concept of stewardship.

Given the prominence with which this concept figures in the materials on which their study is based, the conclusion of the researchers is unsurprising: "the ideology of stewardship constitutes [a] legitimating consciousness" for many persons who have inherited their wealth. Nor is it surprising that the language of legitimation is infused with traditional religious imagery, since the exegetical tradition disseminated categories and terms that have been accommodated and assimilated through many centuries of cultural work. What requires scrutiny, however, is the casual manner in which the traditional religious terminology is deployed, as when, for instance, people talk about what they have inherited from their ancestors as if it had been given them by God. Many people in this study speak as if the meaning of biblical texts is transparent and the implications of those texts are threatening only in ways that they have already managed to tame. "I don't want to arrive at the gates of heaven," says Warner Hundley,

and have a voice of responsibility asking me what I did on earth and I tell him how much money I made for the company and how high sales were, and I had a family of six children and that I think they have good values. I'm afraid that his next question might be, "What did you do that was important?" I want to make sure I have an answer. I mean we're all put here to *do* something.

Hundley is not accusing himself here of not having done something, nor does he seem to fear exclusion when he reaches the gates of heaven. Rather, he offers a criterion for judging his life according to which actions he has already performed are lined up in a credit column. Moreover, with respect to his present life in this world, his comments suggest that traditional religious categories can sometimes prove useful to the wealthy for representing their lives as essentially continuous with those lived by other people, on the assumption that everyone is ultimately accountable to the same God. Thus, also Patrick Lockwood: "If God gives you a little, you ought to do the most you can with a little. If God gives you a lot, you ought to do the most you can with a lot."

At the outset we saw that Lockwood offers a conspicuous instance of how the parable can be explicitly invoked in an attempt to justify one's economic position. "The Bible teaches invest," says Lockwood. "Jesus gave these three guys talents. . . ." It is of interest that when Lockwood then goes on to abstract a general moral from the parable, he accomplishes it by way of a centuries-old practice of fusing it with another biblical text without in any way considering, it seems, that while the two texts are thematically related, they come from different books written hundreds of years apart and in different languages. Lockwood simply borrows language from Genesis to conflate Jesus' parable with what Genesis depicts as God's original command to Adam and Eve: "So I believe," he says, "we ought to be fruitful and multiply what we have." This fusion of texts from the first book in the New Testament and the first in the Old piously ascribes all wealth ultimately to God. It leaves in place an implication that each person's condition in life is God-given. Lockwood also proposes his principle as one that applies equally to all persons, whether or not they are wealthy.

Careful reflection on Lockwood's observations is in order. First, it may be said that they seem to entail a shrewd if unformulated recognition that the parable in Matthew already represents a reinterpretation of the text from Genesis. Such reinterpretations are utterly characteristic of later biblical literature, of course, for it was written by persons thoroughly acquainted with stories from the Torah and steeped in the categories that informed Israel's self-consciousness. Yet Lockwood's use of the texts masks the implications of his own insight that the texts are related. Instead of exploring the interesting differences between the two biblical texts, he proceeds as if they come ready-made to be abstracted from their contexts and belong instead to some trans-historical realm of timeless truth. His assimilation of the parable of the talents to the archetypal story of Adam and Eve neutralizes human history, in which the distribution of wealth is not wholly the work of a benign Maker but is also and more especially a function of agencies that inevitably involve injustices. His appropriation of the parable creates the impression that what he has comes from God, as the Garden of Eden and all its fruits were given to Adam and Eve by their Creator, or as the talents were apportioned by the master in Jesus' parable. Even as he emphasizes his strong sense of obligation—"You're responsible for what God gives you"—he swerves away from the really difficult questions entailed in trying to conceive the relations between socially constructed patterns and systems and what God has given to any particular person in history. Unless one is willing to question whether and in what precise senses biblical texts may be applied in historical circumstances that are radically different from those in which they were created, appropriations of those texts are likely to support rather than challenge the status quo. Yet, as Pheme Perkins has pointed out in Chapter 3, careful scrutiny of the New Testament for an economic "message" turns up a propensity for questioning the configurations of power relations, and in particular whether wealth is being made to serve the interests of the powerful.

In another interview, Dale Jayson draws upon the parable of the talents to present the idea of universal accountability in glowingly positive terms. Yet here there is an implicit if only momentary recognition that something is amiss: "Every human being should have an opportunity," he urges, "to develop his God-given talents. The greatest gift that God gave man is talent. The greatest gift that we can give back to God is the utilization of that talent. . . . Freedom is the cornerstone for growth and self-developing." Every human being should have the opportunity, and yet not all persons are in fact in the position of the three servants in the parable. As Jayson implies, not everyone is free to pursue self-development. There are significant differences between the relatively clear-cut terms in which the master in the parable holds each person accountable "according to his several ability" and the messier inequalities in which we are historically enmeshed.

While there are many points in the interviews when the free-enterprise system is praised in terms borrowed from traditional religious discourse, at other times what is striking in the language is how manifestly inhibiting an undigested appropriation of the biblical categories may be. "I am held accountable," Jayson maintains and then adds,

now just think about what the world would be like if we knew what we'd be like after we die. That fear of what's going to happen after I die is the thing that keeps me on the straight-and-narrow here on earth. That's why I'm not a murderer. That's why I'm not a dope-dealer. . . . Because of the accountability, the fact that some supreme being is saying that what you do here on this earth after you die, you're going to be held accountable for. . . . That fear, that accountability, keeps me going to Church.

The usefulness of presenting oneself as an accountable steward (rather than, say, as an independent agent) becomes more clear when we consider various other implications inherent in the metaphor. Stewardship suggests at once a sense of privilege and a sense of obligation, both of which take into account the different situation of those who (by whatever criteria) are not wealthy. It rests to some extent upon a sense of human community and provides wealthy persons with a basis for thinking that they do not differ in kind, but only in degree, from fellow human beings who, from an economic standpoint at least, might be thought less "fortunate." In this vision no one is more responsible than anyone else for the economic system. The existence of that system is not questioned, while the behavior of individuals within it becomes an object of scrutiny for which there is said to be accountability.

These implications are all suggested in a functional definition of stewardship that appears in another of the interviews: stewardship is "a conviction that if one does well in the world and has more than one can possibly need, one ought to share it and try to influence some of the surroundings and places to which one is loyal or for which one is responsible for the good" (118). We may prescind here from considering whether and under what conditions it may be morally desirable, or necessary, to "influence . . . the surroundings and places to which one is loyal." Such a conception begs for further reflection. It is more difficult to overlook the implication that it is only what one considers a surplus ("more than one can possibly need") that requires to be shared. The fundamental problem comes into better focus when we listen to the idea of stewardship framed in terms that posit not only greater but fundamentally different responsibilities for those in positions of wealth and power:

I was very much raised with the notion that I was very fortunate and it was my responsibility to take my good fortune and make that progress in the classic sense of doing things which one is "called upon to do." . . . It's the classic charitable posture right out of Dickens of the haves acting on behalf of the have-nots. . . . It's a notion that if you have wealth it behooves you, it's your responsibility to do for others, looking out for others, looking out in general for the society.

We ought not to allow ourselves to be distracted by the fact that this utterance is cast in the crude terms of nineteenth-century patriarchal benevolence, spoken, or so it seems, utterly without irony. The problem here is that the principle is enunciated as if its applicability were utterly manifest, as if there was no considerable difficulty in finding dignified and empowering ways of disbursing philanthropy. In this sense, the parable, which is not about those difficulties, is invoked in a way that suggests that those difficulties are irrelevant. The parable counsels action and insists on accountability on the grounds of whether a person has acted or not. When someone invokes it to express a sense of responsibility and to justify actions that have been and continue to be taken, it might be useful to acknowledge the limited scope of the parable and to ask questions about which the parable has nothing to say, including questions about the effects of the actions that have been taken.

Besides presenting themselves as stewards in ways that suggest a sense of solidarity with the less "fortunate," many wealthy persons use this category to distance themselves from other wealthy people, who are said to have wholly different conceptions of the prerogatives of riches. Wealthy people, one philanthropist emphasizes, "should be utilizing their talents for their fellow man rather than running around on their yachts" (120). Here we can see the distinct possibility that a traditional interpretation of the parable, instead of serving the status quo, can provide a continuing challenge to those in positions of powerful influence.

A Revivification of the Monetary Sense of "Talent"

In late twentieth-century America, where there is a considerable amount of Bible study among adults and a fairly wide use of popular commentary on the Bible, many Christians (although I am dubious whether it is a majority) may be more or less aware that the "talents" referred to in Matthew's parable were denominations of money. For those who wish to find in the New Testament economic messages that may be applied to their lives, and especially for those who tend to think that the meaning and implications of biblical texts are easily extracted, the ostensible encouragement to multiply one's wealth may come as a welcome balance, and reassurance, to other New Testament texts that sound more threatening to the wealthy: the story of the rich man and Lazarus (Luke 16), for example, or the saying that "it is easier for a camel to go through the eye of a needle, than for a rich man to enter the kingdom of God" (Mark: 10:25). This is the use made of the text, for instance, by George Weigel, who proposes that the parable provides a "biblical warrant" for his idea that some Christians are certainly "called" to be "entrepreneurs" who will create wealth for the benefit of all.[56]

Just how fully the parable of the talents can be said to have been appropriated for a capitalistic ethic is not clear. At the start of the twentieth century one biblical expert remarked, by way of protesting against what had already become a standard interpretation, that the "use of wealth" was widely regarded as the "leading thought" in the parable, and that people were taking as its lesson that "one ought to strive for riches."[57] If modern readers know that once a "talent" was a denomination of money, they may think that the parable encourages the accumulation of capital. One learned expositor has recently assured his readers that "a safe inference would seem to be that Jesus . . . is not opposed to responsible capitalism. Profit promotes employment and makes possible helping those in need."[58] A more popular commentator invites readers to find here "a very modern parable" about God's great "investment program" and applies the story to his readers' lives by way of a book called *How to Sell Your Way through Life*.[59] The usefulness of the parable to entrepreneurs is perhaps best illustrated, however, by an excerpt from an article of 1922 titled "The Economic Factor in the Messiahship of Jesus":

Jesus knew that the Jewish people had to grow strong. . . . To begin with, there had to be more people. . . . How could they produce enough to support a large population? The only answer to that question is that they must develop and utilize the productive capacity of the people to the maximum. This is primarily a problem of . . . eliminating every form of waste, especially the waste of human energy. . . . Good-will, generous appreciation of the achievements of others, self-discipline to the extent of developing all one's powers and applying them to the doing of useful or life-supporting things—these must take the place of the vices or wasteful habits that generally prevail. . . . Our young Jew set out to accomplish these things, knowing that if he succeeded he would be laying the foundations of national freedom. . . .

As the passage continues, Jesus is made a prophet, many centuries before the development actually took place, of the movement to do away with the prohibition of usury:

Other things had to be done.... The old superstitious taboo against interest had to be removed. In the parable of the talents and the pounds he gave us as clear and definite a justification of interest as is contained in any text-book in economics....

It is ... a waste to have land or any other productive agent in the hands of a poor manager when it might be in the hands of a better manager. In addition to justifying interest, the story of the talents or the pounds teaches this lesson as clearly as it could be taught. Substitute the word "tool" or the word "acre" for the word "talent" or "pound" and you get a most important economic lesson.[60]

Given the leading sense of the word "talent" in modern English, it is not surprising that current readers of the parable generally think that it teaches that each person has a responsibility to develop his or her natural abilities. This line of interpretation renders Jesus' teaching compatible with intense individualism and with the institution of private property. Yet the triumph of those who would appropriate the resources of the biblical tradition to promote the capitalist system remains incomplete. There is a residue, at least, of older assumptions and interpretations of the parable that sometimes appears, as we have seen in the transcripts from the survey on philanthropy, when people enlist the parable to explain their sense of obligation to "contribute to the well-being of the wider community" or even to "share [their wealth] with the church or other institutions." A nagging suspicion that the parable does not, or should not, encourage unbridled capitalism continues to show up, in fact, in scholarly commentaries on the parable. A British commentator, for instance, begins his discussion with an observation designed to unsettle the assumptions that many readers likely bring to the passage: "It is unfortunate," he writes, "that this parable should be generally known as the parable of the talents, for the word 'talent' in contemporary English refers exclusively to the natural aptitude and inherent ability of certain people for certain functions." He goes on to insist that the "parable is in no way concerned ... with those who are 'talented' in this sense. On the contrary, the *talents* in the parable *belong to someone else*, and are entrusted by him to others to be used not only in their interest but in his." Similarly, an American exegete ends nine pages of dense and closely argued commentary with the conclusion that the "talents do not refer to natural abilities; they symbolize opportunities to do good works."[61] These comments, which go against the popular notion that this "very modern parable" teaches us that "God has ... distributed His assets among His people" in a grand "investment program,"[62] preserve a tradition of interpretation that finds in the Bible a good deal of material that challenges ready complicity in modern economic practices. The outcomes of the reappropriation of biblical materials for capitalist ideology are, we might say, mixed, and they are mixed in ways that, try as one might to return to some imagined purity of the past, are inextricably intermingled.

In the early modern period, as we have seen, when the capitalist system was only beginning to emerge, interpreters and exegetes, likely sensing a potential in the parable to be interpreted in ways that would encourage the accumulation of private wealth and the pursuit of what we now think of as personal fulfillment, commonly sought to interpret the parable as an injunction to socially responsible conduct. Undoubtedly, many preachers and divines may have been as ineffectual in their pleas for religious asceticism as Simon Schama represents those of seventeenth-century Holland.[63] Yet we need not suppose that little can be learned from attending to their persistent attempts to make the parable teach lessons that promote the interests of a broad community. Schama has concluded, against what might be expected in light of the Weber thesis, that the Dutch church did not provide "a rationalization for tooth-and-claw capitalism so much as a defense against it" (338). A similar point needs to be made about English prelates and scholars of the same period, even after the fissiparous occurrences of the 1640s, when the church split into a broad variety of denominations and for a time the bishops lost their monopoly on the public practice of religion.

Considered from a twentieth-century perspective that supposes that the parable of the talents teaches the obligation to develop one's natural abilities, what is a particularly telling difference in sixteenth- and seventeenth-century commentary on the parable is this: it yields little evidence that people assumed that what was best for a particular individual was also best for society. The commentators of the early modern era did not appeal to the parable to encourage "healthy competition." Rather, they tended to think that the parable demands sacrifice of one's own interests for the sake of others, on the model of Christ's death. This emphasis kept alive the possibility that the biblical text could be made to stand in judgment against socially unjust behavior. But it could not preserve the parable—no interpretation can—from being appropriated by those in power for the purpose of consolidating their position. As the parable has been transformed over the past three centuries, during which it has been made to produce meanings compatible with capitalist ideology, the traditional emphasis on self-sacrifice has been reduced but not suppressed. In fact, that emphasis has had, from the point of view of those in power, a continuing usefulness. Self-sacrifice can be urged upon workers as a virtue that is ultimately in their own interest. It can also figure as a prominent motif in the autobiographical narratives by which the wealthy legitimate their status. Discipline, hard work, investment and the taking of risks, evidence of productivity—all these features of traditional interpretations of the parable can be made useful in managing the challenges the parable is allowed to pose. Yet it also remains possible that this residue from the tradition may escape the control of those who seek to domesticate the parable in the service of preserving the status quo. If the parable cannot be fixed within the prophetic tradition in which Jesus lived and taught, neither can it be permanently appropriated by those in positions of power—so long as there are interpreters to keep alive the potential in biblical literature for standing in judgment on unjust behavior.

TOWARD A CONCLUSION AND DISCUSSION

What does the history of interpreting the parable tell us about its possible meaning in our time and about the workings of "cultural scriptures" today? Different readers of this history will draw different conclusions, of course. I will venture a few of my own. First, we have seen that through the centuries "talent" has referred to many different phenomena: weight, money, the Scriptures, opportunities for service, natural abilities. In our time the last of these senses has pretty much driven out all the others with the exception, among those who know something about the ancient Mediterranean world, of the monetary sense. Since the seventeenth century the word "talent" has been gradually and almost thoroughly detached from the biblical context that made it generally available in Western Europe long after the monetary designation had passed from use. By the late nineteenth century "talent" had become an important word in the lexicon of the sports page. In the twentieth century it is widely used in the realm of entertainment and the arts. Given the connotations that the word has acquired in these spheres, it is likely that anyone reading or hearing the parable in our time will suppose that it teaches the importance of "being all that you can be," even that it urges as a duty self-cultivation and the pursuit of self-fulfillment. This interpretation depends entirely on the metaphorical sense of "talent" that developed out of allegorical interpretations. To notice all this, however, may be to do little more than to indulge a certain historical curiosity. Historical knowledge offers some controls on the interpretation of the parable; it does not determine its meaning.

I should stress that this historical exercise has not been aimed at policing the boundaries around the meaning of the word "talent," or at forbidding people to import into their understanding of the Bible their experiences with their own language. It does not suggest that either religious practice or ethical economic behavior requires considerable antiquarian knowledge. Nor does it propose that the value of the parable lies wholly in some reconstructed "original meaning," whether this might be thought to reside in the words that Jesus once uttered or in the text of Matthew's gospel, nor that its value may be found in some timeless truth abstracted from the story and established somewhere within the broad historical traditions of Christianity.

By the same token, I do not credit the idea that the parable, which has manifestly been made to mean any number of things through the centuries, can be said to mean anything that anyone wants it to mean. Rather, this chapter has posited a dynamic concept of making "meaning," one that includes a willingness to investigate what the story has meant to various people. This should help to clarify criteria by which people living at the end of the twentieth century may make intelligent and responsible judgments about what they want the parable to mean. In this sense, I think that learning is useful, since it can function as something of a check on interpretations that appropriate authoritative texts as if their meaning is timeless and their application unproblematic. This "genealogy" has shown how in various epochs readers bring different concerns and questions, even radically different assumptions, to the processes by which they produce meaning from the parable. What a survey of the history of the parable can do is to locate a potent residue from earlier meanings that, in our time, continues to contribute to an ideology of stewardship. This ideology often seeks not only to appropriate biblical authority but to tame the complex and challenging "economic messages" in the New Testament. (By "taming" that message I mean to refer especially to ways of reading that close off the possibility that there are serious injustices in the status quo or that excuse readers from entertaining perspectives from which their economic position might be seen to be complicit in unjust power relations.) In the parable of the talents, almost more than in any other biblical text, modern readers are likely to overlook or misconstrue what may be the most challenging implications of the New Testament's diverse teaching on wealth and possessions. This assertion implies that, having read the parable carefully and having surveyed its history, I am willing to take a stand on what I think it can and should mean in our time. This willingness is not merely a function of detached scholarly objectivity. It grows out of convictions that are suspicious of putting religious energies at the service of those in positions of wealth and power. Such convictions are partly the result of study, which can persuade us that the biblical tradition inspires Godlike generosity and human solidarity. The Bible itself, written in particular times and places and languages, can alert us to watch for moments when a lack of generosity and solidarity is masked by those in positions of power. And it can inspire us, in the manner of courageous biblical prophets, to speak and act against injustices.

NOTES

1. The study was sponsored by the T. B. Murphy Foundation Charitable Trust and published by the Social Welfare Research Institute at Boston College (Chestnut Hill, Mass., 1988) as *Empowerment and Beneficence: Strategies of Living and Giving among the Wealthy*. Andrew Herman served as coauthor. Parenthetical references to page numbers refer to this volume. Thanks are due to Paul Schervish and to Ethan Lewis for making available excerpts from the transcripts, in which the names of the persons who were interviewed have been changed.

2. See Chapter 3 in this volume.

3. Simon Schama, *The Embarrassment of Riches: An Interpretation of Dutch Culture in the Golden Age* (Berkeley and Los Angeles: University of California Press, 1988), especially 93–125.

4. A helpful model for studying the relations between linguistic usage and economic realities may be found in the discussion of the word "capitalism" by Fernand Braudel in *Civilization and Capitalism*, vol. 2, *The Wheels of Commerce*, trans. Siân Reynolds (1979; New York: Harper and Row, 1982), chap. 3.

5. "Nietzsche, Genealogy, History," in *Language, Counter-Memory, Practice*, trans. Donald F. Bouchard and Sherry Simon (Ithaca, N.Y.: Cornell University Press, 1977), 151–52.

6. The point had already been made by Samuel Johnson in *A Dictionary of the English Language* (London, 1755). It has often been repeated, and can be found in the *Oxford English Dictionary* at sense 3.

7. The *O.E.D.* traces the modern sense of the English word back to Old French. (The etymologies given in the *O.E.D.* are not, however, wholly reliable.)

8. Sometimes there was more than an analogy. Although bishops did not have income-producing revenues until later in history, from early on they served as the dispensers of charity from the church's collections.

9. Origen, *Homilies on Genesis and Exodus*, trans. Ronald E. Heine (Washington, D.C.: Catholic University of America Press, 1982), 376.

10. *The Stromata: or Miscellanies*, in *Ante-Nicene Christian Library: Translations of the Writings of the Fathers down to A.D. 325*, ed. Alexander Roberts and James Donaldson, vol. 2, *Fathers of the Second Century*, trans. William Wilson (c. 1867; reprint, Grand Rapids, Mich.: Eerdmans, 1962), 299.

11. Letter XLIX to Dracontius, Oxford translation, revised by Miss Payne-Smith, in *A Select Library of the Nicene and Post-Nicene Fathers of the Christian Church*, ed. Philip Schaff and Henry Wace, 2d ser. vol. 4, *St. Athanasius: Select Works and Letters* (1891; reprint Grand Rapids, Mich.: Eerdmans, 1957), 558; Augustine, Sermon XLIV, trans. R. G. MacMullen, also in *A Select Library*, vol. 6 (1887; reprint, Grand Rapids, Mich.: Eerdmans, 1956), 406; and Caesarius of Arles, *Sermons*, vol. 3, trans. Mary Magdeleine Mueller (Washington, D.C.: Catholic University of America Press, 1973), 182–83.

12. John Chrysostom, *Discourses against Judaizing Christians*, trans. Paul W. Harkins (Washington, D.C.: Catholic University of America Press, 1979), 240.

13. Homily LXXVIII [on Matt. 25: 1–30], in *A Select Library of the Nicene and Post-Nicene Fathers of the Christian Church*, ed. Philip Schaff, vol. 10, *Saint Chrysostom: Homilies of the Gospel of Saint Matthew*, trans. George Prevost (1888; reprint, Grand Rapids, Mich.: Eerdmans, 1956), 472. Cf. also *Discourses against Judaizing Christians*, 94, 240–41.

14. John Chrysostom, Homily X, from *On the Incomprehensible Nature of God*, trans. Paul W. Harkins (Washington, D.C.: Catholic University of America Press, 1984), 245.

15. "On Christian Doctrine," trans. J. F. Shaw, in *A Select Library*, vol. 2, *Saint Augustin's City of God and Christian Doctrine* (1886; reprint, Grand Rapids, Mich.: Eerdmans, 1956), 520–21.

16. Cf. Louis Réau, *Iconographie de l'art chrétien*, 3 vols. (Paris: Presses Universitaires de France, 1955–59), 2, 2:343.

17. Cf. Stephen L. Wailes, *Medieval Allegories of Jesus' Parables* (Berkeley: University of California Press, 1987), 11. My summary of medieval allegories of the talents owes a good deal to Wailes's fine work; see 184–94.

18. Ibid., 188–89.

19. Ibid., 189, 194.

20. Gregory the Great, *Forty Gospel Homilies*, trans. Dom David Hurst (Kalamazoo, Mich.: Cistercian Publications, 1990), 127.

21. Homily LXXVIII, in *A Select Library*, vol. 10, *Saint Chrysostom: Homilies on the Gospel of Saint Matthew*, trans. George Prevost, 471–72.

22. Among the more prominent and influential studies are Barbara Kiefer Lewalski's *Protestant Poetics and the Seventeenth-Century Religious Lyric* (Princeton, N.J.: Princeton University Press, 1979), and John King's *English Reformation Literature: The Tudor Origins of the Protestant Tradition* (Princeton, N.J.: Princeton University Press, 1982).

23. R. H. Tawney, *Religion and the Rise of Capitalism: A Historical Study* (New York: Harcourt, Brace, 1926). See Louis Wright, "William Perkins: Elizabethan Apostle of 'Practical Divinity,' " *Huntington Library Quarterly* 3 (January 1940): 182; Christopher Hill, *Society and Puritanism in Pre-Revolutionary England* (New York: Schocken, 1964), 129–30; and C. Hill, *Puritanism and Revolution: Studies in Interpretation of the English Revolution of the Seventeenth Century* (1958; reprint, New York: Schocken, 1964), 229.

24. This work has been summarized by Hartmut Lehmann, "Ascetic Protestantism and Economic Rationalism: Max Weber Revisited after Two Generations," *Harvard Theological Review* 80 (1987): 307–20.

25. This paragraph is indebted to Stevenson's *Praise and Paradox: Merchants and Craftsmen in Elizabethan Popular Literature* (Cambridge: Cambridge University Press, 1984), which provides references (132) to the relevant studies of the writers referred to here.

26. *Puritan Legacies: Paradise Lost and the New England Tradition, 1630–1890* (Ithaca, N.Y.: Cornell University Press, 1987). Cf. Schama's study of the seventeenth-century Dutch, *Embarrassment*, 124–25, 338.

27. Weber's essay first appeared in German in 1904–5 and was translated by Talcott Parsons as *The Protestant Ethic and the Spirit of Capitalism*. The literature on Weber is immense. Bibliographies are available, inter alia, in the volumes edited by S. N. Eisenstadt, *The Protestant Ethic and Modernization: A Comparative View* (New York: Basic Books, 1978), 385–400; and Robert W. Green, *Protestantism, Capitalism, and Social Science: The Weber Thesis Controversy*, 2d ed. (Lexington, Mass.: Heath, 1973), 191–95. See also Gordon Marshall, *In Search of the Spirit of Capitalism: An Essay on Max Weber's Protestant Ethic Thesis* (London: Hutchinson, 1982).

28. John Preston, *The Nevv Covenant, or The Saints Portion*, 2d ed. (London, 1629), 177–79.

29. Elyot, *Dictionary* (1538; reprint, Menston, England: Scolar Press, 1970); Cooper, *Thesaurus Linguae Romanae & Britannicae* (1565; reprint, London, 1584); Marbeck, *A Book of Notes* (London, 1581), 1074–75; Bullokar, *An English Expositor: Teaching the Interpretation of the hardest words used in our Language* (1616; reprint, Menston, England: Scolar Press, 1967); Leigh, *Critica Sacra: Or Observations on all the Radices* . . . , 3d ed. (London, 1650), 258; Phillips, *The New World of English Words*

(London, 1658). See also Robert F. Herrey's "second Alphabet" in *Two Right Profitable and Fruitfull Concordances* [London, 1578?].

30. H. J. Oliver, Introduction, *Timon of Athens*, Arden ed. (London: Methuen, 1959), xxvii. Oliver proposes that Shakespeare may have been drawing on divergent sources—namely, Lucian and Plutarch—who gave high and low estimates of the value of an ancient talent. He also cites the two passages from Matthew (18:24 and 25:14–30) as illustrations of the possibility of giving high and low values to a talent. Terence Spencer glosses the Ventidius episode in the opening scene by way of Matt. 25; see "Shakespeare Learns the Value of Money: The Dramatist at Work on *Timon of Athens*," *Shakespeare Survey* 6 (1953): 75–78. For a dissenting opinion, see Lewis Walker, "Money in *Timon of Athens*," *Philological Quarterly* 57 (Spring 1978): 269–71.

31. See, e.g., Tremellius, *Iesu Christi D. N. Novum Testament* (London, 1580): Matt. 18:24; cf. Munster, in *Critici sacri*, [ed. John Pearson et al.], 8 vols. (Amsterdam, 1698), 6:844–45.

32. *Annotations*, 2 vols. (London, 1683–85), 2: Matt. 25:15.

33. Erasmus, *The First Tome or Volume of the Paraphrase of Erasmus upon the New Testament* (1548), a facsimile reproduction with an introduction by John N. Wall, Jr. (Delmar, N.Y.: Scholars' Facsimiles and Reprints, 1975), fol. xcvi[v].

34. See the Geneva Bible (1560 ed.) marginalia for verses 14 and 29; Calvin, *Commentary on a Harmony of the Evangelists, Matthew, Mark and Luke (1563)*, trans. William Pringle, 3 vols. (Grand Rapids, Mich.: Baker Book House, 1981), 2:442; Joseph Hall, "Paraphrase on Hard Texts," *Works*, 10 vols. (London, 1808), 4:162–63; and Henry Hammond, *A Paraphrase, and Annotations upon all the Books of the New Testament*, 2d ed., enl. (London, 1659), 125. Those who countenanced the possibility that Jesus was encouraging his followers to use their own abilities routinely took occasion then to insist that even one's natural capacities are gifts from God.

35. *A Paraphrase on the New Testament, with Notes, Doctrinal and Practical* (1685; 3d ed., London, 1701), note on Matt. 25:18.

36. Calvin, *Commentary*, 2:443. Cf. Henry Jessey, *A Storehouse of Provision* (London, 1650), 67–68; also, Hammond's treatment of Luke's parable of the pounds (*Paraphrase*, 251).

37. William Perkins, *Works* (Cambridge, 1605), 937.

38. *The Works of Issac Barrow*, 3 vols. (New York: John C. Riker, 1845), 1:561–62; Ezekiel Hopkins, "Death Disarmed," in *Works*, 4 vols. (London, 1809), 4:155–56.

39. See Mario Miegge, *I talenti messi a profitto. L'interpretazione della parabola dei denari affidati ai servi dalla Chiesa antica a Calvino* (Urbino: Argalia, 1969), 115. Miegge has studied Calvin's interpretation of the parable vertically, in its relation to patristic and scholastic precedents, but not horizontally, in relation to other sixteenth- and seventeenth-century interpretations. His claim that Calvin effected a "rivolutione ermeneutica" (126) in the history of interpreting the parable is, in view of other commentary from Calvin's era, somewhat overstated. His belief that his work augments the thesis of Weber is possible chiefly because he has ignored the work of Calvin's contemporaries; the social emphasis in Calvin's interpretation of the parable (Miegge, 6–7, 113–26) was typical of the era and is as readily found among Catholics as Protestants. I should like to thank Professor Christopher Hill for alerting me to this study and Professor John W. O'Malley for help in reading the Italian.

40. See William Sherlock, "The Charity of Lending without Usury" [a sermon preached in Easter week, 1692], in *The English Sermon, Vol. II: 1650–1750, an Anthology*, ed. C. H. Sisson (Cheadle Hulme, England: Carcanet Press, 1976), 213–14.

41. See John T. Noonan, *The Scholastic Analysis of Usury* (Cambridge: Harvard University Press, 1957), especially 365–67. Cf. Charles H. George, "English Calvinist Opinion on Usury, 1600–1640," *Journal of the History of Ideas* 18 (October 1957): 455–74. Calvin makes no appeal to the parable in *De Usuris*.

42. Cf. Calvin, *Commentary* 2:444. The Geneva Bible interprets the Lucan version (19:11–27), to which the marginalia for Matthew's version refers, as a parable against idleness.

43. *First Tome*, fol. xcvi^v.

44. *Critici sacri*, 6:844, 849; Barrow, *Works*, 1:561; Baxter, *Paraphrase*, note on Matt. 25:16, 17.

45. See Matthew Poole's *Synopsis Criticorum*, 4 vols. in 5 (London, 1669–76), 4:599.

46. Grotius's *Annotationes in Libros Evangeliorum* (Amsterdam, 1641) was reprinted in the *Critici sacri* 6:851–54; and Poole's *Synopsis* drew on them extensively in its annotations for Matt. 25:14–30. Besides I Cor. 12:7, 11, and 29, Grotius cited Rom. 12:6 and Eph. 4:11. See also Perkins, *Works*, 937; cf. 906–8.

47. *Critici sacri*, 6:848.

48. See Clarius, *Critici sacri*, 6:848; Zegerus, 6:849. Cf. Bossuet, *Méditations sur L'Évangile*, ed. Me. Dreano (c. 1692; Paris: Librairie Philosophique J. Vrin, 1966), 285–86. Calvin, although he too acknowledged that Matthew envisaged differing responsibilities for different persons, insisted from the start that "we must not inquire anxiously into the number of the servants, or into the sums of money" (*Commentary*, 2:441).

49. *Annotations upon all the New Testament Philologicall and Theologicall* (London, 1650), 68. See also Calvin's polemical remarks incorporated in Augustine Marlorate's *Catholike and Ecclesiastical Exposition of the holy Gospel after S. Mathewe*, trans. Thomas Tymme (London, 1570), 597.

50. The *Critici sacri*, for instance, did not isolate the individual passages but printed each author's commentary on the entire twenty-fifth chapter together.

51. Vavasour Powell, ed., *Spirituall Experiences of sundry Beleevers*, 2d ed. (London, 1652), 160–91.

52. Taylor, *Ductor Dubitantium* (1660), in *The Whole Works*, ed. Reginald Heber, 15 vols. (London: Ogle, Duncan, 1822), 1:395.

53. *Complete Prose Works of John Milton*, ed. Don M. Wolfe et al., 8 vols. (New Haven: Yale University Press, 1953–82), 1:320, 801.

54. *The Poetical Works of John Milton*, ed. H. C. Beeching (Oxford: Humphrey Milford, 1922), 84.

55. Preston, *The Nevv Covenant*, 178–79.

56. George Weigel, "Camels and Needles, Talents and Treasure: American Catholicism and the Capitalist Ethic," in *The Capitalist Spirit: Toward a Religious Ethic of Wealth Creation*, ed. Peter L. Berger (San Francisco: Institute for Contemporary Studies Press, 1990), 81–105, especially 96, 103, and note #41.

57. Orello Cone, *Rich and Poor in the New Testament: A Study of the Primitive-Christian Doctrine of Earthly Possessions* (New York: Macmillan, 1902), 110.

58. William Hendriksen, *Exposition of the Gospel According to Matthew*, New Testament Commentary (Grand Rapids, Mich.: Baker Book House, 1973), 883.

59. LeRoy Lawson, *Matthew*, Standard Bible Studies (Cincinnati: Standard Publishing, 1986), 294–97.

60. T. N. Carver, "The Economic Factor in the Messiahship of Jesus," *The Christian Register* 101 (1922); quoted by Henry J. Cadbury in *The Peril of Modernizing Jesus* (New York: Macmillan, 1937), 12–13.

61. R.V.G. Tasker, *The Gospel According to Matthew: An Introduction and Commentary* (London: Tyndale, 1961), 234; Robert H. Grundy, *Matthew: A Commentary on His Literary and Theological Art* (Grand Rapids, Mich.: Eerdmans, 1982), 510.

62. See Lawson, *Matthew*, 294.

63. See Schama, *The Embarrassment of Riches*, 321–37.

5

Capitalism and Wealth Creation

JOSEPH F. QUINN

All societies develop mechanisms and institutions to deal with the problem of scarcity. Societies always have more goals than they have means to attain them. Decisions must be made about what to produce, how to produce it, and how and to whom to distribute it. A wide range of economic systems have developed to answer these questions. They have differed dramatically in their forms of productive organization, their sources of motivation and incentive, the extent and importance of markets, and the redistributive role of the state.

At one end of the spectrum were early societies where the economic units—the family, tribe, or village—were close to self-sufficient.[1] People gathered, hunted, grew, or plundered the necessities of life, primarily food and shelter. The products were consumed by the group and were generally not for sale, although some trading of surplus did take place. Markets were small, contained, and quantitatively unimportant. There were a limited number of tasks, and the allocation of specific duties was usually determined by custom or by the tribal or village head.[2] Living standards could remain unchanged for long periods of time.

A separate economy did not really exist in these early societies. Production and distribution were not determined by market exchange but were embedded in the overall institutional structure of society. Economic decisions were largely determined by tradition. Many transactions and redistributions were based on social obligations, like gift-giving.[3] The study of these relationships is more what we think of as sociology or cultural anthropology than it is economics.[4]

Intermediate stages developed with some differences and some similarities to the primitive schemes. In the Greco-Roman and medieval eras, the world remained largely agricultural. New economic relationships appeared, such as between masters and serfs and between landowners and renters. Artisan and merchant classes arose, who produced goods and services and sold them to others, and improvements in transportation dramatically increased the geographic scope of these specialized trades. But markets remained relatively unimportant in the aggregate. Land, for example, was generally not for sale, and most people continued to consume primarily what they or those nearby produced.[5]

At the other end of the economic spectrum are modern industrial nations, which bear almost no resemblance to early societies. Because of dramatic technological advances, farming is no longer the primary occupation in the developed world. Most people work for others and consume relatively little of what they produce. Markets are extensive and central to economic life. Goods and services are not bartered but sold for money, often by large business entities. The revenues are used to pay workers and the owners of other means of production, who then buy things made by others. Material living standards have risen dramatically, and daily life today is very different from what it was only a century ago.

Two interrelated developments that separate the slow, intermittent material progress of past millennia from the rapid growth of the past century or two are the Industrial Revolution and the rise of laissez-faire capitalism. The latter developed from the emerging market economies of medieval Europe. Capitalism was nurtured by the writings of philosophers and political economists such as David Hume, Adam Smith, Jeremy Bentham, and John Stuart Mill. It blossomed in nineteenth century England and, in its purest form, suffered a quick demise. Communist revolutions in the early and middle twentieth century prevented its development in the Soviet Union, China, and Eastern Europe, and the disastrous worldwide depression of the 1930s altered it significantly in Western Europe and America. In the former communist world, the fundamental concepts of laissez-faire capitalism were rejected and replaced by a very different economic system based on government ownership of the means of production and extensive central control of nearly all allocation decisions. In the West the role of government also expanded significantly, and modern mixed economies developed.

Despite the wide variety of economic systems that exist in the world today and the difficult transitional problems that many of them are suffering, it is instructive to group them into two camps or philosophies—capitalist and socialist. This does not imply that pure forms of either exist or have existed anywhere. Economies lie along a continuum. But the two camps differ enough in two important elements, the extent of private property and the use of markets, that the simplification is useful.

Economists love markets. This is one of many ways in which they differ from scholars and practitioners in many other fields. To many, markets sound cold, impersonal, and unattractive—poor mechanisms for allocating resources and improving well-being. To economists, they sound cold, impersonal, but extremely attractive—excellent mechanisms for creating wealth and improving the material well-being of members of society. Although material wealth is only one determinant of well-being, it is a very important one. Other determinants become important once basic material needs are met.

Why do economists love markets? What is the attraction? What do markets do well, and under what circumstances? What do markets do poorly, and what can be done about it?

I will argue below that a capitalist economic structure does an excellent job of creating material wealth. Under certain conditions, a competitive market economy will maximize the value of the goods created by a given set of resources. Although these conditions are rarely met in real life, they, like the frictionless plane in physics, provide a useful theoretical model, and one with powerful and surprising characteristics.

I will also argue that the market system does a good job of allocating output, given the distribution of income and wealth. The allocation will then be "efficient," an unfortunately technical and inhumane-sounding concept, but one that becomes very attractive once it is understood.

The major drawbacks of a market economy, and the reason it is long dead in its purest form, are alluded to above. The first is that the conditions necessary for efficiency rarely hold. When they go, so do the most desirable attributes of the system. But this damage can often be repaired. The second drawback is found in the phrase "given the distribution of income and wealth." Unregulated market economies can lead to income distributions that most societies find unacceptable. The pie may be large, but some of the slices are very small. This can also be remedied, but not without some loss of output. In other words, society may well be better off with fewer goods if they are allocated more equally. In fact, nearly all modern capitalistic societies accept this tradeoff and therefore tax and transfer income to various degrees.

In the sections below, I discuss briefly the historical and philosophical foundations of the competitive market economy and try to describe its appeal. I also discuss, in broad terms what can go wrong and what can be done about it. It is not that economists do not like to interfere with markets; rather, they do not like to interfere without a good reason. Fortunately or unfortunately, good reasons abound.

THE PHILOSOPHICAL FOUNDATIONS OF THE MARKET ECONOMY

Adam Smith is generally considered to be the father of capitalism and the free market system, but he was really one of a number of philosophers who were thinking and writing in a similar vein. They were trying to do for social interactions what Isaac Newton had done a century earlier for the physical world—to explain a complex social order with some general "laws of motion" based on simple underlying principles.

The early political economists were advocates of utilitarianism, a philosophy proposed by David Hume, Jeremy Bentham, and James and John Stuart Mill.[6] The central propositions are that individual well-being should be the ultimate end of moral action, and that societal decisions should be evaluated on the basis of their consequences—on whether or not they make people happier. The goal of social action is the maximization of general utility, or, in Bentham's words, "It is the greatest happiness of the greatest number that is the measure of right or wrong." The early proponents assumed that utility, or well-being, could be quantified and measured and therefore added across individuals. This turned out to be a major stumbling block.

What has survived to this day in economics is the basic notion that individual preferences are the starting point of social analysis. Because of this emphasis, utilitarianism was quickly abandoned by the other social sciences, like sociology, where the emphasis is on exactly what economists tend to ignore—the power of social forces and interactions to alter these underlying preferences. What is exogenous to the economist is a major focus of the sociologist.

One of the early social scientists was David Hume (1711–1776). Although his economic essays are only a small fraction of his writings, he anticipated many of the concepts later described by Smith.[7] Based on empirical observations, he concluded that people work in order to satisfy their desires for consumption, challenge, and gain—the last referring to the accumulation of the trappings of success. Since Hume was a utilitarian, he judged the desirability of the commercial and industrial society he saw developing on this basis.

In Hume's view, the emerging capitalist society did well. Economic growth directly addressed workers' desires for consumption and challenge and had favorable noneconomic effects as well. Economic development contributed to the growth of knowledge in the liberal and mechanical arts, enhanced a nation's ability to defend itself, and advanced political harmony.[8] The growth of commerce also encouraged the development of a middle class interested in laws protecting their property, and this, according to Hume, led to parliamentary government and respect for individual liberty. Here is an invisible hand of sorts, but with political rather than economic consequences.

Economists have tended to emphasize only the first of Hume's reasons for work—the desire for consumption. It is worth noting that Hume had a much broader conception of "economic man." He argued, for example, that although people do seek pleasure, they are also driven by instincts, which sometime induce them to do things not directly in their own best interests.[9] Individual welfare depends on much more than individual material wealth.

Adam Smith (1732–1790) was able to synthesize, expand, and popularize much of the rudimentary social science of the time.[10] He was also one of the early systematic analysts of economic growth. When he wrote *An Inquiry into the Nature and Causes of the Wealth of Nations* in the late eighteenth century, he was studying a chaotic social revolution that was disrupting a once orderly society. Millions of peasants had been turned into paupers by Enclosure Laws that had thrown them off land their ancestors had worked for years. Labor and capital were being combined in factories—a new and initially inhumane mode of production. Poverty and unemployment were rampant, and parish poorhouses overflowing. As Heilbroner has written, "The market system . . . was born in agony—an agony that began in the thirteenth century and did not run its course until well into the nine-teenth."[11]

Smith's contribution, borrowing heavily from the insights of earlier and contemporary authors, was to rationalize the chaos he saw and to describe a comprehensive structure for what must have first seemed like hell on earth. He proposed a new set of societal laws of motion—a blueprint of the developing economy—based on a controversial concept of economic man. Motion implies direction, and Smith's direction was forward. He painted a generally optimistic picture of economic growth and progress and fore-cast steadily improving material well-being for the common man.[12]

This new society was to be based on a seemingly untrustworthy main character—a self-seeking (utilitarian) individual motivated by personal gain—and on the revolutionary concept of free markets in both output and in the factors of production: labor, land, and capital.[13] Smith did not describe self-interest as a virtue, but rather as a fact of life and an important economic force. The mechanism to regulate this potentially destructive selfishness was not government but competition, and the ultimate winner would be the consumer.

The key features of Smith's vision are the private ownership of the means of production and the extensive use of markets to determine what gets produced, how it gets produced, and who ends up with it—the central economic questions faced by any society. Individuals, entrepreneurs, and firms are asked only to look out for their own well-being, to do the best they can given the constraints they face. In each market prices adjust to equate supply and demand. Prices tell producers about the preferences of consum-ers and allocate the output among those demanding it. Excess demand raises prices, which induces supply and lowers demand until they are equal; excess supply lowers prices, which does the reverse.

If the number of producers of a particular product is large, no one of them can affect the price, and anyone attempting to charge more than the market price will find no buyers. Profits induce an influx of additional producers, whose competition drives down the market price until the profits are eliminated. The economy is self-regulating in that prices, profits, and costs cannot long depart from their equilibrium values. Consumers end up with the products they want, produced and sold by firms at a price equal to the minimum possible cost of production. Markets deliver the goods.

All this happens without any central planning, and no altruistic behavior on the part of any of the participants is required. As the Lay Commission on Catholic Social Teaching, a particularly pro-capitalist group, has noted, capitalism's "driving force does not depend on extraordinary altruism, but on far more ordinary and statistically more frequent motivations."[14] In Adam Smith's famous words,

It is not from the benevolence of the butcher, the brewer, or the baker that we expect our dinner, but from their regard of their own self-interest. [The producer] neither intends to promote the public interest, nor knows how much he is promoting it. . . . By directing that industry in such a manner as its produce may be of the greatest value, he intends only his own gain, and he is in this, as in many other cases, led by an invisible hand to promote an end which was in no part his intention. . . . By pursuing his own interest he frequently promotes that of the society more effectually than when he really intends to promote it.[15]

Material wealth, in Smith's view, comes primarily from the division of labor—laborers, combined with capital, concentrating on only one small aspect of the productive process. At the very beginning of *The Wealth of Nations*, Smith writes that "the greatest improvement in the productive powers of labor . . . seem[s] to have been the effects of the division of labour."[16] In his famous pin factory example, he suggests that "ten persons . . . could make among them upwards of forty-eight thousand pins in a day. . . . But if they had all wrought separately and independently . . ., they certainly could not each of them have made twenty, perhaps not even one pin in a day."[17]

The key to this kingdom is capital, output that is not consumed but rather saved and reinvested in enterprise.

Whenever capital predominates, industry prevails. . . . Every increase . . . of capital, therefore, naturally tends to increase . . . the real quantity of industry, the number of productive hands, and consequently the exchangeable value of the annual produce of the land and labour of the country, the real wealth and revenue of all its inhabitants. . . . By what a frugal man annually saves, he not only affords maintenance to an additional number of productive hands . . . but, like the founder of a public workhouse, he establishes as it were a perpetual fund for the maintenance of an equal number in all times to come. . . . When we compare . . . the state of the nation at two different periods, and find that the annual produce of its land and labour is evidently greater at the latter than at the former, that its lands are better cultivated, its manufactures more numerous and more flourishing, and its trade more extensive, we may be assured that its capital must have increased during the interval between those two periods.[18]

Without capital accumulation, the gains from the division of labor are short-lived and economic growth nonexistent.

Fortunately, there is no need for government intervention to encourage this essential parsimonious behavior. To Smith, it is natural, and will occur on its own.

The principle which prompts to save is the desire of bettering our condition, a desire which, though generally calm and dispassionate, comes with us from the womb and never leaves us till we go into the grave. . . . An augmentation of fortune is the means by which the greater part of men propose and wish to better their condition . . . and the most likely way of augmenting their fortune is to save and accumulate some part of what they acquire. . . . In the greater part of men . . . the principle of frugality seems not only to predominate, but to predominate very greatly. . . . The natural effort of every individual to better his condition, when suffered to exert itself with freedom and security, is so powerful, that it is alone, and without any assistance, capable of carrying on the society to wealth and prosperity.[19]

According to Keynes, this theory of laissez-faire capitalism seemed to provide

a divine harmony between private advantage and public good . . . [and] . . . gave the notion a good scientific basis. Suppose that by the working of natural laws individuals pursuing their own interests with enlightenment in conditions of freedom always tend to promote the general interests at the same time! Our philosophical difficulties are resolved. . . . The political philosopher could retire in favor of the business man—for the latter could attain the philosopher's *summum bonum* by just pursuing his own private profit.[20]

Smith's view of the future was not entirely rosy, but his central message was. The struggle for personal gain, combined with a just legal system, could hold a society together. It could also provide for steadily improving material well-being, provided that it was not too severely hobbled by "the monopolizing spirit of merchants and manufacturers" or the "impertinent obstructions with which the folly of human laws too often encumbers its operations."[21]

Jeremy Bentham (1748–1832), a contemporary of Smith's, was a committed utilitarian who believed strongly in the natural principle of self-interest. Bentham provided a goal for society (the greatest happiness) and Smith, the means. But Bentham was much less sanguine than Smith that individuals acting in their own best interests would bring about this universal happiness.[22] He thought it necessary to impose sanctions and incentives on people in order to harmonize their private best interests with those of society.

Bentham spent much of his time proposing laws and institutions to do just that. He was an interventionist and envisioned government roles in education, health, insurance, public works, and income redistribution. Modern economists may owe as much to Bentham as to Smith, since many economists' proposals involve not leaving the market system alone, but rather harnessing it to induce people to behave in a way that will make society better off. Tax breaks for homeowners and marketable pollution rights are two simple examples of this—the former long a mainstay of the tax code but the latter still a marginal and unpopular (except to economists) weapon in the defense of the environment.

Capitalism is a popular form of economic organization today, although it has changed dramatically from what Smith observed and described. It dominates the most developed nations of the world and is sought by many as a hope of salvation in the rest.[23] Philosophers, economists, and others have written extensively on its advantages and disadvantages, and they are very much part of the modern political and economic debate.

THE CASE FOR A MARKET ECONOMY

Arguments for capitalism have come from two main sources. The first is political. Some have argued that capitalism is philosophically consistent with political freedom and liberty. If the latter are desirable goals, then this reflects well on the former. The second argument is economic and is really a modern version of Adam Smith's contribution. People who like capitalism like it because it works, and even if it does not always work well, it works better than any of the alternatives that have been tried.

Political Issues

Adam Smith wrote near the end of the Enlightenment, a period of intellectual history that championed the emancipation of the individual from political, clerical, and mercantilist restrictions. From this era grew political systems based on the rights of individuals and an economic system built on their preferences.

Under capitalism the allocation of resources is largely determined by the desires of individual consumers. People speak through markets, and although no single voice can be heard, the combined chorus comes through loud and clear. Firms that produce what the market demands prosper; those that do not either adapt or disappear. Individuals have choice over occupation and location. Although no one would argue that the range of choices is the same for all, the modern capitalist economy is a far cry from the constraining medieval and mercantilist systems that the Enlightenment helped to dismantle.[24]

In the capitalist economy, however, there remains a significant and indispensable role for government. Although Adam Smith is most often quoted for his articulate and often amusing opinions on the shortcomings of government, his economic blueprint required a stable governmental structure within which people could go about their business.

According to the system of natural liberty, the sovereign has only three duties to attend to: three duties of great importance . . . first . . . protecting the society from the violence and invasion of other independent societies; second . . . protecting, as far as possible, every member of the society from . . . injustice or oppression . . . [and] . . . establishing an exact administration of justice; and thirdly . . . erecting and maintaining certain public works and certain public institutions.[25]

Where government was neither needed nor wanted was in the markets for most goods and services, where the preferences of individuals would rule the day.

These economic freedoms are laudable goals in themselves. Adam Smith claimed that the failure to allow individuals to employ their capital and labor as they desire is a salient violation of a sacred right. Milton Friedman wrote that "freedom in economic arrangements is itself a component of freedom broadly understood, so economic freedom is an end in itself."[26] The Lay Commission on Catholic Social Teaching argued that the

market system is validated because it is the only system built upon the liberty of its participants. That it also works better to promote invention and to yield an incredible bounty is a secondary (although not insignificant) advantage. A market system values new ideas, the inventor, the entrepreneur, the creator, and it values the free, individual choices of every worker and participant.[27]

But many have gone further than this and argued that the economic freedom central to capitalism is, at a minimum, highly correlated with political freedom and democracy, or, more strongly, an absolute prerequisite. Friedman claims the latter, that capitalism is a necessary condition for political freedom. Peter Berger is less certain about the causation but notes that "democracy developed precisely in the same Western countries in which modern capitalism unfolded." He claims that all democracies are capitalist.[28] Although capitalist economies that are not democratic are easy to find (Fascist Germany, Greece under the junta, Pinochet's Chile, or South Africa today), noncapitalist democracies are rare if not nonexistent. Berger's reading of history also suggests to him that there is a positive correlation between democracy and respect for human rights, although he admits that there is no logical necessity for that to be the case.[29]

A main connection between capitalism and individual freedom is that capitalism creates a gap (a small one, according to many critics and almost all students of electoral politics) between economic power and political power. It removes many important decisions from the political arena. Heilbroner makes this point nicely.

Capitalism is unique in history in having not one but two centers of authority, one built around the "economic" prerogatives of the business system, and the other around the "political" prerogatives of the governmental system. In all other socie- ties, from primitive to socialist, a single source of authority—village council, king, priesthood, party—makes both the determinations of war, law, and public cere- mony, which we recognize as political, and the decisions on what shall be produced and how it shall be produced, which we call economic. A seamless cloak of authority thus extends over the entire social structure. . . . Under capitalism, this cloak is torn in two. . . . Capitalist governments . . . are excluded from what is elsewhere a first prerogative of rulership—direct command over the material resources on which rulership must depend. . . . Capitalists . . . no longer possess the basic powers that accrue to persons of similar importance under earlier systems; unlike the most minor feudal lords, they cannot try, imprison, or forcibly muster "their" work forces, or enjoy the privileges of a legal code different from that applicable to other groups.[30]

In a similar vein, Friedman argues that "by removing the organization of economic activity from the control of political authority, the market elimi- nates a source of coercive power. It enables economic strength to be a check to political power rather than a reinforcement."[31]

Capitalism and democracy do appear to go together. They both depend critically on choices made by individuals, and these choices have more impact on society than they do in more centralized economic systems. They both have mechanisms that limited the power of central authority, and they are both attractive to those who favor personal freedom and individual rights.

Economic Issues

There are at least two ways to discuss the economic attractions of a capitalist system. The first is to concentrate on some features that seem desirable. The second is to compare the actual record of capitalist societies with those of other systems and draw conclusions about the likely impact of economic and political organization on well-being, material and other- wise. I will concentrate on the former, then mention the latter only briefly.

A capitalist economy tends to produce goods and services that consum- ers are willing to buy. Resources are not wasted on output that people do not want. If calculators are desirable, then calculators will appear. If slide rules become obsolete, then they will disappear. These responses to the changing demands of consumers require no government intervention. Prices provide signals about current preferences, and the potential for profit induces firms to meet them.

In addition, profit-seeking firms are always trying to introduce new and better products and services. The menu of choice is constantly changing. Those new products that sell remain on the menu; those that do not are soon dropped.

To judge this invisible hand desirable, one must respect the underlying individual preferences. Although there are many exceptions (society requires school attendance and Social Security contributions; it outlaws the use of heroin and the sale of vital human organs), economists generally assume that the consumer knows best. These preferences are determined by a myriad of factors, including nature, nurture, education, and advertising. Economists, in the utilitarian tradition, tend to view the final outcome as legitimate and are generally reluctant to override others' preferences with their own.

Output can be produced in many ways. Rice can be grown with lots of land and little labor, or the reverse. Which method makes more sense? Again, the market will decide. Factor prices reflect relative scarcities, which in turn reflect alternative uses of these resources. Resources with valuable alternative uses will be expensive; those without will be cheap. Profit-maximizing firms will choose the least expensive combination of inputs in order to minimize production costs. If the supply of oil decreases, its price will rise. Producers will look for alternatives, not because of any altruistic motivation to share the burden, but because it is in their financial best interests to find a cheaper combination to do the job. These difficult decisions also require no central planning. Producers will do what an omniscient and benevolent dictator would command—produce what the people want at minimum cost.

Profits are an essential mechanism in this system. To an economist, profit refers to economic, or excess, profit—returns over and above opportunity cost, what the entrepreneur could earn elsewhere.[32] In a competitive economy, economic profits are always being driven to zero. Zero profits do not imply that entrepreneurs are earning nothing, only that they are earning no more than they could earn elsewhere. Positive profits induce others into the market, increasing supply, lowering prices, and reducing profits. Negative profits do the reverse. Equilibrium—the only situation in which firms are not being induced in or induced out—occurs when profits are zero. Only the most efficient—lowest cost— firms can make zero profits. Higher cost (inefficient) firms suffer losses.

Inefficiency has a very specific meaning to an economist. A particular allocation of resources is inefficient if it would be possible, by reallocating, to make someone better off without making anyone else worse off. This is a relatively noncontroversial criterion for action. From this perspective

inefficient allocations are really unfortunate, because they imply that someone could have been made better off and was not.

In contrast, an allocation is called efficient if all such reallocations have
occurred—if it is no longer possible to make someone better off without
making someone else worse off. Of course, it is always possible to make
someone better off while making someone else worse off—just take something from the latter and give it to the former. It is much more difficult here
to judge whether society as a whole is better off. This requires quantifying
and comparing the gains and losses of different people.

Under certain circumstances, the allocation of resources that results from
a competitive market economy will be efficient. This can be shown formally,
and this is done in most microeconomics textbooks. It is hard to think of
any other allocation scheme that can make this claim. It is a theoretical
point, but one that has much to do with economists' love of markets.
Markets can do something that no other system can. In a world of scarce
resources, where needs outweigh means, this is an important feature,
although one that might be outweighed by other disadvantages of the
market system, like income distribution.

There are many such efficient allocations, including one where one
individual has all the resources, each associated with a different initial
allocation of wealth.[33] Choosing among them is much more difficult, because this involves comparing someone's loss with another's gain. Of
course, in real life that is exactly what policy decisions involve, so our
efficiency criterion, though relatively noncontroversial, is of limited practical use. What remains is a powerful theoretical point: markets can do
something that no other form of economic organization could possibly
do—allocate scarce resources efficiently. Unless the society has no unmet
needs, this is a credential worth considering. The use of the word "efficiency" to convey this concept may be a poor one. As Thomas Schelling has
written,

Unfortunately, economists use the term "efficiency" to describe this process, and
often distinguish between considerations of "equity" and "efficiency." The word
"efficiency" sounds more like engineering than human satisfaction. . . . If I tell you
that "not efficient" merely means that I can think of something better—something
potentially better from the points of view of all parties concerned—you can at least
be excused for wondering why I use "efficient" in such an unaccustomed way. The
only explanation I can think of is that economists talk mainly to each other.[34]

It is very difficult to summarize the performance of an economy with a
single index or two. A popular summary statistic is output per capita. This
is certainly related to the material well-being of the populace, although it
ignores many relevant dimensions. It generally ignores home production
and underground economies (which tend to be more important in a less
developed country), the value of leisure, the negative externalities (like

pollution) associated with production, the composition of output (e.g., consumer goods versus military material), and the distribution of output (which is discussed below). In addition, the relative standing of nations can change dramatically with changes in exchange rates, since comparisons are made in a common currency. Despite all these caveats, the relative economic performance of capitalist nations along this dimension is so different from that of nations with other forms of economic organization that it is worth mentioning.

The International Bank for Reconstruction and Development estimated 1990 Gross National Product per capita for 125 nations. Of the twenty-four countries in the top category, with GNP per capita ranging from about $10,000 (Ireland) to $33,000 (Switzerland), twenty-two are capitalist societies. The other two (Kuwait and the United Arab Emirates) are oil-exporting nations. The top socialist economies were Hungary, Yugoslavia, and Czechoslovakia, with about $3,000 per capita.[35] This is confirmed by comparisons (casual or otherwise) of East and West Germany or North and South Korea. It is difficult to argue that capitalist nations do not do a better job of producing material wealth than similarly situated socialist neighbors.

THE CASE AGAINST AN (UNREGULATED) MARKET ECONOMY

There are several points that counter the arguments above. The impressive allocative features of a competitive market economy depend on a number of assumptions that are either controversial or unrealistic. When the assumptions fail, so do the allocation conclusions, and government intervention may be appropriate. Also, societies have noneconomic goals, and the use of markets may interfere with some of these. Finally, the attractiveness of an economy depends not only on the size of the pie, but also on its distribution. There is nothing in the theory discussed above that guarantees that the competitive allocation will be equitable, fair, or politically sustainable over time.

Competitive Market Assumptions

The competitive model is built on a number of assumptions—that people know what is best for themselves, that more consumption makes someone better off, and that people behave in their own self-interest. None of these is universally true. We do not allow young children to decide whether to go to school, and we try to prevent certain types of self-destructive behavior in adults. People can be envious and may well be worse off if their consumption goes up while that of another increases even more. People leap on grenades to save others and leave tips in restaurants they will never visit again.

The question is not whether these behavioral assumptions are universally true—clearly they are not—but whether they provide a simple and useful basis for understanding a certain subset of human behavior. Here, social scientists and philosophers can differ. Most economists, following Hume, Smith, Bentham, and Mill, believe that rational self-interest is a useful simple description of the motivation for economic activity, and that it will lead us less astray than other simple explanations. Others disagree, and think that models of rational economic man leave out too much that is essential to human behavior.[36]

The model also assumes much about the state of the world. People are assumed to have perfect information, which they do not, and markets are assumed to clear. Labor markets certainly do not always clear, as many long episodes of mass unemployment make painfully obvious. There must be a sufficient number of buyers and sellers of each good, service, and factor of production so that no one has any influence over any market price. Monopolists and oligopolists, on the other hand, do have market power and can reduce quantities and raise prices above the competitive level. Smith understood this and described the danger in one of his most famous passages. "People of the same trade seldom meet together, even for merriment and diversion, but the conversation ends in a conspiracy against the public, or in some contrivance to raise prices."[37] Competition is the disciplinarian that keeps costs and prices low; without it, the consumer suffers. One of the roles of good government is to prevent agreements in restraint of free trade. Unfortunately, then and now, governments often do just the reverse and encourage anticompetitive behavior.

An unregulated market economy also works poorly in the presence of externalities—situations in which the behavior of one party imposes costs or benefits on another. Pollution is a good example. If some of the costs of production are not borne by the producer (for example, they fall on people living downwind or downstream), then the firm, acting in its own best interests, will not minimize total costs. It will minimize the private costs of production but ignore those downstream. In such cases, too much of the product will be produced and it will be sold too cheaply—at a price that does not reflect its true cost to society. Market intervention is needed, à la Bentham—a tax on the good is a simple solution to raise the cost to the firm to the full social cost. Once these externalities have been internalized to the firm by the imposition of the tax, profit maximization and the (now regulated) market will again promote society's best interest.

Governments must also intervene to regulate natural monopolies (industries in which costs of production are minimized by having only one supplier, like electric power transmission within a community) and to provide public goods—those, in Smith's words, "which it can never be in the interest of any individual . . . to erect and maintain; because the profit could never repay the expense to any individual . . . though it may frequently do more than repay it to a great society."[38]

There are many exceptions to the rule that markets know best. Government intervention is needed to supply certain goods, encourage some, and discourage others. But a regulated market economy, even a highly regulated one, is still a market economy. Prices send signals to producers and consumers, and production decisions are largely determined by consumers' preferences. The point of the regulation is to tinker with, but not eliminate, market incentives to have prices reflect true social costs and to regain the efficiency features mentioned above.

Noneconomic Goals

Most societies have intentionally excluded many goods and services from market exchange. People have rights and entitlements that they are not allowed to sell. Slavery and the sale of children are generally outlawed. It is usually illegal to buy and sell votes, even though both the buyer and the seller would presumably be made better off by this voluntary exchange. In many societies medical care has been removed from the market and provided by a nationalized health service.

A fascinating question—and one that goes well beyond the realm of economics and the scope of this chapter—is what is the appropriate extent of the market? Few would object to a man or woman selling locks of hair to a wig manufacturer. Hair is not essential to life, and it regenerates. Most would object strenuously to the sale of a child. There are many points along this spectrum. What about blood? It is essential to life, but it regenerates. Some societies have active markets in blood, while others, like ours, rely primarily on volunteer donations. What about kidneys? They are essential to life, they do not regenerate, but each of us has a spare. The sale of vital organs is illegal in the United States, even though the volunteer supply is grossly inadequate, and many people suffer and die because of it. If a market in kidneys would increase the supply, would the benefits to the recipients outweigh the ethical concerns? What about paying people now for the right to harvest their organs after death? What about surrogate motherhood? In each of these cases, informed and voluntary market agreements could make both parties in the exchange better off. But society often determines that larger interests supersede economic efficiency, and many goods remain allocated through nonmarket means.

Certain transactions may actually change the nature of the goods or services involved.[39] Some things may have value because they have no price. Purchasing friendship is very different from having a friend. Buying sex changes the nature of the act. A market in pollution rights (an outstanding idea from an economic perspective) may confer legitimacy on pollution and damage societal attitudes toward nature.

Markets are good, but in their place. Where appropriate, they do certain things very well. But they are often inappropriate, and alternative allocative mechanisms are preferred.

Income Distribution

Markets treat some people very poorly. Even Adam Smith feared the eventual impact of his ultimate engine of growth, the division of labor.

The man whose whole life is spent in performing a few simple operations . . . has no occasion to exert his understanding, or to exercise his invention. . . . He naturally loses, therefore, the habit of such exertion, and generally becomes as stupid and ignorant as it is possible for a human creature to become. . . . In every improved and civilized society this is the state into which the labouring poor, that is, the great body of the people, must necessarily fall, unless government takes some pains to prevent it.[40]

Capitalism puts workers at the mercy of changing markets. An advantage of market allocation is that production automatically rises and falls with consumer demands. But shifting preferences, technological change, and recessions cause unemployment, and the transitional costs to individuals and locales can be severe. Capitalism can create insecurity and instability.[41] Although improved macroeconomic policies have reduced the magnitude of the fluctuations, and welfare policies, to varying degrees in different countries, have reduced their impact, business cycles remain serious problems.

In a market economy earnings depend on one's resources, including labor and human capital, and the returns they earn in the market. Because both the distribution of endowments and their returns are unequal, the resulting income distribution can be highly skewed. Adam Smith anticipated this and its impact: "Whenever there is great property, there is great inequality. For one very rich man, there must be at least 500 poor, and the affluence of the few supposes the indigence of the many. . . . No society can surely be flourishing and happy, of which the far greater part of the members are poor and miserable."[42]

In the United States, for example, the richest 20 percent of the households has nearly half (47 percent in 1991) of the total pretax income, while the bottom 20 percent has less than 4 percent. In fact, the top 5 percent has nearly 5 times the aggregate income (18 percent) as the bottom 20 percent.[43] U.S. wealth data tell the same story. In 1988 the poorest 20 percent of all households, measured by income, had 7 percent of the total household net worth in the country; the top 20 percent had 44 percent.[44]

Table 1 shows analogous income data for seven capitalist countries around 1980.[45] While the United States does have the largest ratio of the quintile percentages, the other ratios, with the exception of Sweden, are

Table 1
Distribution of Gross Pre-tax Family Income, by Quintile, around 1980

Country	Highest Quintile	Lowest Quintile	Ratio
Canada	4.6%	41.4%	9.0
United States	3.8	44.5	11.7
United Kingdom	4.9	40.8	8.3
West Germany	4.4	46.9	10.7
Sweden	6.6	38.9	5.9
Norway	4.9	39.8	8.1
Israel	4.5	43.6	9.7

Source: O'Higgins, Schmaus and Stephenson (1989: table 2).

Table 2
Distribution of Net After-tax Family Income, by Quintile, around 1980

Country	Lowest Quintile	Highest Quintile	Ratio
Canada	5.3%	39.7%	7.5
United States	4.5	41.0	9.1
United Kingdom	5.8	39.5	6.8
West Germany	5.0	45.8	9.2
Sweden	8.0	36.9	4.6
Norway	6.3	36.7	5.8
Israel	6.0	39.5	6.6

Source: O'Higgins, Schmaus and Stephenson (1989: table 2).

similar. The pretax cash income of the richest 20 percent of the families ranges from eight (or from six, including Sweden) to twelve times that of the poorest 20 percent. This is already a tempered version of the capitalist outcome, because these income data include cash transfer payments from the government.

When after-tax family income is considered (Table 2), the ratios are all lower.[46] Sweden stands out at one end, the United States and West Germany at the other. But the fact remains that the income distribution in capitalist countries is very unequal.

Another way to assess economic standing is through poverty measures—the number and percentage of people living in households that fall below some poverty threshold.[47] Poverty in America remains extensive, especially among certain subgroups. In 1991, for example, over 14 percent

Table 3
Relative and Absolute Poverty Rates around 1980

Country	Relative	Absolute
Australia	12.2%	13.2%
Canada	12.6	7.4
West Germany	5.6	8.3
Norway	5.2	8.6
Sweden	5.3	5.6
Switzerland	8.5	5.8
United Kingdom	9.7	11.8
United States	17.1	12.7
Unweighted average	9.2	9.5

Source: Smeeding, Torrey and Rein (1988: table 5–2).

of all Americans (36 million people) were officially poor. Among blacks and Hispanics the percentages were 33 and 29 percent. Over 20 percent of all American children (under age 18) are in poverty households; this includes nearly half (46 percent) of all black children and 40 percent of all Hispanic children.[48] Even when all the noncash government transfer programs (like Medicare, Medicaid, food stamps, and housing allowances) are included, plus an imputed return on owner-occupied housing, 10 percent of all Americans (and over 20 percent of all blacks and Hispanics) live in poverty households.[49]

Smeeding, Torrey, and Rein have attempted some cross-national comparisons of poverty rates in eight capitalist countries around 1980 using both an absolute and a relative standard.[50] The absolute figures use the U.S. poverty threshold, translated to other currencies; the relative standard uses one-half of each country's median income as its poverty line. As seen in Table 3, the poverty rates average about 9 percent by either measure. A significant minority is left behind, although the social safety nets in some of these countries have reduced the poverty populations to about 5 percent. The United States is at the other end of the spectrum.

In a relatively recent article, Richard Barnet called attention "to the problems of American capitalism—falling standards of living, inadequate education and health care, shameful poverty amid glitzy affluence, crime, addiction, the shadow of environmental catastrophe, and the seeming paralysis of the political system in responding to these multiple challenges."[51] But problems are relative. Our poverty thresholds would define a wealthy family in much of the less developed world. As Adam Smith said, with only a bit of exaggeration,

Observe the accommodation of the most common artificer or day laborer in a civilized and thriving country. . . . The accommodation of an European prince does not always so much exceed that of an industrious and frugal peasant, as the accommodation of the latter exceeds that of many an African king, the absolute master of lives and liberties of ten thousand naked savages.[52]

But comparisons can go both ways. O'Higgins, Schmaus, and Stephenson estimate that in the United States, cash government transfers account for about 8 percent of aggregate gross income. In Sweden, another capitalist country with private ownership of property and extensive market allocation of resources, transfers are nearly 30 percent.[53] The results are not surprising: as we have seen, their income is much more evenly distributed than ours. The overall Swedish poverty rate is less than half of that in America. It is less than a third of ours for children and about one-eighth for the elderly.[54]

There is a trade-off between the size of the pie and its distribution. Generous income maintenance programs can diminish work incentives and decrease labor supply. Although there is little debate about the sign of these effects, there is great disagreement about their magnitudes. In an exhaustive survey of American income transfer programs, Danziger, Haveman, and Plotnick conclude that the aggregate labor supply effect is modest. They estimate that if all public transfers were eliminated, aggregate labor supply would increase by less than 5 percent.[55] Because not all of those looking for work would find it, and because income transfer recipients tend to have lower than average market wage rates, the increase in total earnings would be even less—about 3.5 percent.[56]

Charles Murray, on the other hand, argues that the long-run effects of American social welfare programs have been devastating to those they were designed to help.[57] According to him, they have destroyed incentive and self-confidence among the poor, eliminated any sense of personal responsibility for one's condition, and created a dependent and self-perpetuating underclass.

Arthur Okun invented a useful analogy—the leaky bucket—to describe the income redistribution trade-off:

This program [to transfer income from the wealthy to the poor] has an unsolved technical problem; the money must be carried from the rich to the poor in a leaky bucket. Some of it will simply disappear in transit, so the poor will not receive all of the money that is taken from the rich. . . . Suppose 10 percent leaks out. . . . Should society still make the switch? If 50 percent leaks out? 75 percent? Even if 99 percent leaks out, the poor still get a little benefit. . . . Where would you draw the line?[58]

Danziger, Haveman, and Plotnick found this analogy useful, and estimated that the leakage due just to the lower earnings of income transfer recipients equals about a quarter (23 percent) of the transfer. For every dollar transferred, the income of the poor rises by about seventy-seven cents. Is 23 percent too large to make the transfer worthwhile? Or is this a price worth paying to reduce income inequality in a capitalist society? There is no right answer. The trade-off is there, and whether to accept it depends on one's own views (which will certainly be influenced by the end of the bucket brigade at which one stands) and, in the aggregate, on the nation's political judgment.

CONCLUSION

Like economies, attitudes toward capitalism are cyclical. In the depths of the Great Depression, Adam Smith would have been a tough sell. Several years ago, with the collapse of the former Soviet Union and the fall of the Berlin Wall, he was the toast of the town. Currently, as the costs of transition from a planned to a market economy become clear, many citizens in these transitional economies are having second thoughts—some about the final goal and others about the route to achieve it.

Adam Smith synthesized a number of valuable insights. A system of private property, free enterprise, and competitive markets, within a stable political and legal structure, provides fertile soil for economic growth and development. Individuals working in their own best interests often do work in society's best interests as well. Often, but not always. Government intervention is essential to prevent monopolistic power, to make firms consider the full cost of their activities, and to provide public goods. Unregulated market economies simply do not perform well in these areas.[59]

Nor is the distribution of income that unregulated market economies would generate acceptable to most developed nations. Significant income redistribution occurs in Western capitalist countries, more so in Europe than in the United States. According to both Berger and Heilbroner, the debate today is not about capitalism versus socialism, but rather about the appropriate extent and means of government intervention and redistribution.[60] The irony is that the superior wealth-generating characteristics of a capitalist system provide the means for a more generous welfare state. How generous is best? During the 1970s the European experience seemed superior to the stagflation in America. In the 1980s, however, the reverse was true, and the U.S. economy rebounded while Europe suffered from high unemployment and Eurosclerosis, partly because of well-meaning social programs that inhibited labor market flexibility.

The main threat to capitalism, in my view, is not the external threat of a vastly different socioeconomic structure, but rather the internal tensions of the divergent standards of living that our version of capitalism generates at home, and, according to Heilbroner, "our indifference, bordering on hostility, to the large and wretched underclass that has appeared in recent years."[61] Although the current situation depends on much more than our choice of an economic system, I believe that changes within the system could alleviate much of it. Our political philosophy is based on equality and our economic philosophy on inequality. True, the poor here may have more than the middle class elsewhere, but this is cold comfort to those at the bottom of the heap.

Despite these serious problems of equity and justice, I must agree with Heilbroner that

capitalism organizes the material affairs of humankind more satisfactorily than socialism; that however inequitably or irresponsibly the marketplace may distribute goods, it does so better than the queues of a planned economy; however mindless the culture of commercialism, it is more attractive than state moralism; and however deceptive the ideology of a business civilization, it is more believable than that of a socialist one.[62]

In Jacob Viner's words, if the mixed economy—the capitalist welfare state—is worth fighting for, "it is because, despite its imperfections in theory and in practice, in the aggregate it provides more promise of preserving and enlarging human freedoms, temporal prosperity, the extinction of mass misery, and the dignity of man and his moral improvement than any other social system."[63]

It is appropriate to end with the most prominent and important economist of this century, John Maynard Keynes, who concluded in *The End of Laissez-Faire* that "capitalism, wisely managed, can probably be made more efficient for attaining economic ends than any alternative system yet in sight. Our problem is to work out a social organization which shall be as efficient as possible without offending our notions of a satisfactory way of life."[64]

NOTES

I would like to thank my colleagues Frank McLaughlin, Harold Petersen, and the members of the interdisciplinary faculty seminar who produced the chapters in this volume for very helpful comments on an earlier draft of my work.

1. Manuel Gottlieb, *Comparative Economic Systems: Preindustrial and Modern Case Studies* (Ames: Iowa State University Press, 1988). Gottlieb identifies eleven different modes of production, of increasing complexity, from primitive domestic through public, the latter denoting an extensive government presence. His list has been telescoped considerably here.

2. Adam Smith wrote that in ancient Egypt "every man was bound by a principle of religion to follow the occupation of his father, and was supposed to commit the most horrible sacrilege if he changed to another." Robert L. Heilbroner, *The Worldly Philosophers* (New York: Simon and Schuster, 1953), 10.

3. George Dalton, *Primitive, Archaic and Modern Economies: Essays of Karl Polanyi* (Boston: Beacon Press, 1968), xxiii–xxiv.

4. Heilbroner has argued that this is the reason that economists did not exist before the eighteenth century. "As long as the problem of survival was handled by tradition or command, the economic problem never gave rise to that special field of study called economics . . . economics waited upon the invention of a third solution to the problem of survival . . . the 'market system.' " Heilbroner, *Worldly Philosophers*, 11.

5. Ibid., 19.

6. I have drawn liberally on C. B. Welch, "Utilitarianism," in *The Invisible Hand*, ed. John Eatwell, Murray Milgate, and Peter Newman (New York: W. W. Norton, 1989), 257–70.

7. This section draws heavily on Eugene Rotwein, "David Hume," in *The Invisible Hand*, 134–42.

8. This point is similar to one made much later by Lester Thurow. It is much easier to keep competing groups happy in an era of economic growth than it is when each group's gain implies an equal loss by another. Lester Thurow, *The Zero-Sum Society* (New York: Basic Books, 1980).

9. This point is the main focus of Robert Frank's book *Passions within Reason: The Strategic Role of Emotions* (New York: W. W. Norton, 1988), whose first chapter is entitled "Beyond Self-Interest." Frank argues that many of these actions that are not in one's rational self-interest benefit society as a whole—again, a noneconomic invisible hand at work.

10. In a recent and very comprehensive book, Hutchison makes it very clear that many of the ideas developed by Smith were very much alive as long as a century before. He argues persuasively that to describe political economic thought before Smith as mercantilist is grossly unfair to a large number of creative thinkers and writers who were debating many of these same topics. Terrence Hutchison, *Before Adam Smith: The Emergence of Political Economy 1662–1776* (Oxford: Basil Blackwell, 1988).

11. Heilbroner, *Worldly Philosophers*, 24.

12. Richard John Neuhaus argues that capitalism's emphasis on the production of wealth was really a new phenomenon. In prior societies wealth was much more a zero-sum concept. One's gain, through gathering or plunder, was another's loss, and therefore there was a fundamental conflict between the rich and poor. The ideas behind Smith's invisible hand, as well as the title of Neuhaus's book, *Doing Well and Doing Good: The Challenge to the Christian Capitalist* (New York: Doubleday, 1992), suggest that this is no longer the case. Through increased output, all can be made better off (172).

13. By no means did Smith think that personal gain was the only motivation of individuals. He wrote at great length, especially in *The Theory of Moral Sentiments*, of the natural bonds of sympathy or empathy between people. "How selfish soever man may be supposed, there are evidently some principles in his nature, which interest him in the fortunes of others, and render their happiness necessary to him, though he derives nothing from it, except the pleasure of seeing it." For this quote (the opening lines of *The Theory of Moral Sentiments*) and for an entire chapter on this topic, see Thomas Wilson, "Sympathy and Self Interest," in *The Market and the State: Essays in Honour of Adam Smith*, ed. Thomas Wilson and Andrew S. Skinner (Oxford: Clarendon Press, 1976).

14. *Toward the Future: Catholic Social Thought and the U.S. Economy* (New York: American Catholic Committee, 1984), 23–24.

15. All the Smith quotes are taken from Robert Heilbroner, *The Essential Adam Smith* (New York: W. W. Norton, 1986), this one from pages 169 and 265. According to Heilbroner, this is the only direct reference to the invisible hand in *The Wealth of Nations*.

16. Ibid., 161.

17. Ibid., 162.

18. Ibid., 237–42.

19. Smith did not think that this frugality characterized the landlord class. However, he thought that the industry of entrepreneurs was sufficient to offset the behavior of "the greater part of rich people, [whose] chief enjoyment of riches consists in the parade of riches, which in their eyes is never so complete as when they appear to possess those decisive marks of opulence which nobody can possess but themselves." Heilbroner, *Essential Adam Smith*, 240, 322, 324.

20. John Maynard Keynes, *The End of Laissez-Faire* (London: Hogarth Press, 1926) 10–11. My colleague Frank McLaughlin points out that the *summum bonum* that Keynes refers to is different from the *summum bonum* of most philosophers. Few of the latter would argue that constantly increasing consumption necessarily makes people better off. At some point it may well interfere with improved well-being. But from Smith's perspective, when living conditions for the masses were a far cry from what they are in advanced industrialized societies today, it is hard to argue that more material possessions would not have been a good start toward improved happiness. I would argue that the same is true today for the bottom end of the American income distribution.

21. Heilbroner, *Essential Adam Smith*, 323–24.

22. For a succinct summary of Bentham's thought, see Ross Harrison, "Jeremy Bentham," in *The Invisible Hand*, 53–60.

23. The economic restructuring proposed in many former communist countries involves a much more extensive use of markets than they traditionally have had, but much of it is still a far cry from the mixed economies in the West today. The main difference, according to Kirkland, is the lack of a clear legal right to own property. If "private enterprise" involves leasing property owned by the government, then the experiment is basically socialist, not capitalist, at heart. Richard I. Kirkland, "Can Capitalism Save Perestroika?" *Fortune*, July 30, 1990, 137–44.

24. Reisman gives a number of examples from Adam Smith's time where state restrictions on individual behavior misallocated resources and reduced societal well-being. These included export subsidies, regulated trading companies (monopolies), settlement and apprenticeship laws (which reduced geographic and occupational mobility), and maximum wage laws. The reader will be excused for thinking that some of these examples are drawn from the 1990s, not the 1790s! David A. Reisman, *Adam Smith's Sociological Economics* (London: Croom Held, 1976), 211–23.

25. Heilbroner, *Essential Adam Smith*, 289.

26. Milton Friedman, *Capitalism and Freedom* (Chicago: University of Chicago Press, 1962), 8.

27. Lay Commission, *Toward the Future*, 26.

28. Berger's definition of a democracy is a simple one—a political system in which governments are formed by majority votes in regular and uncoerced elections. Peter Berger, *The Capitalist Revolution: Fifty Propositions about Prosperity, Equality and Liberty* (New York: Basic Books, 1986), 73–74.

29. Lindblom finds this entire discussion of capitalism and democracy vague, sterile, and unenlightening. Capitalism involves markets (the use of the price system) and private enterprise (private ownership of the means of production). He suggests that, to the extent that there is a connection between democracy and capitalism, it is the use of the price system that is key, not private enterprise. He sees no contradiction between public ownership of enterprises (for example, certain British industries or American public utilities) and democratic government. In any case, Lindblom thinks that the relevant policy questions revolve around the political impact of incremental changes in economic structure (e.g., more or less public ownership), not on debates about ends of the spectrum (e.g., capitalism vs. communism). Recent news from Eastern Europe, however, suggests some of the increments may be substantial! Charles E. Lindblom, *Democracy and Market System* (Oslo: Norwegian University Press, 1988).

30. Robert L. Heilbroner, "The Triumph of Capitalism," *The New Yorker*, January 23, 1989, 102–3.

31. Friedman, *Capitalism and Freedom*, 15.

32. Suppose a self-employed individual had revenues of $150,000, out-of-pocket costs of $100,000, and could have earned $40,000 elsewhere if not self-employed. Although accounting profits would be $50,000, economic profits would be only $10,000—the difference between the $50,000 earned and the $40,000 forgone by not working elsewhere. Positive economic profits—in this case, $10,000—would attract people to this field.

33. If one person has all the resources, then any reallocation will make this person worse off. Hence, the initial allocation of resources was efficient in the economists' sense; it is not possible to make anyone better off without making someone worse off. Since each efficient outcome is associated with some initial allocation of resources, one can theoretically choose any of these outcomes by controlling the initial allocation. If this could be done costlessly (through "lump sum" taxes and transfers that did not affect people's behavior), then there would be no trade-off between equity and efficiency. (Joseph Stiglitz, "The Invisible Hand and Modern Welfare Economics," National Bureau of Economics Research, Working Paper no. 3641, March 1991.) This is an interesting but not particularly useful theoretical point, since real-world reallocations do involve real costs, as discussed below.

34. Thomas Schelling, "Economic Reasoning and the Ethics of Policy," in *Choice and Consequence* (Cambridge: Harvard University Press, 1984), 17.

35. International Bank for Reconstruction and Development, *World Development Report 1992* (New York: Oxford University Press, 1992), table 1.

36. Frank (*Passions within Reason*, xi, 256), has offered what he calls a friendly amendment to the self-interest model. He describes many examples of behavior that do not appear to be in one's narrow self-interest—the grenade and restaurant examples, for example, voting when it will make no difference, giving anonymous gifts, or not cheating when the infraction would go undetected. He argues that passions are also an important behavioral determinant and that a motive nobler

than self-interest—moral behavior and commitment to others—"confers material benefits on the very individuals who practice it." Being motivated by emotions can actually be an advantage. Self-centered people are often excluded by others and can be very unhappy. Frank argues that the rational self-interest model is popular, not because it is accurate, but because it is precise. "Many of its predictions are wrong, but at least it makes predictions." According to some, this should be the economists' credo: rarely right, but never in doubt!

37. Heilbroner, *Essential Adam Smith*, 322.

38. Ibid., 289.

39. Steven Kelman has written persuasively on this topic, especially with regard to environmental issues, in *What Price Incentives? Economists and the Environment* (Boston: Auburn House, 1981). Karl Polanyi lamented the rapid development of markets nearly a half century ago in "Our Obsolete Market Economy," *Commentary*, February 1947, 109–17.

40. Heilbroner, *Essential Adam Smith*, 302. The pains alluded to were the establishment of schools to educate the common people. Smith proposed private schools subsidized by the government.

41. Charles E. Lindblom, *Politics and Markets* (New York: Basic Books, 1971) 82–84.

42. Heilbroner, *Essential Adam Smith*, 203, 294.

43. U.S. Bureau of the Census, Current Population Reports, Series P-60, No. 180, *Money Income of Households, Families and Persons in the United States: 1991* (Washington, D.C.: U.S. Government Printing Office, August 1992), table B-3. These estimates are based on pretax money income and include cash government transfers. When government cash and noncash transfers (like food stamps, housing allowances, Medicare, and Medicaid) are included along with taxes and an imputed rent on home equity, the income share of the top quintile drops slightly (to 44 percent in 1989) and the share of the bottom quintile rises slightly (to 5 percent in 1989). U.S. Bureau of the Census, Current Population Reports, Series P-60, No. 169-RD, *Measuring the Effect of Benefits and Taxes on Income and Poverty: 1989* (Washington, D.C.: U.S. Government Printing Office, September 1990), table B.

44. U.S. Bureau of the Census, Current Population Reports, Series P-70, No. 22, *Household Wealth and Asset Ownership: 1988* (Washington, D.C.: U.S. Government Printing Office, December 1990), table B.

45. These data are taken from Michael O'Higgins, Guenther Schmaus, and Geoffrey Stephenson, "Income Distribution and Redistribution: A Microdata Analysis for Seven Countries," *The Review of Income and Wealth*, 35, no. 2 (June 1989): table 2.

46. Ibid.

47. It is worth noting that U.S. poverty thresholds are low. The 1991 cutoff for a family of four was $13,924 per year—less than $10 per person per day. U.S. Bureau of the Census, Current Population Reports, Series P-60, No. 181, *Poverty in the United States: 1991* (Washington, D.C.: U.S. Government Printing Office, August 1992), table A-3. The food allocation (a third of the total) is therefore about $1 per person per meal. Poverty families are those that are below—and sometimes considerably below—these thresholds. In addition, another twelve million Americans are near-poor, below 125 percent of the poverty threshold (table 5).

48. Ibid., tables 1, 3.

49. U.S. Bureau of the Census, Current Population Reports, Series P-60, No. 182-RD, *Measuring the Effect of Benefits and Taxes on Income and Poverty: 1979 to 1991* (Washington, D.C.: U.S. Government Printing Office, August 1992), table 2.

50. Timothy Smeeding, Barbara Torrey, and Martin Rein, "Patterns of Income and Poverty: The Economic Status of Children and the Elderly in Eight Countries," in *The Vulnerable* (Washington, D.C.: Urban Institute Press, 1988).

51. "Defining the Moment," *The New Yorker*, July 16, 1990, 46.

52. Heilbroner, *Essential Adam Smith*, 154.

53. O'Higgins, Schmaus, and Stephenson, *Review of Income*, table 1. The U.S. estimates are based on 1979 data, the Swedish on 1981.

54. These are comparisons based on 1979 and 1981 data. Ibid., table 5.2.

55. Sheldon Danziger, Robert Haveman, and Robert Plotnick, "How Income Transfer Programs Affect Work, Savings, and the Income Distribution," *The Journal of Economic Literature*, 19 (September 1981), 1019.

56. Ibid., 1020. Even these modest numbers may be overestimates since, to some extent, private transfers (intra-family and employer-provided) would replace some of the public transfers, and these would have their own work disincentive effects. On the other hand, these estimates do not include the effects of the work disincentives on those who pay the taxes that fund the transfer programs.

57. *Losing Ground: American Social Policy 1950–1980* (New York: Basic Books, 1984).

58. In Okun's words, "the leak represents an inefficiency. The inefficiencies of real world redistribution include the adverse effects on the economic incentives of the rich and the poor, and the administrative costs of tax collection and transfer programs." Arthur M. Okun, *Equality and Efficiency: The Big Tradeoff*. (Washington, D.C.: Brookings Institution, 1975), 91–92.

59. Neither, it should be noted, do socialist countries. For example, the environmental destruction in the former Soviet bloc is far more severe than in the West.

60. Berger, *Capitalist Revolution*; Heilbroner, *Triumph of Capitalism*.

61. Heilbroner, *Triumph of Capitalism*, 109.

62. Ibid., 98.

63. Quoted in Moses Abramovitz, *Thinking about Growth*. (Cambridge: Cambridge University Press, 1989), 370.

64. Pp. 52–53.

6

In Another Time: Statements of American Reformers Regarding Wealth and Privilege

CAROL MORRIS PETILLO

PLACEMENT AND METHODOLOGY

Persuaded by the current wisdom that "where you stand depends on where you sit," I will begin this chapter with a personal statement of position, or placement.[1] Born in 1940, I grew up as the only child of two adults whose major shaping experience was the grinding poverty of the Great Depression of the 1930s. While World War II brought an unexpected upward mobility to their lives, as it did for many Americans, their adult point of view remained essentially unchanged. In their experience, life in the United States held the possibility of great material deprivation, and their identification was with those who, like themselves, suffered most in that situation: the less-educated farmers and workers who comprised the society's majority. Although their perspective did not lead to radical political participation, the values they conveyed to their only child were those built on the assumptions of the New Deal: government action was required to balance the inequities of the marketplace. They believed that 1929 had unquestionably proven that unbridled capitalism and its practitioners could or would not provide economic security for the majority. Put differently, this fundamental value system of my childhood corresponded closely to the view described by Paul Schervish and Andrew Herman that led in some instances to "structural guilt," a belief that "wealth is accumulated largely through the exploitation of others . . . [or] 'them that has gets.' "[2] My extended family, comprised of mill workers, small farmers, and housewives, and the small West Virginia mining towns where I grew up provided a culture that confirmed these values for me.

Supplementing this fundamental value system was a superstructure of what I would call "Baptist democracy." Without going into too much detail, my moral training outside the home was first received in the Sunday school classes of our local Baptist church. Fundamentalist in theology, these churches in the 1940s and early 1950s, at least in West Virginia, were ardently independent and firmly on the side of the scriptural argument that warned about camels and eyes of needles.[3] Each church decided its own fate, largely outside of any centralized organization, and in this process democratic pluralism often led to passionate arguments and schisms. Each church member was encouraged to seek his or her own salvation according to the light God provided and through individual study of the Bible. In church governance, majority rule was a value always sought if not always achieved, and strengthened by a perhaps simplified, but passionate belief that all were equal under God.

I left that environment in the late 1950s to become the first member of my family to go to college. The 1960s intervened, but the lessons learned in those years did not, for the most part, contradict the values of my childhood. Ideas about democratic pluralism and the necessity for redistribution of wealth and power appeared only to have wider application in areas concerning international relations, race, and gender than I had earlier perceived. I learned, during an educational process that involved two widely separated stints in college, interrupted by and intermixed with the marrying of two husbands and the raising of four children, to call myself a pacifist, a feminist, and a populist. These labels allowed me to build upon my training as a professional historian and its subsidiary intellectual propensity to categorize and engage in a more widely shared discourse. They did not, however, essentially change my earlier vision.

Since 1979, when I received my Ph.D. in American history, I have taught U.S. diplomatic and military history, as well as a general survey of American history, at Boston College. During the past decade, I have had the opportunity to observe more closely than ever before the hierarchical structure of the Roman Catholic church and the workings of a moderately large, and thus necessarily increasingly bureaucratic, university. These observations occurred within the context of Ronald Reagan's presidency, a historical era characterized at least in part by a neoconservative ideology, a restructuring of tax policies, and by a backlash against the governmental activism that developed in the 1960s and 1970s.[4] According to recent discoveries this period has also witnessed a widening of the gap between the rich and the poor and a proliferation of related social problems. No doubt due in part to the perspective I brought to the events, my assessment of the last ten years is one that includes (but is not limited to) rejection, rage, and increasing alienation. To deny these reactions would be to make the presentation of what follows less honest.

Throughout the past two years, the contributors to this book have met to discuss topics related to the accumulation and use of wealth as well as to its changing meanings as they have been shaped by history, culture, and various scholarly disciplines. Ostensibly we sought a wide-ranging examination of wealth and its uses over time, as viewed from our specific areas of specialization. From the outset, however, I sometimes heard a subtext that sought to confirm the merits of the capitalist system and which seemed to assume that somehow that economic approach not only effectively increased wealth, but also was the best available way to improve the lives of those working within it. As we talked, a little voice inside my head kept whispering. "Yes, but what about the homeless, no longer just the de-institutionalized, but whole families, and lots and lots of children? Or the underemployed who have lost their health benefits as factories in this country have closed and their jobs have moved to Mexico or Korea? Or the deaths of more and more infants in the inner cities? What about the widening gap between the rich, often with several homes and cars and increasingly lavish life-styles, and the average American family which must have the income from two full-time workers just to hold onto one house and provide its children with apparently deteriorating educational opportunities?"

As this ongoing, but largely unarticulated dialogue continued within me, it increasingly took on a historical dimension: I was reminded, again and again, of the period of rapid industrialization that followed the Civil War and of the similar problems and debates it spawned. Then, too, those who supported the capitalist system in the United States argued that a laissez-faire approach to the marketplace would ultimately benefit all. Then, too, the proponents of capitalism refused to measure the human sacrifices it demanded. It seemed to me that while the last century had brought amazing changes in technology, and while much more money passed through the hands of most Americans now than in earlier decades, many of these terrible problems of the late nineteenth century had not been solved. In fact, the 1980s seemed in many ways to repeat the economic tragedies of the 1890s or the 1920s, and yet no one in our discussions pointed this out. Were we aware of the parallels? Would the words of critics and social reformers from that earlier period remind us of the haunting similarity between then and now? As a U.S. historian myself, I decided to reexamine those years and some of that debate to see what it might bring to our current concerns. I would let some of those from that earlier period with whom I identified make the argument I had suppressed during our discussions.

Obviously, within the limits imposed by one chapter in this book, I could not recapitulate the vast literature historians have produced in their study of what has come to be known as, successively, the eras of Reconstruction, Populist revolt, and Progressive reform. I could, however, locate some of the discourse of that period as it reflected concerns about wealth, poverty, reform, and philanthropy as they were defined within the available culture. For reasons to be further explained below, I decided to study the autobiographies of certain women progressive social reformers to learn what they had said about these topics.

The first methodological issue must then concern itself with the nature of autobiography as source.[5] Without doubt, self-presentation is a problematic method for discovering whatever truths can be known about attitudes and motivations of either men or women, although each gender may require a different analysis. Whether the narrative construction tells a story of journey or self-abnegation or follows another trajectory altogether, the fact that most autobiographies fall into discernible patterns requires that we continually ask what has been omitted or reshaped to fit these constructs.[6] Comparing our autobiographical sources with relevant biographies and social histories may help to counteract the distortions in the self-created picture, and to whatever extent this has been possible, I have tried to follow this course in my research. The primary focus of my analysis, however, is on the words chosen to convey the story, rather than on the question of whether or not the words tell the fuller truth as other observers have interpreted it. I have sought a specific "culture" as it is retrievable from a small sample of my selection. The examples in the main body of the chapter hopefully will make these distinctions more clear. I admit to the methodological weaknesses of this approach, but believe that since the women examined were recognized "movers and shakers" in their time, what they thought they thought has some relevance. I have tried to be respectful of what these women believed they knew, while remaining aware that their stories were undoubtedly framed by certain narrative conventions as well as by the overwhelmingly powerful societal mores that shaped the vision of women even as unusual as these.

Finally, my decision to study exclusively the autobiographies of women progressive social reformers rather than to include some of the many men with whom they participated in their activities must be explained. This is a choice based on my other current scholarly concerns. At present, my research interests involve reading the diaries, letters, and memoirs of another set of women for another study entirely. Since my previous work in military and diplomatic history has not often given me the opportunity to consider women, I hoped to learn more about my new subject in general (both in terms of theory and concrete example) as I went about the researching and writing of this work. To what extent I have actually accomplished this goal remains to be seen. In any event, let me state unequivocally here that it is my suspicion that had I chosen to study both men and women defined as progressive social reformers, I would have found that while the outlines of their stories might have differed in many ways, their attitudes toward wealth would have resonated profoundly with each other.

HISTORICAL CONTEXT: THE SETTING FOR THE STORIES

Originating in the early nineteenth century and based on a legal system which from the earliest days of the Union had supported business interests, the nascent industrial system of the United States blossomed in the decades following Appomattox. Encouraged by laws passed by the radical Republicans during the Civil War and by the demands of war for the increased production of materiel, several substantial changes aided the development of industrial capitalism: transcontinental railroads to transport manufactures from factory to port; a nationally rationalized banking system to ease the buying, selling, and financing of these products; policies encouraging the settlement of western lands; and a set of land-grant colleges to provide an educated work force for the new factories all contributed to the process. Extraction of fossil fuels and other minerals increased markedly, and research and development facilities found new uses to which they might be put. Businesses expanded, seeking efficiency of production and maximization of profit through horizontal and vertical integration. Soon these processes led to monopolization and the involvement and subsequent control by investment bankers of significant portions of American industry.

Described as the "Gilded Age" by Mark Twain, the era provided the context for a generation of potential entrepreneurs and investors recovering from the pain and disruption of the Civil War and determined to seek "the main chance" economically within the new "window of opportunity" the war and reconstruction government had provided. Despite their substantial and long-standing influence on and support by government, these business leaders pinned their arguments for capitalism on the inviting ideology of Adam Smith and the more recent Social Darwinism: a laissez-faire market, guided somehow by a "hidden hand" produced wealth "naturally" if left alone, and ultimately that wealth benefited everyone, although certainly, those most fitted to survive would benefit most. Some of them, later labeled "robber barons," achieved great wealth and power although frequently without much concern for the price paid by those who contributed to their accumulation.[7]

At first enhanced by this postwar expansion, the U.S. economy soon suffered periodic capitalist "boom and bust" cycles in dimensions previously unknown. While producing more millionaires, this expanded manufacturing system also required, attracted, and then incorporated increasing numbers of immigrant workers from Europe, Asia, and the rural areas of America. Once each decade in the 1870s, 1880s, and 1890s, recessions developed with painful economic consequences for the majority in the society unprotected by private wealth. As Ann J. Lane explains,

If America produced more millionaires than anywhere else, it also produced slums, class inequities, cyclical depressions, social unrest, and rural and urban suffering. . . . Great cities rose in which enormous wealth was produced, but the impoverished, exploited working populations suffered hideously. . . . It was a world in which only success counted, in which the central goal was wealth, and there is never enough wealth if that is the primary goal. The earlier vision of a good society was fading. The problem was not a handful of powerful, evil men who built an industrial empire but saw no need to contribute to the public welfare. The problem, as viewed by many, was that the moral center of the nation was in jeopardy.[8]

By 1893, when the first "great depression" in U.S. history occurred, conditions among workers were unbearable.[9] By then, violent strikes were commonplace, and efforts to establish labor unions widened. Cries for help and reform mounted. Soon a full-fledged social and political force, known as the Progressive Movement, would organize nationally, seeking to wrest from the grasp of the business interests political power with which to remedy these conditions. Two of the women who serve as the focus for this study, Jane Addams and Charlotte Perkins Gilman, emerge as public figures within this context.[10]

Relieved somewhat by early Progressive reforms at the local level and even more by the economic upswing encouraged temporarily by the election of McKinley in 1896 and the Spanish-American War that followed two years later, the situation in the United States remained unevenly chaotic in the years between the mid-1890s and World War I. Industrial conditions continued to spur labor unrest, while Progressive laws intermittently allowed union activity to expand, most frequently along the traditional capitalistic lines followed by the American Federation of Labor, but occasionally incorporating the more radical, socialistic program of such organizations as the Socialist Party and the syndicalism of the Industrial Workers of the World (the Wobblies, as they were more commonly known). Intellectual ferment built on the Social Darwinist debates of earlier decades began to incorporate other more homegrown theories such as the Nationalism of Edward Bellamy, Fabianism imported from Great Britain, and anarchism associated with the unrest in Russia. By 1920, following U.S. entry into World War I, the Bolshevik Revolution, and the tragedy of Versailles, the Progressive reformers of the late nineteenth century had been joined by other political activists who urged a more radical economic restructuring of the U.S. system, and for what seemed to most a revolutionary movement toward the left. Elizabeth Gurley Flynn, the remaining activist examined here, moved onto the public stage during this period and in this way. For Addams and Gilman, the greatest part of their activism was over by the early 1930s. Still, each was born and shaped by one era of reform and lived to see its extension during the New Deal. Flynn, more radical in her activism and analysis, lived on into the 1960s and saw a "second great awakening" in her final years. In the face of my alienation described above, I take consolation from the fact that despite the current ascendancy of neoconservatism, the twentieth century has seen some continuity in its efforts at reform as witnessed in the lives of these three women. In an attempt to understand the foundations upon which their philosophies were based, and how they themselves understood their beliefs, we will examine their discussions of wealth and privilege as they saw it during their lives.

THE STORIES: THREE WOMEN SPEAK

Of the eleven women studied, all but one were born in the nineteenth century and died in the twentieth, the vast majority (eight) born during the period of the enormous industrial upheaval of the late 1800s.[11] While none came from great wealth, two (Addams and Vorse) might be categorized as belonging to the upper middle class, six to the middle class (Bloor, Dorr, Gilman, Livermore, Phelps, and Sanger), and three to the working class (Flynn, Goldman, and Dennis).

While only Addams and Dorr had what in modern terms might be called a college education, all were more educated than was generally the case for women of their class and time. Most (Bloor, Gilman, Livermore, Phelps, Sanger, and Vorse) achieved this status through some special formal schooling. Bloor, Livermore, and Phelps attended what might today be referred to as finishing schools. In those years, these schools often provided the only opportunity for young women to acquire the rough equivalent of the education available to men. Gilman and Vorse studied art, briefly in professional schools and independently as well. Sanger attended a woman's college for a while and then formally trained as a nurse. Not surprisingly, the three working class women (Dennis, Flynn, and Goldman) had the least formal education, although Dennis did attend college for a short period, and Goldman briefly received nurse's training in Vienna. All, especially Flynn and Goldman, read widely.

Most women in nineteenth-century America (and indeed twentieth-century America as well) did not expect to prepare for careers outside the home. Although the women in this study were all exceptional in that they ultimately had such careers, their expectations as young women were set within this traditional domestic context. Only three (Gilman, Sanger, and Vorse) had any idea of preparing for a specific career, and of those three, only one, Sanger, achieved her career goal. The other upper middle- and middle-class members (Addams, Bloor, Dorr, Livermore, and Phelps) found themselves facing uncertain futures as women with education but without much opportunity. After casting around for possibilities, Livermore taught for a while before marrying and then helped nurse Union soldiers during the Civil War; Dorr and Phelps ultimately became professional writers, as did Gilman and Vorse. Of this group, only Bloor and Addams (and to a certain extent Gilman and Vorse) became social reformers outright. All three women from the working class ultimately supported themselves variously while working almost full-time as labor organizers and members of radical political movements.

Finally, in their personal lives, these women encompass all the available possibilities. Of the eleven, only one, Livermore, had a conventional, long-term, heterosexual marriage. Another, Phelps, married in midlife, and although unhappy, remained in the marriage until her death. Addams is the only one of the group never to marry, although it is now assumed that her long relationships with Ellen Starr and Mary Rozet Smith fulfilled for her whatever companionate needs she had. Of the eight others, each married at least once (Dorr, Flynn, and Goldman) and some twice (Bloor, Dennis, Gilman, Sanger, and Vorse). Of these, Dennis, Gilman, Sanger, and Vorse found happiness in their second marriages; the others (Bloor, Dorr, Flynn, and Goldman) ultimately rejected monogamous relationships as unrealistic. All except Addams, Goldman, and Phelps had at least one child (Dorr, Flynn, and Gilman) and the majority more (Bloor, Dennis, Livermore, Sanger, and Vorse). All those with children wrestled with the difficult arrangements necessary to combine both a career and a family. Most write about these struggles in formulaic and yet fascinating ways—but that is the subject of another study. The focus here will now shift from generalization to three individual actors, selected as representative of the broad categories that emerged from the larger study, and what each perceived as the reasons for living her life as she did.

Jane Addams

Jane Addams is undoubtedly the most well known of the women examined in this study. Safely domesticated and sanitized, her activities as the "angel of Hull House" are nearly always described in grammar and high school textbooks as an example of the way women participated in U.S. history. Usually this brief treatment is accompanied by her picture, taken in later years, reflecting a plump figure in dark Victorian garb, her gentle, smiling face surrounded by hair drawn back in a conventional knot—everybody's vision of a benign, grandmotherly nurturer. Her own words in her widely read autobiography, *Twenty Years at Hull-House*, do not contradict this vision significantly. She never saw herself as radical, and she believed that she achieved her most important goals through diplomacy rather than confrontation. And yet, as a pacifist in the years around World War I, she was labeled "the most dangerous woman in America" by the U.S. attorney general, A. Mitchell Palmer. Only after receiving the Nobel Peace Prize more than a decade later would Addams be welcomed back into the pantheon of American heroes, her work for international peace largely left unexamined.[12]

Born in Cedarville, Illinois, on September 6, 1860, only months before the beginning of the Civil War, Addams grew up in the small-town middle America whose values she would always try to replicate.[13] The youngest living child of her father's first family, she was raised primarily by his second wife, who entered her life when she was seven and brought to the family two sons from a previous marriage. Addams was not particularly fond of her stepmother, always maintaining that her father, a prosperous miller, banker, and community leader, was the central influence on her life. "Jane Addams grew up believing in the American dream of democracy, equality, and equal opportunity for all. She was aware, of course, that her father was the wealthiest and most prominent person in the village, that her house was bigger than all the other houses, that she had advantages that many other children did not have."[14]

In 1877 Jane entered the Rockford Female Seminary as her father wished, although she herself had hoped to attend Smith College. While there, Rockford became a degree-granting institution, and Addams's strongly held desire for a real college education was fulfilled when she graduated in 1882 at the head of her class. Rockford was primarily a training school for Christian missionaries, but Addams refused to move in this direction, choosing instead to prepare for a career in medicine and then work among the poor.

For the next decade Addams followed a not uncommon pattern among the women social reformers of this era. Convinced that her education and situation demanded that she contribute to society, she yet could not settle into a position that seemed effective. After her father's death in 1881, at which time she received a comfortable inheritance,[15] she tried and rejected medical school, suffered through two long and debilitating physical illnesses, soul-searched, and ultimately joined a Protestant church. She traveled in Europe and, at the urging of her stepmother, considered and then rejected the idea of marriage to her stepbrother. Ultimately, in the late 1880s, while on a second trip to Europe, she found a focus. She would return to the United States and, using some of the money her father had left her, begin a settlement house patterned after those she had visited in England. In 1889 she and Ellen Starr, a former classmate from Rockford and a lifelong friend and companion, moved into Hull House in Chicago's 19th Ward, an area peopled heavily with the European immigrants who now made up three-fourths of Chicago's urban population.

Although Addams herself always argued that she and her fellow settlement house workers received as much as they gave from their neighbors and the work they did among them, it was for her contributions to the Chicago immigrants themselves that she became known. In less than five years, Hull House was sponsoring more than forty activities and provided educational, recreational, and health-care support systems for immigrant children and their parents. Originally financed almost exclusively by Addams, this expansion, coupled with the depression of 1893, forced her to appeal for funds from outside sources. Perhaps as an outgrowth of her complex and diverse family experience, she showed particular skill in gathering talented people around her and drawing from them significant contributions, both financial and otherwise, to the programs she envisioned.

Before long, as the excesses of industrialization increased in correlation with the economic collapse of 1893, it became apparent that individual enterprises such as Hull House could not solve the broader problems facing their constituency. At this point, Addams and her fellow Hull House workers became involved in local and then state politics, working for such reforms as a factory inspection act and later child labor laws, laws to limit the working hours of women and to allow for increased labor organizing, improved welfare procedures and industrial safety, and compulsory education. Although various Hull House workers contributed significantly to these different struggles, Addams remained at the center of the efforts, raising funds, writing explanatory articles, and unifying the programs for greater efficiency.

By the first decade of the twentieth century, Addams had become a national figure, writing about the reforms Hull House had achieved in Chicago and lecturing widely. Everywhere Progressivism was ascendant, and Addams was perceived as an effective mentor for the movement. Important people, both American and otherwise, visited Hull House regularly, and Addams was invited abroad to spread her gospel. In 1912 she seconded the nomination of Theodore Roosevelt for the presidency on the Progressive Party ticket. When her autobiography, *Twenty Years at Hull-House*, first appeared in 1910 it achieved immediate success and ultimately sold 80,000 copies during her lifetime alone.

Nonetheless, Addams was not without her critics, particularly among those most familiar with the specifics of her programs. It must be remembered that the Hull House activities described thus far coexisted in a city shaken by labor unrest, most effectively represented by the Haymarket Riot and subsequent trials. By 1900 Chicago industrialists strongly criticized her labor activism, and her support of a wrongly imprisoned anarchist at the time of McKinley's assassination brought heavy political criticism. Her insistence that all ideas deserved an equal hearing often led to invitations to Hull House for people whom her more conventional supporters considered dangerous. While her work as a suffragist in this period drew little criticism from her traditional support group, the other national political effort of her later career was vehemently attacked. It was as a pacifist in the years around World War I that Addams's proud public persona suffered most.

As she moved into national political activity after 1912 and international politics after 1914, Addams argued that her new concerns grew out of her previous work with the poor. Again and again she explained that the internationalism of her immigrant neighborhoods in Chicago proved that different national groups could cooperate, and that the money and energy spent on war could be better spent to solve the economic problems of the poor. These problems, she argued, ultimately contributed to the causes of war anyway. Serving both as chairman of the U.S. Woman's Peace Party and president of the International Congress of Women at The Hague, as well as the president of the Women's International League for Peace and Freedom (WILPF) after 1919, she worked increasingly for peace from 1914 until the early 1930s, when her health failed. Despite the gradual abandonment of most of her fellow pacifists after the U.S. entered the war in 1917, Addams refused, uncharacteristically and in this effort alone, to compromise. Attacked widely for her positions during the war, her efforts were more appreciated in the 1920s, although she still found herself the target of tirades from the Daughters of the American Revolution and the American Legion. Disheartened by what she believed was increased intolerance in American life brought on by the war, she helped to found the American Civil Liberties Union in 1920 and continued her social service activities both nationally and internationally throughout the decade. In 1931 she was awarded the Nobel Peace Prize, immediately donating the $16,000 she received to the WILPF. Increasingly honored near the end of her life, but suffering from a variety of ailments, Addams died in 1935 at the age of seventy-four.

Although not as a medical doctor, as she had originally planned, Addams remained remarkably consistent in her early decision to work among the poor. In the words of her primary biographer, "Jane Addams never became a radical in religion, in economics or in politics, but she did become a social reformer, a defender of organized labor, and she did come to believe that her main task was to eliminate poverty rather than to comfort the poor."[16] First at the local level in Chicago, then in national and international forums as her opportunities and responsibilities expanded, she steadily rejected security, both emotional and economic, that might have been hers had she chosen a more conventional life. Certainly the fame she achieved provided some compensation for these sacrifices, and it cannot be argued that Addams's life was one of great financial difficulty. Still, had she married into her own class, as her stepmother wished, and reinvested her inheritance in traditional channels, as was generally expected, she would likely have ended her life wealthier and certainly less subject to public attack. Her choices made the difference, and it is to her own explanations for those choices that we now turn.

As suggested above, throughout her entire life Jane Addams believed that the lessons taught her by her father were most significant in shaping her value system. She gives a detailed illustration of how this worked early in her autobiography:

Although I constantly confided my sins and perplexities to my father, there are only a few occasions on which I remember having received direct advice or admonition; . . . I can remember an admonition on one occasion, however, when, as a little girl of eight years, arrayed in a new cloak, gorgeous beyond anything I had ever worn before, I stood before my father for his approval. I was much chagrined by his remark that it was a very pretty cloak—in fact so much prettier than any cloak the other little girls in the Sunday School had, that he would advise me to wear my old cloak, which would keep me quite as warm, with the added advantage of not making the other little girls feel badly. I complied with the request but I fear without inner consent, and I certainly was quite without the joy of self-sacrifice as I walked soberly through the village street by the side of my counselor. My mind was busy, however, with the old question eternally suggested by the inequalities of the human lot.

Only as we neared the church door did I venture to ask what could be done about it, receiving the reply that it might never be righted so far as clothes went, but that people might be equal in things that mattered much more than clothes, the affairs of education and religion, for instance, which we attended to when we went to school and church, and that it was very stupid to wear the sort of clothes that made it harder to have equality even there.[17]

At another point a little later in the autobiography, Addams proudly recounts comments made at her father's death that while there were lots of people who refused bribes during the period of high corruption in government following the Civil War, her father, as a member of the Illinois legislature, had never even been offered one "because bad men were instinctively afraid of him." She goes on to tie this more closely to her own experience by remembering her chagrin when in later years, while working for the factory inspection law, Hull House was offered $50,000 to curtail its activities. "What had befallen the daughter of my father that such a thing could happen to her?" she asked, distraught that someone might think it even possible that she would consider such an offer.[18] Clearly, the image of her father's high standards shaped Addams's responses to wealth.

As one might expect, her own inherited wealth presented Addams with a problem. In the difficult period following her father's death, when evidence suggests that she was working through many serious life questions and while the country was in the throes of the farm failures of the 1880s, the uses to which her own money was being put required her consideration. As she tells the story,

[I]n one of the intervening summers between these European journeys I visited a western state where I had formerly invested a sum of money in mortgages. I was much horrified by the wretched conditions among the farmers, which had resulted from a long period of drought, and one forlorn picture was fairly burned into my mind. A number of starved hogs—collateral for a promissory note—were huddled into an open pen. Their backs were humped in a curious, camel-like fashion, and they were devouring one of their own number, the latest victim of absolute starvation or possibly merely the one least able to defend himself against their voracious hunger. The farmer's wife looked on indifferently, a picture of despair as she stood in the door of the bare, crude house, and the two children behind her, . . . appeared but half-human. It seemed to me quite impossible to receive interest from mortgages placed upon farms which might at any season be reduced to such conditions, and with great inconvenience to my agent and doubtless with hardship to the farmers, as speedily as possible I withdrew all my investment.[19]

During her first years at Hull House, Addams had many opportunities to meet and work with those holding wealth and power. Gradually, she began to understand that those with power were not necessarily well-intentioned. She recounts that her first insight in this direction occurred while on her second trip to London: "I think that up to this time I was still filled with the sense . . . that somewhere in Church or State are a body of authoritative people who will put things to rights as soon as they really know what is wrong. [I believed] that behind all suffering, behind sin and want, must lie redeeming magnanimity. [I could] imagine the world to be tragic and terrible, but [not] that it may be contemptible or squalid or self-seeking."[20] Later, she would point out that just as religion or political power did not necessarily lead to wisdom and generosity, wealth itself seldom redeemed its possessors. "One of the most discouraging features about the present system of tenement houses is that many are owned by sordid and ignorant immigrants. The theory that wealth brings responsibility, that possession entails at length education and refinement, in these cases fails utterly."[21]

As she sought to help her Hull House constituency achieve some measure of material security, her analysis of the system upon which they depended sharpened. She came to question some of the basic assumptions of capitalism. Commerce, she argued, used devices to control and manipulate the workers just as had the powerful institutions of other periods in history, and the causes of nineteenth-century capitalist economic growth could not be separated from its inherent exploitative practices. As she explained in 1907,

[I]n so far as commerce has rested upon the successful capture of the resources of the workers, it has been a relic of the mediaeval baron issuing forth to seize the merchants' boats as they passed his castle on the Rhine. . . . As its prototype rested upon slavery and vassalage, so this commerce is founded upon a contempt for the worker and believes that he can live on low wages. . . .

America is only beginning to realize, and has not yet formulated, all the implications of the factory system and of the conditions of living which this well-established system imposes upon the workers. . . . If the wonderful inventions of machinery, as they came along during the last century, could have been regarded as in some sense social possessions, the worst evils attending the factory system of production—starvation wages, exhausting hours, unnecessary monotony, child labor, and all the rest of the wretched list—might have been avoided in the interest of society itself. All this would have come about had human welfare been earlier regarded as a legitimate object of social interest.

But no such ethics had been developed in the beginning of this century. Society regarded machinery as the absolute possession of the man who owned it at the moment it became a finished product, quite irrespective of the long line of inventors and workmen who represented its gradual growth and development. Society was, therefore destined to all the maladjustment which this century has encountered. . . . The possessor of the machine, like the possessor of arms who preceded him, regards it as the legitimate weapon for exploitation. . . .[22]

The harshness of factory life was one aspect of the immigrant experience to which Addams and others like her never became inured. Gradually, she came to believe that the conditions she decried would not be changed willingly by the owners. She described this realization in these words:

During the same winter three boys from a Hull-House club were injured at one machine in a neighboring factory for lack of a guard which would have cost but a few dollars.

When the injury of one of these boys resulted in his death, we felt quite sure that the owners of the factory would share our horror and remorse, and that they would do everything possible to prevent the recurrence of such a tragedy. To our surprise they did nothing whatever, and I made my first acquaintance then with those pathetic documents signed by the parents of working children, that they will make no claim for damages resulting from "carelessness."[23]

At last, this daughter of an American businessman with high ideals finally came to comprehend that what had perhaps been true for her father was not universally a fact. After a long struggle against those whom she ultimately referred to as "the aggressive captains of industry,"[24] she came to believe firmly in governmental involvement in the relief of poverty: "One of the . . . lessons we learned at Hull-House was that private beneficence is totally inadequate to deal with the vast numbers of the city's disinherited. We also . . . came to realize that there were certain types of wretchedness from which every private philanthropy shrinks and which are cared for only in those wards of the county hospital provided for the wrecks of vicious living or in the city's isolation hospital for smallpox patients."[25] Needing perhaps to find heroes somewhere, Addams transferred her admiration to the government officials with whom she often worked and who had, in her words, "accepted without question and as implicit in public office, the obligation to carry on the dangerous and difficult undertakings for which private philanthropy is unfitted, as if the commonality of compassion represented by the State was more comprehending than that of any individual group."[26]

Her ultimate vision of the world and how it should work was perhaps best expressed at the end of the autobiography, where she described a visit she made to Oberammergau to watch the Passion Play in 1900:

The peasants who portrayed exactly the successive scenes of the wonderful Life, who used only the very words found in the accepted version of the Gospels, yet curiously modernized and reorientated the message. They made clear that the opposition to the young Teacher sprang from the merchants whose traffic in the temple He had disturbed and from the Pharisees who were dependent upon them for support. Their query was curiously familiar, as they demanded the antecedents of the Radical who dared to touch vested interests, who presumed to dictate the morality of trade, and who insulted the marts of honest merchants by calling them "a den of thieves." As the play developed, it became clear that this powerful opposition had friends in Church and State, that they controlled influences which ramified in all directions. They obviously believed in their statement of the case and their very wealth and position in the community gave their words such weight that finally all of their hearers were convinced that the young Agitator must be done away with in order that the highest interests of society might be conserved. These simple peasants made it clear that it was the money power which induced one of the Agitator's closest friends to betray him, and the villain of the piece, Judas himself, was only a man who was so dazzled by money, so under the domination of all it represented, that he was perpetually blind to the spiritual vision unrolling before him. As I sat through the long summer day, seeing the shadows on the beautiful mountain back of the open stage shift from one side to the other and finally grow long and pointed in the soft evening light, my mind was filled with perplexing questions. Did the dramatization of the life of Jesus set forth its meaning more clearly and conclusively than talking and preaching could possibly do as a shadowy following of the command "to do the will"?

The peasant actors whom I had seen returning from mass that morning had prayed only to portray the life as He had lived it and, behold, out of their simplicity and piety arose this modern version which even Harnack was only then venturing to suggest to his advanced colleagues in Berlin. Yet the Oberammergau folk were very like thousands of immigrant men and women of Chicago, both in their experiences and in their familiarity with the hard facts of life, and throughout that day as my mind dwelt on my far-away neighbors, I was reproached with the sense of an ungarnered harvest.[27]

Written a decade after the event and twenty-four years before her death, these words, perhaps as well as any that she ever spoke, conveyed the worldview that had shaped Addams's actions since her childhood. She was neither inexperienced nor overly idealistic, and her practical achievements in the arenas of politics and economics were substantial. Yet she saw the world through a prism of experience that began to take shape during an early walk to Sunday school with her father, sharpened during her daily interactions with the rich and powerful at Hull House, and found full expression as she watched a world-famous theatrical event more than thirty years later. It had broadened, but not essentially changed, and consistently it rejected the argument that wealth and power deserved admiration, or that left to themselves, the wealthy and powerful could be relied upon to care for their fellow humans without the intercession of the state. No ideas about "a thousand points of light" would have seduced Jane Addams.

Charlotte Perkins Gilman

Jane Addams and Charlotte Perkins Gilman had much in common. Both were born in 1860 and both died in 1935. Both came from white, Anglo-Saxon, Protestant families which had deep roots in the history of the United States. Gilman visited Addams at Hull House and drew sustenance from the community of women she found there. Each admired the work of the other, both in terms of the reforms they sought and the ideas they publish-ed. Yet since their deaths, the uses to which their memories have been put have differed greatly. Addams, whose radical visions were almost imme-diately denied, quickly joined the long list of safe patriots the establishment would offer as role models to future generations. Gilman, on the other hand, was simply forgotten, not to be resurrected until the 1960s, when her radical feminist vision once again resonated with the cultural needs and experiences of an era.[28]

Born in Hartford, Connecticut, on July 3, 1860, Charlotte Perkins Gilman took great pride in her relationship with the famous Beecher family long connected to the intellectual and reform life of New England.[29] Although her own family life was both economically deprived and emotionally barren after the early separation of her parents, her values and worldview were sharply influenced by the status and acomplishments of her extended family. Their kindnesses to her, although sparse and inadequate, provided some opportunity for an intellectual vision and development that might otherwise have been unavailable.

After her parents' separation in Charlotte's early childhood (they di-vorced thirteen years later), Charlotte, her mother, and brother were forced to rely on the charity of family and friends for most of their livelihood. In Gilman's first eighteen years, the family moved nineteen times, and there was little opportunity or money for sustained education. The funds pro-vided by her errant father over and above those needed for mere survival were used to educate her younger brother, Thomas, who attended various preparatory schools and finally M.I.T., from which he was not graduated. Although after occasional secondary schooling she did briefly attend the Rhode Island School of Design, Charlotte always felt great inadequacy regarding her education, and sought with incredible energy and determi-nation to counter its weaknesses with ardent autodidacticism. Although her intellectual development as reflected in her writing reveals the gaps and spaces often accompanying such self-training, it also illustrates an originality and power of thought that might have been lost had she been more conventionally educated.

Charlotte also suffered emotionally. While her father did not entirely disappear from her life, he remained a distant, cold figure until after the death of her mother, when Gilman was already a parent herself. Her mother, determined that they not be hurt by human attachments as she felt she had been, denied her children any physical signs of affection while they were awake. Since she did allow herself an occasional caress while they slept, Charlotte often pretended to be asleep to experience her mother's love. Cut off from the stimulation of education and normal family life, Gilman took charge of her own late adolescence through rigid discipline, including philosophical self-examination, arduous exercise, and jobs outside the home to contribute to the family income. Although remarkably attractive, she rejected traditional feminine interests, firmly expecting not to marry and hence not to have to face the difficult life her mother had known.

All this discipline and planning came to an end in 1884 when, after a long struggle with herself, she decided to marry the young artist Charles Walter Stetson. Ten months later their only child, Katherine Beecher, was born. By all accounts, including Charlotte's, Stetson was a thoughtful and considerate husband, yet after only a few months Gilman was suffering from exhaustion and depression which did not improve after the birth of the child. Despite great effort on the part of both husband and wife, her condition deteriorated into a serious nervous breakdown. An extended stay at the clinic of neurologist S. Weir Mitchell did not help. Soon it became apparent that her only recoveries occurred when she traveled away from Stetson. In 1888 they agreed to a permanent separation, and Charlotte and Katherine moved to Pasadena, California. Four years later the Stetsons divorced, and Charles married a close friend of Charlotte's. The three remained friendly, and shortly before the actual wedding, Charlotte sent her eight-year-old daughter to live with the new couple. For the individuals involved, the solution seemed to work for the most part. But Gilman, who during the intervening years had achieved some public prominence, found herself pilloried in the popular press for her unconventional family arrangements. Nonetheless they held, and she and her daughter would live together only infrequently thereafter. Charlotte never fully recovered from the trauma of these years, but her retreat from the traditional feminine responsibilities of home and family gradually restored her abilities to think and write.

Professionally, Charlotte gradually began to build a life as a writer. She first published poems in magazines after her arrival in California in the late 1880s. Her 1890 poem "Similar Cases" caught the attention of William Dean Howells, who began to support her work. In 1892 she published a short story, "The Yellow Wall-Paper," about her nervous breakdown, which has become her best known work. In 1893 she published her first book, *In This Our World*, a collection of poetry. In these early years she argued the case for a progressive evolution that might result in an ultimate solution to the problems of humankind. In this she was strongly influenced by the sociologist Lester Ward and the utopian nationalism of Edward Bellamy. As Ann Lane explains, "She took the prevailing belief in evolution, the process of growth and change, and constructed a full-scale historical and sociological analysis of men and women in history and society."[30] Although firmly outside the Marxist camp, Gilman rejected the harsh realities of capitalism and supported the goals of socialism, particularly in its nonviolent, Fabian manifestation, throughout her life. Just as Addams had argued that the attitudes of earlier periods needed to change and that the technological advances of nineteenth-century industrialization should be thought of as "social possessions," Gilman urged

union; the organic social relation, the interchange of functional service, wherein the individual is most advantaged, not by his own exertions for his own goods, but by the exchange of his exertions with the exertions of others for goods produced by them together. We are not treating here of any communistic theory as to the equitable division of the wealth produced, but of a clear truth in social economics,—that wealth is a social product.[31]

Unable to support herself solely through her writings, Gilman joined the significant lecture circuit of the day.[32] She soon found that she was good at it, coupling logical argument with an ironic humor and attractive demeanor. Audiences across the country and in Europe paid to hear her, and although during these years she was never able to have a home or many comforts, her lecture fees kept her from starving. As Lane tells us, "It was not money Charlotte sought, it never was; it was the opportunity to have her message heard."[33] The lectures also provided her with an opportunity to work through ideas that she would later publish in the books that made her even more famous in the years before World War I. In 1898 her most famous nonfiction work, *Women and Economics*, appeared. Arguing for female economic independence both as an advantage for women and society in general, it struck a sensitive nerve in a period when more and more literate women were taking jobs outside the home. Eventually translated into seven languages, it sold widely and firmly established Gilman's reputation.[34] In the following years she published several more such treatises, including *Human Work*, which she considered her most important effort. None would achieve the accolades of *Women and Economics*, but Gilman's reputation was sustained by her lecturing and public persona well into the 1920s.

In 1900 Charlotte finally agreed to marry her first cousin, George Houghton Gilman, who was seven years her junior and apparently willing to support Charlotte's career while making few demands on her domestically. Their relationship, which lasted until his death in 1934, was by all accounts very satisfactory. As Gilman herself described it in her autobiography, *The Living of Charlotte Perkins Gilman*, "we were married—and lived happy ever after. If this were a novel, now, here's the happy ending."[35] Thereafter, supported by his small law practice and the income from her books and continuing lectures, Charlotte wrote steadily. Between 1909 and 1916 she published her own journal, *Forerunner*, for which she did almost all the writing. Never financially self-sustaining, it nonetheless allowed her editorial control over her material and provided a forum for much of her work.

Although primarily a lecturer and writer addressing feminist issues, Gilman also participated in the suffrage and peace movements in the years before 1920. With the franchise, however, feminism faded somewhat, and Gilman's audience diminished. Although she continued to make national lecture tours during the 1920s and to maintain contacts with the thinkers and reformers of earlier years, her public career gradually declined. As Lane sensitively explains,

[I]t was not an easy or reassuring old age that Charlotte Gilman entered. She had been respected, admired, and widely acclaimed, and now she was none of these. She must have hoped and longed to spend her declining years in comfort; if not in material comfort, which she never had nor much coveted, then in spiritual comfort, a sense of having accomplished much and having been heard and understood.[36]

By the late twenties, she was settled into a private life in Norwich, Connecticut, where she and Houghton shared a small home with his brother. Early in 1932 she found that she had breast cancer and, characteristically, determined to handle the crisis rationally. She refused to burden either her husband or her daughter with the slow death that failed treatments left as the only option. So she accumulated enough chloroform for a painless suicide, wrote her autobiography for posthumous publication, and, after her husband's sudden death in 1934, moved to California to be near her daughter. In August 1935, when the pain finally outweighed the pleasure, she ended her life as she had planned.

Recognized by such diverse figures as George Bernard Shaw and Woodrow Wilson as significant to the intellectual life of the United States, Gilman achieved great prominence in the years central to this study. That the end of her life did not sustain this influence speaks as much to the reactionary nature of the 1920s as it does to the quality of her work. The questions her arguments sought to answer declined briefly, only to reemerge a quarter of a century after her death more clearly asked and more demanding of a fully developed vision. For this, the writings of Charlotte Perkins Gilman provided a fertile resource.[37]

As Gilman's major biographer reminds us, "All her life she was poor."[38] In her autobiography Charlotte makes this generalization painfully specific as she recounts how "she [her mother] sold her piano when I was two, to pay the butcher's bill, and never owned another. She hated debt, and debts accumulated about her, driving her to these everlasting moves."[39] A few pages further on she reprints a letter written to her father when she was twelve: "Dear Father, Will you please send the money for July, August, and September?" it begins.[40]

In the face of these deprivations, one might expect Gilman to seek wealth in her later life, and as an exceptionally attractive young woman, well-connected to New England society, she might very well have achieved it in the only way most women were able to in that era: through marriage into a rich family. Just the opposite occurred, as she explained while describing her life at age sixteen: "The lack of money never impressed me at all. Not only were we used to it, but in the literature we fed on, as Louisa Alcott, Mrs. A.D.T. Whitney, the *Youth's Companion*, etc., the heroes and heroines were almost always poor, and good, while the rich people were generally bad. It was many years before I was wholly assured that rich people could be just as good as poor ones."[41] And indeed, when she first married, it was to an artist, handsome, romantic, and nearly as poor as she.

When her health and marriage collapsed, Charlotte once again relied on the kindness of friends for small loans to pay for the Weir treatment and, later, to travel to California for relief from her nervous collapse. She began her second life in Pasadena with Katherine on a financial shoestring, amazed at the fact that she could buy grapes and other fresh fruit so cheaply and rent a cottage for $10 each month. "For ten cents I could buy a rambling collop they called a mutton chop, big enough to make two meals for an invalid woman and a small child."[42] And it was ever such; when the fees she earned for her poetry no longer were sufficient, she moved north to San Francisco, where she worked on various journals and, for a while, ran a boarding house. Finally, after the press attacked her for sending Katherine to Charles, she could no longer find employment at all and set out to travel the country and lecture in friendlier environs. Still, she remained steadfast. As she explained, "Failures were nothing, debts were nothing—didn't most business have to have credit? I was alive and had my work to do; I was escaping from the foulest misrepresentation and abuse I have ever known, and I had a wholly reliable religion and social philosophy."[43]

During the next five years she would live this nomadic life, building a following of women and men who saw in her social vision one that they too could embrace. Still, her concern with her own welfare remained minimal.

For years I lived on that basis, as propertyless and as desireless as a Buddhist priest, almost, though needing something more than a yellow robe and begging bowl. Once I preached in Battle Creek, Michigan. My pay was to be the collection. The sermon was on heaven, and never did I give a better one, making them see how near it was, our heaven on earth, how real and practical, how well within our power to make. When it was ended the congregation sat breathless, eager, deeply moved. I gave them a benediction and the meeting was over.

I quite forgot the collection. If I had remembered it, I would not have broken the spell that was on them for any money.

Two good old people were entertaining me, and next morning my host asked me, "Do you believe in missionaries?" I said I did, some kinds. "Do you think they ought to be supported?" I agreed that they had to be. Then he told me that they thought I was a missionary, and his wife wanted him to give me ten dollars. So I was paid, even without the collection.[44]

Deriving her worldview from her family situations, her childhood experiences, and her failed attempt at a conventional marriage, Gilman extrapolated from the personal to the political, widening her intellectual focus to what she saw as the central problems of American industrial society—great excesses of wealth and poverty, and the unbridled competition of late-nineteenth-century capitalism.[45]

In her most successful work, *Women and Economics*, Gilman takes on the issue of wealth from a theoretical, rather than experiential, point of view. She expressed her major argument in these words: "Rudely classifying the principal fields of human difficulty, we find one large proportion lies in the sex-relation, and another in the economic relation, between the individual constituents of society. To speak broadly, the troubles of life as we find them are mainly traceable to the heart or the purse."[46] In answer to the many social and economic inequities she saw in the United States in the 1890s, she stated this position:

Civilization, be it understood, does not consist in the acquisition of luxuries. . . . A civilized State is one in which the citizens live in organic industrial relation. The more full, free, subtle, and easy that relation, the more perfect the differentiation of labor and exchange of product, with their correlative institutions,—the more perfect is that civilization. To eat, drink, sleep, and keep warm, these are common to all animals. . . . But to serve each other more and more widely; to live only by such service; to develop special functions, so that we depend for our living on society's return for services that can be of no direct use to ourselves,—this is civilization, our human glory and race-distinction.[47]

Arguing firmly that "wealth is a social product," dependent on "highly specialized skilled labor" working cooperatively, Gilman concluded that "this failure to recognize or, at least, to act up to a recognition of social interests, owing to the disproportionate pressure of individual interests is the underlying cause of our economic distress."[48] From this foundation, she derived the central point of her philosophy:

To make the sexual gain of the male rest on his purchasing power puts the immense force of sex-competition into the field of social economics, not only as an incentive to labor and achievement, which is good, but as an incentive to individual gain, however obtained, which is bad; thus accounting for our multiplied and intensified desire to get,—the inordinate greed of our industrial world. . . .

The contest in every good man's heart to-day between the "ought to" and the "must," between his best work and the "pot-boiler," is his personal share of this incessant struggle between social interest and self-interest. For himself and by himself he would be glad to do his best work, to be true to his ideals, to be brave in meeting loss for that truth's sake. But as the compromising capitalist says in "Put Yourself in His Place," when his sturdy young friend—a bachelor—wonders at his giving in to unjust demands, "Marriage makes a mouse of a man." To the young business man who falls into evil courses in the sex-relation the open greed of his fair dependant is a menace to his honesty, to his business prospects. On the same man married the needs of his wife often operate in the same way. The sense of the dependence of the helpless creature whose food must come through him does not stimulate courage, but compels submission.

The foregoing distinction should be clearly held in mind. Legitimate sex-competition brings out all that is best in man. To please her, to win her, he strives to do his best. But the economic dependence of the female upon the male, with its ensuing purchasability, does not so affect a man: it puts upon him the necessity for getting things, not for doing them. In the lowest grades of labor, where there is no getting without doing and where the laborer always does more than he gets, this works less palpable evil than in the higher grades, the professions and arts, where the most valuable work is always ahead of the market, and where to work for the market involves a lowering of standards. The young artist or poet or scientific student works for his work's sake, for art, for science, and so for the best good of society. But the artist or student married must get gain, must work for those who will pay; and those who will pay are not those who lift and bear forward the standard of progress.[49]

After further describing the debasement of a Veblenesque "conspicuous consumption" that middle- and upper-class women suffer in this situation, and its subsequent impact on the poor due to the unfair distribution of wealth in the capitalist system, Gilman reaches the obvious conclusion that women should have economic independence, not just for themselves, but for the general good of society. Derived from her earliest experiences both in her families of origin and of marriage, this vision was first fully articulated by Gilman in *Women and Economics* in 1898, and continued to form the basis for all that followed. In other works, she would go on to describe in great detail the living arrangements that might allow women to support themselves while still fulfilling their maternal roles and maintaining satisfying relationships with men. As a road to these reforms, she embraced suffrage and peace programs, arguing convincingly in both her lectures and later writings that all of these processes and issues were interrelated and necessary for the achievement of a fair and equitable life for all. As Ann Lane concludes:

Women and Economics is an extraordinary and important book. . . . Her issue is gender. She pays inadequate attention to class or race or ethnicity, and her argument is thereby weakened. But what she had to say about gender is still startling today, ninety years later.

Her major assertion that the "sexuo-economic" relationship is the central fact of human relationships is a brilliant formulation. She built on the labor theory of value, but extended it to the issue of gender. She did the same with evolutionary theory, giving new life to both widely held notions by that extension. Gilman used the accepted "scientific" wisdom of her time but infused it with a feminist angle of vision, and thereby transformed it profoundly, offering a view of gender relationships that appears obvious after she says it, but that is deeply original. Like other theorists committed to the theory of evolution, she used it to explain and insist on the desirability of change. What she wanted changed was hers alone: women's work, home, marriage, child-rearing.[50]

Much more of what Gilman said in the remaining years of her life is of great interest to twentieth-century social reformers but is not centrally germane to this study. We can conclude, however, that the vision of wealth and privilege she extracted from her own personal experiences and those of the society within which they occurred—a vision that concerned itself with the place of women in a capitalist economy and sought consistently to understand how the ideology which supported that economy was flawed at its center—led to her most significant work and to the conveyance of a vision of social change still a part of the struggle today. That more than fifty years after her death her country could still be engaged in a debate about affordable child care would have amazed Gilman. That the argument still reflected a fight for basic economic power that was both gender- and class-connected would not.

Elizabeth Gurley Flynn

Elizabeth Gurley Flynn was born on August 7, 1890, thirty years after Addams and Gilman and certainly into different circumstances. The eldest child of working-class Irish immigrants, Flynn's early years were, in absolute terms, more impoverished than Gilman's, although she had the advantage of a loving, supportive, and undivided family.[51] Certainly the urban, immigrant culture of her childhood differed greatly from the experience of either Addams or Gilman.

Both parents were socialists, and throughout her life, Flynn explained her own radicalism as the result of her Irish and family traditions. As she argued in the early pages of her autobiography, *Rebel Girl*: "By birth I am a New Englander, though not of Mayflower stock. My ancestors were 'immigrants and revolutionists'—from the Emerald Isle. . . . There had been an uprising in each generation in Ireland, and forefathers of mine were reputed to be in every one of them."[52] In a further connection of her own value system to that of her family's, she explained that her father

was suspended from college [the Thayer School of Engineering at Dartmouth] for a short interval because he refused to give the names of those attending a secret meeting of Catholic students who were organizing to protest the denial of their right to attend Catholic services. The New York *World* of that day had an article commending his stand; the student body supported him, and he was reinstated. I thought proudly of this family precedent in December 1952, over 65 years later, when I entered the Women's House of Detention in New York City to serve a 30 days' sentence for contempt of court for refusal to "name names" [in the McCarthy era].[53]

During Elizabeth's early childhood in the 1890s, the Flynn family moved frequently as her father sought work in the mills and as an itinerant civil engineer. But in 1900 the family settled in the Bronx, where they would remain for twenty-seven years in an apartment that frequently offered safe haven to Elizabeth during her first long stint of labor organizing. This location allowed the elder Flynns to rejoin a socialist community and their serious eldest daughter to come into contact with such figures as Emma Goldman, and the written work of Charlotte Perkins Gilman and Edward Bellamy as well as the classic socialist and anarchist writings of the day, including those of Friedrich Engels, August Bebel, and Peter Kropotkin.[54]

Flynn enjoyed public speaking in school and soon found herself invited to participate in a local street meeting at the Harlem Socialist Club on the subject of women under socialism. Her lecture was well received, and more importantly, Gurley, as she came to be known in this period, found that she enjoyed the work. She left school, and by 1907 she was an active participant in the socialist lecture circuit. Her passionate delivery, attractive appearance, and dramatic skills not only made her popular with New York audiences, but called her activities to the attention of nationally circulated newspapers. Soon she was invited to address radical organizations across the country, particularly those connected to the I.W.W. (International Workers of the World), which she had joined in 1906.[55] Necessarily, her public speaking for the Wobblies (as members were known) led to actual involvement in the wide-ranging strikes of the period.

Like most Wobblies she viewed labor as the measure of people's power and creativity. Most IWW members were foreigners, migrant workers, and women and therefore ineligible to vote; political franchise was irrelevant to them. Economic democracy, that is, decent wages and working conditions, and the right to organize were the vital demands.[56]

Among her many activities in this period, Flynn worked in the Mesabi Iron Range (Minnesota) strike of 1907 and the textile strikes in Lawrence, Massachusetts, in 1912 and Paterson, New Jersey, in 1913. She also led successful free speech fights in Montana and Washington in 1909. During the same period, Flynn met and married John Jones, a labor organizer also associated with the I.W.W., and in 1910 her only child, Fred, was born. The marriage failed at about the same time, and Flynn never married again. She did, however, maintain a long, intimate relationship with Carlo Tresca, an Italian-American anarchist, which lasted until the mid-1920s. Both relationships failed, as relationships do, for a variety of reasons, but one central complaint voiced by Flynn concerned the fact that both men wanted her to stop organizing, while they were unwilling to make the same sacrifice. Thereafter, her personal relationships were varied but short-lived. She was a passionate woman, and part of the lure of the life of an organizer was no doubt the freedom it gave her—freedom unavailable to most women of that era, and which would have been difficult for her as well, had she not been able to rely on her mother for child care during the months she spent on the road.

Like the other reformers examined here, Flynn's concerns expanded during the years before World War I, when, like nearly all the others, she staked out a pacifist position. This argument, coupled with her ongoing syndicalism and support of the Bolshevik Revolution in 1917, led to her arrest, along with 169 other activists, for violation of the Espionage Act. Although the charges against her were eventually dropped, this experience only foreshadowed what was to come during the postwar "Red Scare" and again in the 1950s. Like Addams, she helped found the American Civil Liberties Union in 1920 to defend against the growing intolerance of political variety in the United States, but unlike Addams, Flynn had neither the popular support, reputation, nor economic resources to come through the struggle relatively unscathed. By 1926 she was both physically and emotionaly exhausted by the struggle, and at only thirty-six, she was diagnosed to have a heart condition and forced to retire, at least for a while.

For the next ten years, Flynn lived in retirement, sharing the home of an old friend, Dr. Marie Equi, in Portland, Oregon. Equi, a physician and radical in many regards, remains essentially shrouded in mystery. But Flynn's papers reveal that the relationship became increasingly difficult to sustain by the early 1930s. Finally, believing her health restored, a mature, substantial, middle-aged Flynn returned to labor organizing, inspired by New Deal programs and the promise of a newly invigorated Communist Party, which she now joined.[57] Her career as a columnist also began at this time when she joined the *Daily Worker*, where she would publish for the next twenty-six years.

Although her reputation suffered because of her Communist Party membership after the signing of the Nazi-Soviet pact, it regained momentum during World War II, when the alliance between the United States and the Soviet Union lent some respectabilty to homegrown communism. In 1942 Flynn ran for U.S. Congress from New York and received 50,000 votes, largely basing her campaign on issues around women's role in the war effort. Riding out the chaotic internal schisms within the CPUSA during and immediately after the war, Flynn later organized groups to defend party members arrested under the Smith Act. Soon she too was under indictment, and after a long trial she was convicted "for conspiring to teach and advocate the overthrow of the United States government by force and violence." For this she served two and one-half years in a federal penitentiary.

In 1957, finally freed from prison, Flynn reentered CP activities, refusing to bow to the ongoing terror waged by the United States Government. As her primary biographer explains the situation, "During these scoundrel, trying times, she kept her spirits up and courageously fought for her party, while the government took a sledge hammer to squash an ailing gnat."[58] Denied her passport, she took the case to the Supreme Court and won. Soon thereafter she made her first visit to the Soviet Union. Belatedly, she labeled

Stalin a "madman" but remained loyal to the communist vision.[59] She would return to the Soviet Union twice more, finally dying there in 1964.

Popularized in her early years by the Wobbly songwriter Joe Hill as the "Rebel Girl," Elizabeth Gurley Flynn continued her rebellion throughout her long life. Proud of her Irish revolutionary traditions and the contributions she had made to ameliorate the harsh conditions of workers in the United States before World War I, Flynn saw the international communist movement between the wars as but an extension of these earlier concerns. Disappointed by its failures both at home and abroad after 1945, she nonetheless remained loyal to its ideals throughout her life. We may question her judgment here, but not her motives. From her early years in the factory towns of New Hampshire until the end in Moscow, Elizabeth Gurley Flynn's loyalty was to the worker with whom she strongly identified, wherever that worker struggled.

How did Flynn express her own dismay at the conditions into which she was born in 1890? At some level, everything she ever spoke or wrote responded to the questions about wealth and privilege that this chapter addresses. To read her articles in the *Daily Worker* or her autobiography, *Rebel Girl*, is to find an overabundance of evidence.

In the early pages of *Rebel Girl*, Flynn paints an idyllic picture of her early childhood in Concord, New Hampshire. Perhaps in contrast to this small town first scene, she then expresses the shock of later experiences in powerful terms:

Indelible impressions were made upon me as a child of working-class life and poverty in the textile towns of Manchester, New Hampshire, and Adams. . . . The change from the pleasant clean little city of Concord, to the drab bleak textile center of Manchester, was sufficient to impress even a five-year-old child. We lived there nearly three years. The gray mills in Manchester stretched like prisons along the banks of the Merrimac River; 50 per cent of the workers were women and they earned one dollar a day. Many lived in the antiquated "corporation boarding houses," relics of the time when the mills were built. Our neighbors, men and women, rushed to the mills before the sun rose on cold winter days and returned after dark. They were poorly dressed and poverty stricken. The women wore no hats, but shawls over their heads. The "mill children" left school early to take dinner pails to their parents. The mothers took time off in the mills to nurse their babies who were cared for by elderly relatives.

The mills would slow down or shut down for no apparent reason. "Bad times," it was called. Then I saw mill children eating bread with lard instead of butter. Many children were without underwear, even in the coldest weather. A young woman mill worker, showing her hand with three fingers gone due to a mill accident, shocked me immeasurably. Safety devices were still unheard of. Once, while we were in school in Adams piercing screams came from the mill across the street. A girl's long hair had been caught in the unguarded machine and she was literally scalped. My first contact with a jail was watching a policeman put a weeping old man, "a tramp" he was called, into a "lock-up" in Adams. He kept assuring us children he had done no wrong, he had no job and no money and no place to sleep. This episode caused me anxiety about all old people. Would it happen to Grandma? Would it happen to all of us when we were old? Yet in Adams, the old millowner lived in a great mansion in the center of the town, drove around in a fine carriage with beautiful horses, and was once visited by President McKinley.[60]

And it was not just as an observer that Flynn understood the harsh realities of poverty. After the move to New York, the Flynns experienced the living conditions of the poor at first hand.

We were horrified, too, at the conditions we had never met in our travels else-where—the prevalence of pests in the old slum houses, mice, rats, cockroaches and bedbugs. . . .

On cold winter days we'd huddle in the kitchen and shut off the rest of the house. We would do our lessons by a kerosene lamp when the gas was shut off for nonpayment. . . . Bill collectors harassed my gentle mother—the landlord, the gas man, the milk man, the grocer. Once she bought us an encyclopedia on the install-ment plan. But she couldn't keep up the payments and our hearts were broken when we lost the beautiful books we treasured so highly. . . .

There were many small factories, veritable sweatshops, in the neighborhood, where children went to work as early as the law allowed and even younger. . . . Mothers worked too and many children were left alone. . . . The wife of the corner saloonkeeper made huge kettles of soup for free lunch and sent bowls of it around to the poorest families. People helped each other as best they could. Truly, as some philosopher said, "Poverty is like a strange and terrible country. Only those who have been there can really speak of it with knowledge."[61]

Later, as her major biographer explains, "Flynn claimed that her reason for becoming a socialist was a change in her family's economic circum-stances: her father, in spite of winning a lawsuit against his employer, was not paid for two years of contracted labor." She recalled:

During two consecutive winters we suffered from the misery and crushing, but sometimes revolutionizing poverty. I became ill, lost six months from school and had time to read, think and reflect carefully. I had theories: here was a condition that did not coincide with my theories; the theories had to go. I began to see the hypocrisy and dishonesty surrounding me and became an iconoclast and a utopian of an anarchist trend. As I studied the evolution of society, of class struggle and economic factors and their power over our lives, I demanded principles more practical and organized or scientific and yet revolutionary. I became and am now a class conscious Marxist socialist. My economic conditions had changed and in many cases, my ideas changed in rapid order.[62]

While this explanation may seem a bit too neat, and certainly precocious for one not yet eighteen, it nonetheless reflects a very real connection between Flynn's life and beliefs central to the questions asked by this study.

As Flynn moved into the broader arenas as a labor organizer, her day-to-day work confirmed her earlier vision. As she got to know the striking workers in Montana, Lawrence, and Paterson, her childhood experiences and the theories of her early radicalism took on more specific weight.

By 1914 I had been in daily contact with workers and their struggles for eight years. I saw their honesty, modesty, decency, their devotion to their families and their unions, their helpfulness to fellows, their courage, their willingness to sacrifice. I hated those who exploited them, patronized them, lied to them, cheated them and betrayed them. I hated those who lived in idleness and luxury on *their* sweat and toil. More and more the iron was driven into my soul. In my youth I lived through a long period of ruthless brutal force, of terror and violence against workers. Private guards, armed thugs, sheriffs, police, state troopers, militia and judges from justice of the peace to the Supreme Court, were at the command of the employers—North, South, East and West. I heard stories of all this wherever I went. I became more and more strong in my hatred of all these evil things. I became in my youth and I remain now, at 64, "a mortal enemy of capitalism"—to paraphrase Karl Marx's description of himself.[63]

As Lane told us of Gilman, through all her life, Flynn, too, was poor. When arrested in 1917, it was difficult to find the money to get to Chicago where she and her codefendants had to appear for arraignment. Finding funds to pay the lawyers took months and posed nearly insurmountable problems. As Flynn explained:

We were all very poor. There was no type of defense organization then in existence. A group of women organized a special committee for me, and we also set up a general defense fund for ourselves. We raised and spent about $5,000. I recall a conversation I had the first day I was out on bail with Fola La Follette, the daughter of Senator La Follette, who said: "I have no money for bail. But here's a little for your expenses." She never knew, I am sure, how much I appreciated that $5.00![64]

Little changed in the next forty-odd years. After the struggles of the 1920s, Flynn, like Gilman, found herself forced to accept the kindness of friends when she became ill. When she returned to labor organizing in the 1930s, there was still no money. Even in the 1950s, when she served as chairman of the CPUSA, she suffered actual physical deprivation to maintain the position. As Baxandall poignantly describes it, "[I]n the late 1950s, as the Party became smaller, there were fewer celebrations, picnics, and events; the social world of the Party shrunk. Although Flynn loved good food and drink, low brow movies, and music, she did not have the money to go out; Communist party funcitonaries were paid bare minimum wages."[65]

At the end of her life, with few financial resources to draw on, Elizabeth Gurley Flynn traveled once more to the Soviet Union, where she hoped to find relief and the time to finish the second volume of her memoirs. Instead, she became ill once again, and hospitalized at the expense of the state, she died soon afterward. The Soviets used her death as an opportunity to honor the American communist movement, while in the United States her memory was both eulogized and vilified, as she had been during her lifetime. Baxandall concludes, "To die in a foreign country, although a Communist one, which treated her better than her own country, seemed an unfitting end. She was an American rebel. It was in America that she stirred millions, fought bravely, and tried, even if she often fell short, to live a revolutionary life."[66] And it was her American experience of poverty, wealth, and privilege that led to this revolutionary life. Although her personal possibilities had declined when she died in 1964, Flynn had lived long enough to see a new wave of concern for the inequities of capitalism developing in her own country. That this surge too would ultimately be countered by the neoconservatism of recent years would not have surprised her. A veteran of the late Progressive era and the hopeful New Deal, as well as the repression that followed both, "Gurley" would have counseled a continued solidarity with the workers from whose numbers she came.

CONCLUSION

From the outset, the contributors to this volume have read about and collectively discussed wealth: its accumulation, its distribution, its cultural meaning, and the uses to which it is put. We have examined this topic from various historical and methodological perspectives. Our discussions have been framed not only by what we consciously bring professionally and intellectually to the debate, but by our personal histories and our resultant complex and often contradictory value systems as well. While we seemed fully aware of the importance of historical and geographical specificity as we discussed wealth in certain contexts, our historical awareness seemed less definite when we discussed the present or even the recent past in the United States. In my perception, we have occasionally suffered from the currently popular assumption that our present economic circumstances and ideology are beyond history—that with the apparent collapse of Marxist-Leninist communism as it was practiced by the Soviet Union, the world has reached "the end of history."

On one level, then, this chapter is an attempt to remind readers of part of that recent past. By its use of certain examples from the late nineteenth and early twentieth centuries, it seeks to illustrate a different reaction to wealth and private philanthropy than is current here and now. Also by alluding to the situations to which these historical figures were reacting and attempting to ameliorate, this study suggests that a century has not made all that much difference in the relative experiences of the rich and the poor in the United States. Its central assumption is that Ronald Reagan's America strongly paralleled Ulysses Grant's "Gilded Age," and that the neoconservative ideology that underpinned its policies is only a somewhat more sophisticated "take" on the brutal Social Darwinism of Herbert Spencer. The recent "discovery" of the corruption within the U.S. Government, the environmental destruction and the savings and loan debacle resulting from deregulation,[67] and the enormous social tragedies of homelessness and drug abuse not remedied by voluntary philanthropy mirror the context within which these social reformers originally experienced outrage and then began to act. In the intervening century, other social activists have attempted many reforms, achieved some, and faced waves of regressive reaction such as that of the 1980s.

That said, it is not the intention of this effort to oversimplify. Attitudes and actions, as they have been illustrated by the lives of the three women most carefully studied here, evolve in complex circumstances.[68] For them (and for us) personal experiences blend with intellectual and political understanding to emerge as firmly held philosophies. When depressions and wars are going on all around us, they teach lessons not as painfully learned in other eras. Historical actors choose different forums within which to convey these philosophies and lessons. Some, the vast majority, remain mute and convey their perspective through actions—actions such as bread riots, the shutting down of a factory, draft resistance or fragging in combat. Others, blessed with literacy and more given to debate, speak or write. And the format they select also shapes the argument, particularly when it is as all-encompassing a focus as autobiography.[69] With this in mind, I have tried to let my subjects speak in their own voices as fully as possible, so that their manner of self-representation as well as the substance of their arguments can be evaluated.

Clearly, the central focus of those arguments is that capitalism and the philanthropy it spawned did not in the experience of Jane Addams, Charlotte Perkins Gilman, or Elizabeth Gurley Flynn much relieve the suffering of the majority upon whose efforts it was built. It is the contention of this writer that the situation in the United States has not changed much since they spoke. Despite the reforms of the Progressive, New Deal, and New Society eras, recent conservative policies have re-created much of the horror of the late nineteenth century. More significantly for the purposes here, the excess wealth created by these policies has not "trickled down" to those from whose labor it has been drawn. As Teresa Odendahl has recently argued, "[A]bout half of philanthropy [in the U.S.] is donated by multimillionaires. Most of this money goes to groups that sustain the culture, education, policy positions and status of the well-to-do. . . . Contrary to popular belief, less than a third of nonprofit organizations serve the needy. In much of their charitable giving, in fact, the wealthy end up funding their own interests." Additionally, much of the allocation of public funds is influenced by the wealthy who serve on the boards of the organizations through which it is channeled and in the legislatures that make the dispersal decisions. Finally, and particularly significant within the context of the recent national debate over taxation, the rich who give to their favorite philanthropic organizations also gain important income and estate tax benefits. Odendhal concludes, "[F]or nearly ten years, two Republican presidents have extolled the virtues of charity and volunteerism. They have claimed that charity will make up for deep cuts in federally funded human service programs. Before our philanthropic system can take on more burdens in response to Federal cutbacks, it's going to need some fundamental changes."[70]

While arguing for cuts in human service programs, these administrations have also sought to shift those resources to the wealthy through incentive programs to encourage further entrepreneurial development. Private enterprise defined within a classic capitalist context has been offered as the penultimate solution to humanity's problems. Recent geopolitical changes have been used as evidence to prove the point. Based on their close observation of late-nineteenth- and early-twentieth-century circumstances, Addams, Gilman, and Flynn would have vehemently disagreed and seen the situation in much more complex and sophisticated ways. This chapter is my attempt to make an argument similar to theirs for the here and now.

NOTES

1. The concept of placement, or "some tracking of individuals, some delineation of their histories—akin to time-lines for issues" is defined in Richard E. Neustadt and Ernest R. May, *Thinking in Time: The Uses of History for Decision Makers* (New York: Free Press, 1986), chapter 9.

2. Paul G. Schervish and Andrew Herman, *Empowerment and Beneficence: Strategies of Living and Giving among the Wealthy*. Final report on the Study on Wealth and Philanthropy (Chestnut Hill, Mass.: Social Welfare Research Institute at Boston College, 1988), 84–85; see also 114, 188.

3. In my Sunday school classes, we were never taught that the "eye of a needle" referred to the "small pedestrian gate of a walled city" [Schervish and Herman, 207] and indeed, in my mind's eye today, the imagery remains that of the child who first heard the aphorism and saw it in reality-based terms.

4. By this I refer to the arguments of trickle-down economics and neo-conservativism, and to some extent "productive philanthropy" as discussed in Schervish and Herman, pp. 168–70.

5. The literature about autobiography as a narrative form and the problems emerging from its use as a source for history is abundant, and I do not claim to have mastered more than a small portion of it. My awareness as reflected in this discussion owes much to two works: Carolyn G. Heilbrun's *Writing a Woman's Life* (New York: W. W. Norton, 1988) and Estelle C. Jelinek's *The Tradition of Women's Autobiography: From Antiquity to the Present* (Boston: Twayne, 1986).

6. I find it interesting to note how often my subjects also "construct a narrative around the conquest of constraints by the application of virtue." [Schervish and Herman, p. 201] In fact, I suspect, nearly all autobiography follows this pattern.

7. Matthew Josephson best described and analyzed this group in his classic study, *The Robber Barons: The Great American Capitalists, 1861–1901* (New York: Harcourt,Brace and World, 1934; reprint, 1962).

8. *To "Herland" and Beyond: The Life & Work of Charlotte Perkins Gilman* (New York: Pantheon Books, 1990), 10–11. The reader should note the similarity of this description to the world described by Tom Wolfe in *Bonfire of the Vanities* (New York: Farrar, Straus and Giroux, 1987).

9. Mary Hill points out that

[i]n 1890, approximately seven-eighths of American families controlled only one-eighth of the national wealth, and in the land of opportunity, the annual income of all nonagrarian wage earners averaged only four hundred and eighty-six dollars. Factory workers' weekly hours averaged about sixty. Nearly two million children below the age of fifteen were wage earners. At least 15 percent, possibly 20 percent, of the wage-earning population was out of work. Prices were relatively low, the cost of living rather stable, but vast numbers of Americans—even by the standards of the day—could be considered poor. . . . [I]t has been estimated that an income of $1,500 to $2,000 a year, provided one exercised economy, was enough for a family to live quite comfortably as members of the middle class. Ten, even five, thousand dollars a year enabled one to live with few major economic worries. An income of $486, however, the average annual income of nonfarm workers, was not adequate to provide even the basic necessities of food, shelter, or clothing.

Mary A. Hill, *Charlotte Perkins Gilman: The Making of a Radical Feminist 1860–1896* (Philadelphia: Temple University Press, 1980), 167–68.

10. During the research for this chapter, I read the autobiographical writings of eleven women born between 1860 and 1910: Jane Addams, Ella Reeve Bloor, Peggy Dennis, Rheta Childe Dorr, Elizabeth Gurley Flynn, Charlotte Perkins Gilman, Emma Goldman, Mary Livermore, Elizabeth Stuart Phelps, Margaret Sanger, and Mary Heaton Vorse. From that group, I selected three—Addams, Gilman, and Flynn—as most representative in terms of their long-term historical recognition, the various classes from which they came, the issues they addressed, or the language with which they expressed their concerns. Although this work examines only three of those studied, many of the points I have chosen to emphasize here were clarified by my reading of the other material.

11. It is interesting to note that all of these women lived into ripe old age, and all but one achieved at least the seventy-year life span the ancients considered desirable. Specifically, their chronologies are as follows: Addams, 1860–1935; Bloor, 1862–1951; Dennis, 1909–; Dorr, 1866–1948; Flynn, 1890–1964; Gilman, 1860–1935; Goldman, 1869–1940; Livermore, 1820–1905; Phelps, 1844–1911; Sanger, 1879–1966; Vorse, 1874–1966.

12. For an interesting discussion of the creation and re-creation of the Addams myth, see Allen F. Davis, *American Heroine: The Life and Legend of Jane Addams* (New York: Oxford University Press, 1973), 282–94.

13. Although I read biographies of each of the three women central to this study (see bibliography), the brief life summaries that precede my discussion of the autobiographical explanations of each of the subjects rely heavily on the convenient

sketches in Edward T. James and Janet Wilson James, eds., *Notable American Women, 1607–1950: A Biographical Dictionary* (Cambridge: Belnap Press of Harvard University, 1971). Emphasis and interpretation are for the most part my own. The interested reader is directed to this remarkably helpful source for further information.

14. Davis, *American Heroine*, 8.

15. Ibid., 31.

16. Ibid., 74.

17. Jane Addams, *Twenty Years at Hull-House with Autobiographical Notes* (New York: Macmillan, 1911), 13–14.

18. Ibid., 32–34.

19. Ibid., 79–80.

20. Ibid., 81–82.

21. Ibid., 100. Others in this study arrived at the same conclusion. See for example, Elizabeth Stuart Phelps's fictional version:

"It is proverbial of men with my history," said Garrick, slowly,—"men who have crawled on their hands and knees from the very quagmires of life,—men who know, as no other men can know, that the odds are twenty to one when a poor man makes a throw in the world's play—...

"Twenty to one," said Stephen Garrick, in a dry statistical tone, "against poverty, always. It is proverbial, I say, that men who know as God knows that it is by 'him who hath no money' that the upright, downright, unmistakable miseries of life are drained to the dregs,—that such men prove to be the hardest of masters and the most conservative of social reformers."

Elizabeth Stuart Phelps, *The Silent Partner* (Ridgewood, N.J.: Gregg Press, 1967), 145.

22. Jane Addams, *A Centennial Reader*, ed. Emily Cooper Johnson (New York: Macmillan, 1960), 213–17. As did many others of the period, Addams often used the words "commerce" or "the factory system" interchangeably to refer to the capitalist economic system of the day.

23. Ibid., 198–99. Crystal Eastman, a labor organizer of a slightly later period, expressed her reaction to a similar situation in these words:

When great unforeseen disasters like the San Francisco earthquake come upon humanity by act of God, we can be thrilled and uplifted by the wave of generous giving which sweeps over the country—we can be comforted by contributing a little ourselves to aid the survivors. And when we are thinking of the deadly list of unpreventable work accidents—the blast furnace explosions, the electric shocks, the falls—it appeases our sense of right a little to realize that we are working away as hard as we can for a law which will assure a livelihood to the children of the victims. But when the strong young body of a free man is caught up by a little projecting set-screw [here she is referring to an accident reported in a recent newspaper article], whirled around a shaft and battered to death, when we know that a set-screw can be countersunk at a trivial cost, when we know that the law of the state has prohibited projecting set-screws for many years, then who wants to talk about "three years' wages to the widow," and "shall it be paid in installments, or in lump sum?" and "shall the workman contribute?" What we want is to put somebody in jail. And when the dead bodies of girls are found piled up against locked doors leading to the exits after a factory fire, when we know that locking such doors is a prevailing custom in such factories, and one that has continued in New York City since those 146 lives were lost in the Triangle Waist Company fire, who wants to hear about a great relief fund? What we want is to start a revolution.

Blanche Wiesen Cook, ed., *Crystal Eastman on Women and Revolution* (New York: Oxford University Press, 1978) p. 281, quoting from an article entitled "The Three

Essentials for Accident Prevention," originally in *American Academy of Political and Social Science Annals*, July–December, 1911.

24. Addams, *Twenty Years*, 207.

25. Ibid., 310.

26. Ibid., 311.

27. Ibid., 391–93.

28. In 1966. at the beginning of her rediscovery, American historian Carl N. Degler described her former achievements:

Today her [Gilman's] name is almost unknown, even among historians of American social thought. Yet in the first two decades of the twentieth century her books ran through numerous editions and were translated into half a dozen foreign languages. Her views on the place and future of women were sought, commented upon, and avidly discussed in this country and in Europe. Her dozens of articles appeared in popular and scholarly journals alike, and as a lecturer she was in great demand in the United States, England, and on the continent.

Introduction to the Torchbook Edition of Charlotte Perkins Gilman, *Women and Economics: A Study of the Economic Relation between Men and Women as a Factor in Social Evolution* (New York: Harper and Row, 1966), vi.

29. Gilman's father, Frederic Beecher Perkins, was the grandson of the theologian Lyman Beecher and nephew of Henry Ward Beecher, Catherine Beecher, and Harriet Beecher Stowe. Her mother, Mary A. Fitch Perkins, traced her ancestry to Roger Williams, founder of Rhode Island and the Baptist church in America. Gilman herself was born a Perkins, married first to Charles Walter Stetson, later to George Houghton Gilman. Since she published as both Charlotte Perkins Stetson and Charlotte Perkins Gilman, much confusion surrounds the tracing of her work. For the purposes of this paper, she will be referred to as Charlotte Perkins Gilman, her last and best known name.

30. Lane, *"Herland" and Beyond*, 6.

31. Gilman, *Women*, 100–101.

32. As Rosalyn Fraad Baxandall explains with reference to Elizabeth Gurley Flynn, "Being a skilled speaker in the early 1900s was equivalent to being a movie star, a media hero today. Before the advent of radio and television, all mass communication depended on either the printed word or unaided spoken words. For radicals these two modes were closely associated, for the main source of sales of their literature was at open-air meetings." Rosalyn Fraad Baxandall, *Words on Fire: The Life and Writing of Elizabeth Gurley Flynn* (New Brunswick, N.J.: Rutgers University Press, 1987), 10.

33. Lane, *"Herland" and Beyond*, 209.

34. Degler recounts (introduction to Gilman, *Women*, xiii):

the book that established her reputation in the United States and Europe was *Women and Economics*, which appeared in 1898 after several months of intensive writing; it was almost immediately republished in 1899. The book attracted wide attention; ultimately seven editions appeared in the United States and Great Britain and it was translated into several languages, including Japanese, Russian, and Hungarian. As a result of this book, the ideas of which she endlessly expounded in other books, articles and lectures, Charlotte Gilman became the leading intellectual in the women's movement in the United States during the first two decades of the twentieth century. The *Nation* went so far as to pronounce *Women and Economics* "the most significant utterance on the subject [of women] since Mill's *Subjection of Woman*" which had appeared over thirty years earlier. Although she published four other books in the next ten years, none achieved the acclaim of *Women and Economics*. Part of the reason was that her subsequent books had all been adumbrated in that first effort; those that followed largely elaborated a position already clearly staked out, even if not thoroughly explored.

35. Charlotte Perkins Gilman, *The Living of Charlotte Perkins Gilman: An Autobiography, with Foreword by Zona Gale* (New York: D. Appleton-Century, 1935), 281.

36. Lane, *"Herland" and Beyond*, 344–45.

37. Since 1980 two biographies have appeared (see bibliography), and much of her writing has been reprinted. In addition, "The Yellow Wall-paper" has been dramatized for public television.

38. Lane, *"Herland" and Beyond*, 3.

39. Gilman, *The Living*, 9.

40. Ibid., 22.

41. Ibid., 35.

42. Ibid., 107–8.

43. Ibid., 180.

44. Ibid., 186.

45. There is reason to believe that Gilman was influenced by economist Richard Ely, "founder of the American Economic Association, and a leading proponent of the 'new school of political economy' [which argued] that current inequalities were ethically unjust and economically unsound; [and] that economic theory should be responsive to human needs." Hill, *Charlotte Perkins Gilman*, 245.

46. Gilman, *Women*, 25.

47. Ibid., 75.

48. Ibid., 101, 105.

49. Ibid., 111–14.

50. Lane, *"Herland" and Beyond*, 251.

51. Flynn's father, Thomas, was actually second-generation Irish and had worked with his father in the granite quarries of Maine before moving to the factories in New Hampshire. Her mother, Annie Gurley Flynn, was the actual immigrant in the family, arriving in America in 1876. Still, both parents identified strongly with the Irish nationalist movement, and Flynn liked to say that "Papa is more Irish than Mama and he never saw Ireland!" Elizabeth Gurley Flynn, *The Rebel Girl: An Autobiography, My First Life (1906–1926)*, rev. ed. (New York: International Publishers, 1973), 29.

52. Ibid., 23–26.

53. Ibid., 32.

54. Baxandall (*Words on Fire*, 7) lists these authors. She goes on in the same passage: "Her sister Kathie described her at this time as 'deadly serious' . . . she seldom laughed or even smiled. . . . Later we [Kathie and EGF] agreed that poverty is bound to make older children super-serious" [ellipses and inserts in original]. Flynn herself explained her seriousness this way: "Needless to say, I was a terribly serious child for my years, the oldest of a poor family, sharing the miseries of the parents. When a family suffers poverty, when children hear their mother and even their father weep sometimes from despair over how to feed their children, when all around are other suffering families—children cannot be light-hearted and happy. We saw 'some way out' in the struggles of the labor movement and rejoiced in them." *Rebel Girl*, 45. In an article published near the end of her life, Flynn explained the influence of Charlotte Perkins Gilman on her thinking and

described Gilman's economic philosophy in these words: "Mrs. Gilman built her arguments for Socialism around the inequalities, exploitation, dependence, and degradation of women under capitalism." "Women in American Socialist Struggles" (1960), reprinted in Baxandall, *Words on Fire*, 174.

55. Baxandall tells us: "Her speeches took the audience (in many places, two-thirds non-English-speaking) to the precipice of every human emotion and left them ready to fight. Even unions hostile to the I.W.W. like the United Mine Workers, enlisted Flynn to speak to their members." Mary Heaton Vorse, in her autobiography, *A Footnote to Folly: Reminiscences of Mary Heaton Vorse*, ed. Annette K. Baxter (1935; reprint, New York: Ayer, 1980), described it this way:

When Elizabeth Gurley Flynn spoke, the excitement of the crowd became a visible thing. She stood there, young, with her Irish blue eyes, her face magnolia white and her cloud of black hair, the picture of a youthful revolutionary leader. She stirred them, lifted them up in her appeal for solidarity. Then at the end of the meeting, they sang. It was as though a spurt of flame had gone through the audience, something stirring and powerful, a feeling which has made the liberation of people possible, something beautiful and strong had swept through the people and welded them together, singing.

Reprinted in Baxandall, *Words on Fire*, 11, 17.

56. Ibid., 100.

57. Flynn had sought membership in the CPUSA as early as 1926, when she saw in it a home after the demise of the I.W.W. Her membership application was not processed however, and her long hiatus away from politics postponed involvement until the mid-1930s, essentially the heyday of American communist activity. After making her commitment, Flynn, although occasionally critical of party policy, never wavered in her loyalty, and later became the first female chairman of the U.S. organization. Baxandall, *Words on Fire*, 1.

58. Ibid., 61.

59. "Flynn followed the Party line and never articulated an alternative. She told her friends that she was no theoretician, merely an agitator and popularizer. The I.W.W. had scored theory as highfalutin dribble, and Flynn had a touch of this Wobbly anti-intellectualism." Baxandall, *Words on Fire*, 40.

60. Flynn, *Rebel Girl*, 35–36, in an entire section entitled "I Hate Poverty," 35–39. It is interesting to compare this passage with the writing of Eastman and Phelps, cited above.

61. Ibid., 38.

62. Elizabeth Gurley Flynn, "How I Became a Socialist Speaker," *Socialist Woman*, no. 3. August 1907, quoted in Baxandall, *Words on Fire*, 6.

63. Flynn, *Rebel Girl*, 191.

64. Ibid., 236.

65. Baxandall, *Words on Fire*, 241.

66. Ibid., 71–72.

67. A particularly effective discussion setting other effects of deregulation into a broader perspective may be found in Pat Broderick, "A Fed-Up Pilot Speaks Out," *Newsweek*, April 23, 1990, 8.

68. A helpful description of these complex circumstances may be found in Schervish and Herman, 156, where sociologist Anthony Giddens is explained and quoted in these words: "A social structure is the compilation of interrelated social positions, cultural meanings, and behavioral conditions which . . . serve as both

the 'medium and outcome' of individual or group practices. As such, a social structure is both 'constraining and enabling.' It is a field or terrain that provides both limits and barriers to action as well as resources and opportunities for changing the structure itself. It produces rules for social action, which in turn become the objects of production." No better description of the context within which the women studied here worked could be written.

69. One of the problems inherent in women's autobiographies of this era involves what the period defined as behavior socially acceptable for women. As Carolyn Heilbrun (*Writing*, 24) argues, "Well into the twentieth century, it continued to be impossible for women to admit into their autobiographical narratives the claim of achievement, the admission of ambition, the recognition that accomplishment was neither luck nor the result of the efforts or generosity of others." Given the nature of what the women in this study did as their life's work, this constraint must have been particularly difficult.

70. Teresa Odendahl, "A Thousand Points of Light," *New York Times*, July 21, 1990, OpEd page. See as well, Odendahl, *Charity Begins at Home: Generosity and Self-Interest among the Philanthropic Elite* (New York: Basic Books, 1990).

7

The Moral Biographies of the Wealthy and the Cultural Scripture of Wealth

---

PAUL G. SCHERVISH

It seems like there's no work at all involved, in fact there is a lot of work of different sorts to be able to deal with [money].

—Malcolm Hirsch

I'm free, you know. I'm free of financial restrictions. It's wonderful. What more could I want? I have money that I can do things with—for myself and for the causes I feel are important. My next career could be anything. I have that freedom and I'm not afraid to sort of think, "Well, maybe you *could* do that."

—Allison Randall

THE NORMATIVE INNER WORLD OF WEALTH

The autobiographies of the wealthy are moral biographies of wealth. The rich understand the forces that shape their lives, define what they want to accomplish, and interpret their dealings with others in reference to culturally dictated normative canons of wealth. Through a series of narrative procedures they explain how it is possible for them to be rich and good at the same time. My purpose in this chapter is to make theoretical sense of how the wealthy make moral sense of their lives. I examine how they assemble the events of their lives into moral biographies and what these personalized morality plays reveal more generally about what I call the underlying cultural scripture, or normative environment, of wealth. I base my analysis on interviews with 130 millionaires. These interviews were conducted in twelve metropolitan areas from 1985 to 1987 as part of the Study on Wealth and Philanthropy sponsored at Boston College by the T. B. Murphy Foundation Charitable Trust.[1]

Moral Biography and the Cultural Scripture of Wealth

I refer to the autobiographical narratives of the wealthy as moral biographies. By "moral" I mean a mode of self-understanding rather than a doctrine of ethics. It is the normative consciousness with which the wealthy define a virtuous identity in relation to money. This does not mean that the wealthy ever cleanly separate what they have to do from what they like to do, especially since the most distinctive attribute of the wealthy is their ability to shape the world according to their desires.[2] It does mean, however, that they seldom if ever describe events simply as a matter of getting what they want. Rather, they are constantly learning and aligning themselves to a range of normative standards—and telling us about it. As G. K. Chesterton writes, "The only two things that can satisfy the soul are a person and a story; and even a story must be about a person."[3] When the story is about the person who is telling it, we must expect to hear an edifying story about the moral quality of that person's soul.

Why the wealthy choose to follow one standard rather than another is due to a number of reasons, including their personal predilections. Still, the fact remains that their choices are normatively directed. The very act of making normatively directed choices lends justification as well as magnitude to their lives, and recounting the moral character of their lives is the organizing principle of their personal narratives. As chroniclers of their own lives, the wealthy place themselves in the company of David Copperfield, who invites his readers to learn to what extent "I shall turn out to be the hero of my own life." These biographies of course are never simply descriptions of factual happenings. They are constructed and sometimes even contrived stories in which the personal quest for riches is told as a quest for a richer life. Yet each in its own way turns out to be, in effect, a contemporary gospel of wealth. Picking up where Andrew Carnegie left off, each provides an exemplary story of riches in the service of virtue.[4]

In addition to shedding light on the meaning of moral biography, the narratives serve as a lens through which to view the shared meanings and sentiments of wealth embedded in our collective consciousness.[5] The moral self-understanding of each wealthy individual is connected to the culturally available meaning of wealth. Each biography in its own way grows out of and supports a general cluster of shared sentiments about the use of wealth and the moral identity of the wealthy—hence, the term "cultural scripture" of wealth. The word "scripture" emphasizes that the various social meanings competing to shape our lives are each symbolically coherent "scripts" or "texts" that become inscribed in our consciousness. We do not learn discrete ideas or attitudes, as theories of culture and ideology often imply. Rather, we learn a way of life, a sequence of causality, an ordering of events. Lionel Trilling says that the characters in nineteenth-century European novels are noteworthy because they present "class traits modified by personality."[6] Although none of the respondents is as celebrated or prototypical as Carnegie, their biographical accounts teach us just as much as Carnegie about the worldly asceticism of wealth. In fact, because these oral histories speak with a voice that is only partially self-reflective, they may offer an even more fertile opportunity for discerning the under-girding cultural logic or "class traits" that shape the wealthy as a group and that the wealthy as individuals tailor into a personalized doctrine of riches.

In this chapter, I examine two aspects of the moral biographies of modern millionaires and explore what these aspects reveal about the cultural scripture of wealth. The first facet of lived morality is the dialectic of fortune and virtue that turns dealings with money into financial asceticism. The wealthy tell of how they apply themselves to make more of their lives and of their circumstances by improving on what was given them by fate. The second component of the moral biography of money is the way the wealthy fashion their stories into morality plays, equating stages of economic progress with stages of personal development. Money looms so large in their development (although not necessarily by choice) that they define their episodes of adversity and their archetypal experiences of initiation, learning, forgiveness, and healing as economic dramas. Their personal troubles and triumphs coincide narratively with economic ones. In the final section I tie together the findings and sketch out the contours of the cultural scripture of wealth that are revealed by the biographical analysis.

Issues of Interpretation

Before taking up the analysis, I want to discusses three issues of inter-pretation that are important in clarifying my argument. I want first to say a bit more about the distinction between the ethical and sociological use of the word "moral." To consider the narratives of the wealthy as moral biographies does not mean that the wealthy demonstrate what philoso-phers or social activists would consider "correct living." The highly charged cultural atmosphere surrounding wealth often results in the ten-dency for commentators to either criticize or defend the ethical status of the wealthy. Whether these commentators take a position for or against the wealthy depends largely upon their understanding of how wealth affects poverty. Those who believe that the creation of wealth entails the impov-erishment of others tend to take a critical stance toward the wealthy. In their view, the wealthy are, at worst, self-serving, exploitative, and greedy; at best, they are well-meaning folk who remain unwilling to abandon their privilege in order to improve the lot of others. In contrast, those who believe that wealth is the remedy of poverty tend to defend the wealthy and justify the concentration of wealth in private hands. This perspective considers the wealthy as agents of economic growth promoting, rather than imped-ing, the economic improvement of the masses.[7]

Rather than pursuing such evaluative conceptions, I employ "moral" in the specifically "sociological" sense of "normatively oriented thinking."[8] I seek not to improve upon existing formulations of financial ethics or, for that matter, upon the lives of the wealthy. Instead, I work inductively, looking at how the wealthy construct themselves as moral agents in their day-to-day dealings with money. The biographies are moral because the wealthy formulate self-justifications and self-criticisms within a framework of culturally determined normative sentiments of what is right to do and what ought to be done. The wealthy make a case for themselves, but not just in the sense of trying to deceive or foist on others a self-serving interpretation of their lives (although this sometimes happens). The case they make for themselves is generally the same one they have come to make to themselves. What they talk about publicly reflects the fact that they have learned to experience money in terms of dedication, obligation, responsibility, and merit. Their biographies are moral not because we hear what is to us an acceptable ethical content. They are moral because the wealthy experience and express their lives, and especially their dealings with wealth, as meeting normative commands rather than meeting personal desires. For this reason, their accounts contain expressions of duty and social concern as well as being replete with legitimations and self-justifications. Like the rest of us, they create a story with themselves in the center, a story that instructs themselves and others about how things are and how they ought to be. Despite temptations to the contrary, then, a crucial first methodological principle is that the wealthy should neither be adulated nor attacked, but studied for the way they make myth out of their lives.

A second issue of interpretation concerns the problem of truth in self-reported life histories. It is not just that "people are always telling stories about themselves," says Anne Beattie in an interview; but that what they tell are "stories that put them in a good light." Some people, she explains, "truly believe those stories. Others tell stories without meaning to be truthful."[9] It might seem, then, that it is crucial to figure out when people are telling the truth and when they are being deceptive. Fortunately, to understand what is going on in the biographies of the wealthy does not require that we discern authorial intentions or distinguish whether words are objectively true or false. I agree with James Olney: "When it comes to autobiography, the truth of falsehood is a deeper and truer concern than the falsification of truth."[10] It is as Picasso said, "Art is a lie that tells the truth." For my purposes, the task is to locate the structure or grammar of morality that resides equally in both the truth and falsehood of what the wealthy say. Certain attitudes and activities are rewarded, others sanctioned; some produce a happy marriage of riches and life, others do not. As Erving Goffman says, "Whether an honest performer wishes to convey the truth or whether a dishonest performer wishes to convey a falsehood, both must take care to enliven their performances with appropriate expressions, exclude from their performances expressions that might discredit the impression being fostered, and take care lest the audience impute unintended meanings."[11] Similarly, what interests me is not the veracity of what the wealthy say but how, in making a case for what it means to be rich and good in America, they calibrate their consciousness to a moral code.

A third and related issue concerns the representativeness of whom we interviewed and of what they said. The sample was obtained through a branching procedure whereby members of the study's advisory board as well those we interviewed recommended family members, friends, and associates for subsequent interviews. In addition to the general tendency for people to tell stories that "put them in a good light," our procedures have probably resulted in an oversampling of those who have something "good" to report. However, this turns out to be rather easily resolved, and less important than a second issue of sampling I will address momentarily. The fact is, at the structural level at which I am working, those who have something good to say do not tell it in a way significantly different from those who have something "bad" to say. We did interview a limited number of respondents who value-oriented critics might classify as materialistic or exploitative. However, it is not possible to identity a distinctive moral code that distinguishes so-called jet-setters and robber barons from "ordinary" millionaires. Despite our prodding, these "less moral" individuals persist-ed in framing their stories within the same moral categories as those who espoused conventionally recognized philanthropic or humanitarian im-pulses. Thus the lack of representativeness of the sample, in this regard, turns out to be less significant than it first appears to be.

A more telling problem surrounds a second form of sampling bias: the fact that each respondent engages in a form of self-sampling in choosing what to say. Here I do find differences in the content of normative orienta-tions which I have distinguished elsewhere under the rather nondescript rubric of first and second level psychological empowerment.[12] But these differences tend to occur within as well as between biographies. The first level is generally characterized by a normative orientation aimed at pursu-ing one's interests, while the second level is characterized by a normative discourse of concern about the quality of those interests. It turns out that this is one important way financial security transforms the consciousness of the wealthy. Once again I find that at both these levels of psychological empowerment the wealthy continue to adhere to a common underlying moral discourse in the sociological sense I am using the term here. Even respondents who readily admit they have taken advantage of others or lived decadently during certain periods of their lives describe these periods with the same normative logic that they use to portray the less "reprehen-sible" phases of their lives. They construct their moral biographies out of the "shadow side" of their lives as much as they do out of episodes of unerring moral rectitude. Those who tell of their failings do so as part and parcel of formulating the subtext that living with wealth always involves living with norms. The point is that the wealthy—no matter how we, or they, might characterize their "objective" moral statute—tell a moral tale in the sense of living under the influence of a normative consciousness. We arrive, finally, at a more fundamental definition of the problem of sampling bias: it is not so much a question of which respondents we have chosen to interview as what these respondents have chosen to say.[13] We arrive as well at the central purpose of the study: to uncover the underlying structure of moral consciousness by examining what the wealthy have chosen to say and how they have chosen to say it. "Novelists spin stories aimed at the penetration (by writer and reader alike) of the many layers of truth," claims Robert Coles, "whereas liars spin stories meant to deceive, mislead, trouble, harm."[14] Ultimately, in telling their stories, the rich are more novelists than liars. More often than not they spin a lofty tale about who they are, but do so in an effort to make meaning rather than to mislead. What, then, are their narrative strategies?

TURNING DAILY EVENTS INTO FINANCIAL ASCETICISM: THE DIALECTIC OF FORTUNE AND VIRTUE

One way the wealthy turn the daily events of their lives into financial asceticism is by telling about the interaction of fortune and virtue. A temporal sequence of events becomes a moral tale in which virtue takes on both the blessings and curses of wealthy. Our respondents invariably portray their lives as a recurring moral exercise of virtue in which they enhance or counter what was dealt them by fate. They recite a litany of their costs of discipleship and express gratitude when fortune bequeaths an inheritance or bestows breaks. But through it all, what most makes their dealings with wealth a salutary accomplishment is disciplined self-sacrifice and a general strength of character.

Disposed over by Fortune

The personalized story of entering into a life of money begins for most of our respondents with vignettes detailing their encounters with fortune. Some mainly talk about overcoming misfortune while others express gratitude for good fortune. But most have a mixed story of fate as sometimes a curse and sometimes a blessing. As it turns out, the underlying theme is that the wealthy are willing and able to handle whatever comes their way. They face the challenges of life with the resoluteness of Thomas Bastard's medieval epigram: "I pray thee fortune, (fortune, if thou be)/Come heere aside, for I must braule with thee."[15]

The starting point of morality is virtue; but the starting point of virtue is fortune. What is fortune and why does it have such moral consequence? Fortune is that with which we "braule" to make more of life. For Durkheim, it is the ensemble of collective representations we face as facticity.[16] For Giddens, it is social structure, defined as the limitations and opportunities we address as agents.[17] For our respondents, it is also a moral test, a visiting angel, the Goddess Fortuna.

The Goddess Fortuna, says Howard Patch, was the only pagan deity to survive the advent of Christianity.[18] Made less sovereign than in her Greek and Roman days, she endures in Boetheus, Dante, and Machiavelli as the relatively autonomous servant of Providence. She imposes fate as starting point and opportunity rather than inexorable destiny. Instead of eliminating the possibility of morality, Fortuna becomes its midwife. For instance, says Patch, both St. Augustine and St. Thomas Aquinas adopt the Aristotelian argument "that chance is necessary in order to make room for free-will."[19] The imagery of Fortuna in medieval literature also indicates the moral challenge offered equally by fortune and misfortune. Fortuna has two faces to symbolize her changing moods: one beautiful or smiling, the other ugly or frowning. Fortuna is blind or blindfolded "to show that she has no regard for merit [or station]." Her two hands represent good and evil fortune. She is "light-fingered in her ability to take back again;" "she has wings because she is fleeting;" and she stands on a ball or a wheel to symbolize her "unsteadiness."[20]

Virtue and *Virtu*: The Practice of Will to Remedy Fortune

Despite the prominence of fortune in setting the terms of life, it still "make[s] room for free will." The practice of will to remedy and amend fortune, says Patch, surfaces whenever people reject the idea that "the most you can do is to take what comes your way." For the Romans, efforts to limit the powers of Fortuna took many forms: "One way to be successful in this was to show courage. Another was to oppose reason to her unreason, to live a life of wisdom; and another, less widely used, perhaps, was to devote one's self to those concerns in which Fortuna had no part—the activities of virtue."[21] For the children of the Enlightenment, however, the practice of virtue has become the life of wisdom and reason as Benjamin Franklin exemplifies in the ascetic regime he devised for self-improvement.

Virtue is the capacity to combat or exploit the vagaries of fortune. Parents, mentors, and life itself teach the efficacious practice of virtue, what Thomas Aquinas defines as the habit of doing good and what one respondent, Dale Jayson, defines negatively as "the habit of doing the things that nonsuccessful people aren't doing." (Dale Jayson is not his real name. Throughout the chapter, I have used pseudonyms to identify all the respondents and similarly have changed all references by respondents to names, places, and activities to insure anonymity.) Whether fortune offers rags or riches, obstacles or opportunities, the wealthy invariably frame their lives in terms of what they contributed to make more of life than what was given.

As in the emergence of what the historian Gordon Rattray Taylor calls the "Puritan personality,"[22] the key is not just the accumulation of specific traits but of character in general. For Machiavelli, fortune is given vitality so that the strong may wrest their triumph. Fortune is like a raging river that "shows her power where there is no force to hold her in check; and her impetus is felt where she knows there are no embankments and dykes built to restrain her."[23] "Fortune yields, not to goodness, nor yet to wisdom, but to power" or *virtu*.[24] *Virtu* is not just one more specific virtue and certainly not to be equated with physical power. It is a special strength of character, an embodied moral power armed with which one sets out to master fortune. It is the capacity of a disciplined self to exercise agency in shaping the world. To build a business becomes not just a way to earn a living or become financially secure but a daily moral test. To receive an inheritance becomes not just a way to recapitulate the involvements of parents or live emotionally secure but a burning challenge to demonstrate independent abilities.

The Exercise of Virtue and the Morality of Money: "There Is a Lot of Work"

The wealthy in our study invariably highlight their struggles to overcome poverty or their achievements to improve their inheritance. To legitimate their acquisition of wealth and to justify emotionally being comfortable with their current status, they tell how they did not like or want every hand that was dealt by life. Making their way through the obstacles of life is the cause of a satisfactory life of wealth. They make themselves moral by the way they obtain and handle their money. "It seems like there's no work at all involved," explains heir Malcolm Hirsch. "In fact there is a lot of work of different sorts to be able to deal with [money]."

Entrepreneurs: The Exercise of Virtue to Make Fortune a Friend

It is the frowning face of fortune that dominates the early years of both the earned and inherited. We learn that fortune eventually comes to smile upon them in the form of breaks and assistance; but their stories begin with accounts of adversity and how they worked to transform the countenance of fortune.

"I crawled here." Entrepreneurs and professionals recount their first encounter with fortune as modest beginnings that often slip into family hardship. Chicago contractor Raymond Wendt experienced the precarious nature of fate as a child growing up in Cleveland. Just as his immigrant father was becoming "fairly successful," first as a bricklayer and later as a self-employed construction contractor, "the Depression hit and he lost everything." The effect on his father was dramatic: "That sort of kicked the legs from under him, and down he went. I don't think he ever really recovered and I think . . . [this] eventually caused his death."

The effect on the ten-year old Wendt was also dramatic and typical. "It caused some fear in me that I didn't have a father and I didn't know what was going to happen to me. I saw my mother go to work and we struggled." Wendt remembers times when his mother had only five dollars for the entire week. "At a young age that makes a very deep impression on you," he explains. Life is changed, lessons learned, and virtue set in motion: "I always told myself that wasn't going to happen to me. I was going to make sure that I would be successful in some way. . . . It made me strive to get ahead, overcome things that maybe some people don't have in their lives, or don't have as a goal to accomplish. But it was exciting."

Looking back on his life as a successful athlete and builder, Wendt is proud that people will never say, "He's a broken-down athlete." He encapsulates the meaning of *virtu* as strength of character: "I crawled here; and I got here just to prove the point that I could do it, and I did it." Wendt is wealthy not because he is selfish but because he wants to prove himself and shield his family from the ravishes of poverty.

"Sleep was something other people did." Many others lose parents— either to death, emotional depression, or alcohol—and experience hard times growing up. The shadow side of fortune also continues throughout later life as marriages fail, children disappoint, and business ventures go sour. St. Louis magazine publisher Allison Arbour wakes up one day to discover that one of her two partners has been pocketing money rather than paying the bills. When confronted, the partner agrees to quit the firm, leaving behind a million dollars worth of bills. "I mean how about that for brilliance," quips Arbour, now realizing that all this did was let their wayward partner off the hook. But soon she learns that her second partner is secretly squirreling away kickbacks from a supplier. She confronts him, and once again ends up responsible for outstanding debts that she faithfully works to repay. Still her misfortune continues. Just as the debt is nearly erased, an impatient creditor forces her into the bankruptcy she had so far assiduously avoided.

What Arbour says next exemplifies an important aspect of how a series of events becomes a moral biography. She treats this bankruptcy as a positive opportunity rather than as an adversity she must overcome with virtue. Up to this point, she has viewed Fortuna as an adversary; now, even in the guise of calamity, she recognizes Fortuna as a benefactor. In her new way of thinking, good fortune is bred from bad fortune. This was "probably the best thing that ever happened to me," says Arbour. "I kept growing, I kept growing and finally got out of it as much as I could," she remarks, leaving it appropriately ambiguous as to whether she is referring to her business or herself. As the lessons are learned and virtue applied, fortune becomes an ally instead of a foe.

How does she come to this realization? Exemplifying the general characteristic of *virtu*, Arbour has developed the habit of struggling within the
realm of Fortuna rather than avoiding it. First, you have to learn "everything by doing it," she counsels, reflecting what many entrepreneurs say
about "the school of life" being more important than formal education. "I
had to get my hands dirty. I didn't have enough educational background
to comprehend things . . . [so] everything I learned, I learned by doing."
Next, you have to have the gumption to "hustle big": "When I think back,
I think 'My Lord, did I have courage.' I was never afraid of my working
ability. I knew that I could work hard. I knew I could make money. There
were times when I had maybe three jobs. I just was never afraid to work. I
was a hard worker." Eventually, Arbour becomes so accustomed to working
hard that it becomes downright invigorating—"a thrill." Heeding Dale
Jayson's injunction to do what the "nonsuccessful people aren't doing,"
Arbour reports that "sleep was something other people did. I never slept,
never slept. I didn't need to. I was never tired." In the moral biography of
wealth, virtue first counters fortune and then makes it a friend.

Looking back on forty years in the business, Arbour suggests one more
confirmation of the fact that dedication to virtue makes life moral. In
addition to countering and taming fortune, virtue makes life successful. As
it tames fortune, virtue makes life successful as well. Arbour discovers that
the goddess also smiles, bestowing not just luck and opportunity but
beneficial outcomes as well: "It's been a wonderful life," she concludes. In
a secularized version of the Calvinist logic of salvation, financial success
and happiness serve as "proof" of a moral life. This does not make Arbour
proud, however. The wealthy seldom express that stereotypical cockiness
we have been taught to expect from those who become masters of destiny.
Doing so would betray the moral character of their story. Instead, we
discover that the more they have struggled to make their way, the more
they honor the blessings of fortune.

I've really been through a wonderful era. I'm very lucky, I think. Someone said,
'How do you think you got those opportunities?' I really think it was sort of after
World War II that everything [fell into place]. They needed help and all the boys
weren't back yet. And if they weren't short-handed I don't think they would have
given me, a young kid, especially a female, an opportunity. Of course I was a worker.
I think I worked like ten men, frankly. I'm not saying some guys didn't do the same
thing, but I know I worked very hard for everything I got. But the opportunity was
to take the job that was there. There weren't that many people back then who could
fill [the jobs]. So I think, in that sense I was lucky. I was there at the right time and
you know, there's a great deal to that.

Inherited Wealthy: Virtue and the Hidden Injuries of Wealth

The inheritors too tell about their "braules" with fortune. They always
acknowledge their advantaged financial circumstances, but they always

deny being particularly privileged or spoiled in their youth. They recall scenes of childhood embarrassment, the pain of stigma, and the imposition of expectations. Some are alienated—lamenting the over-imposition of the rules and responsibilities of money. Others are anomic—regretting their isolation from the norms of wealth and how this prolonged their economic adolescence.

"We really do pay." Especially among men, the inheritance of money coincides with the inheritance of the duty to recapitulate family expectations, financial responsibilities, professional directions, and business obligations. These duties are translated into stark psychological burdens that weigh heavily on their minds. Their privilege induces feelings of guilt, the need to prove that they can be successful in their own right, and a yearning for relationships cleansed of the complications of wealth. In a word, wealth like poverty is something to "deal with." This is true in all kinds of ways says Malcolm Hirsch, thirty-nine, whose experience captures the onus of second- and third-generation wealth. He explains, "It's been hard," not because wealth is itself a problem, but because of what comes with it:

There are things about my life that have been harder due to the fact that I grew up the way that I did, not so much having money but all the accoutrements. There are all the sort of, there are more social expectations. There is a lot of frivolous stuff that comes with having money, a lot of garbage, a lot of confusion. But you know, that was just what I got dealt, that's the hand I got dealt. The hand I got dealt had pluses and minuses. Money is something I count up as being both. It's not one or the other.

One thing for sure, explains Hirsch, is that fortune exacts a price before bestowing the blessings. "My own experience and my experience with other people who inherited money is that they really do pay—we really do pay." They pay in many ways, first as children and then as adults, but almost always in reference to the underlying ambiguity about wealth in an achievement-oriented society. The cultural scripture of wealth imputes not just a consciousness but an array of sentiments that are stored or "hidden away" in memory. Among the feelings hidden away are the various costs of wealth that are exacted by fortune in what Hirsch refers to as "currencies." One is the currency of "shame" resulting from "isolation in the culture." In an ironic reversal of the adage, the cultural scripture mandates a form of loving the sin and hating the sinner:

This culture again has really ambivalent feelings about money. Obviously, in many ways it worships money but it doesn't like people [who are wealthy]. The Puritan ethic also worships work. So it has very ambivalent feelings—on the one hand respecting the money that people have when they inherit it, but on the other hand resenting the fact that they didn't work for it. So there is a certain amount of shame and I think you start to pick these things up from the time you are quite young. I have stories that I have heard again repeated by many friends of mine, for example, wanting to be driven to school in a Cadillac and wanting to be dropped off a block from school. So you don't pull up in this fancy machine and just, again, feel separated from all your friends. I can remember feeling things like that, really from the time I was probably ten, and that's just my first memories. There are probably traces of it hidden away.

A second cost is exacted in the currency of guilt, says Hirsch, expanding on the most commonly voiced burden imposed by fortune. "Guilt is just something that I think that anyone who has money with any conscience at all has to really deal with. It was certainly some piece of the motivation for my . . . feeling like I wasn't an okay person." For many, this guilt comes from having inherited "dirty money." But this was not Hirsch's problem because he "didn't have any particularly dirty investments to begin with." While the paper company his father owned "wasn't a particularly clean investment in terms of pollution and stuff, it wasn't a particularly awful one either." Instead, his guilt comes from the "extraordinary extremes of wealth and poverty" that he saw all around him as he grew up in New York. He remembers visiting his family's black maid at her apartment and thinking, "Boy, she sure does live differently from me." As the inherited repeatedly tell us, such experiences lead not to arrogance but to humility. Again, virtue shifts the countenance of fortune. Hirsch, for instance, realizes that "I wasn't a better person than she was" and carries this lesson with him as he invests his wealth in philanthropic ventures until, as he puts it, "I put myself down to little enough money."

"Another currency that you pay for [wealth] is in friendships," continues Hirsch. "You're never sure to what extent your friendships are based on people's wanting something from you." Worse, however, is the currency of deteriorated family relationships. When large amounts of money—and family heritage—are at stake, parents become ready agents of fortune. Money is just "another lever that parents have that makes the relationship not clean":

My mother, for example, at various times when she was having trouble with me when I was a rebellious teenager, said "Well, if you don't do so and so, or if you do do so and so, I am going to disinherit you." Which was heavy; it was stupid of her too. But first of all it wasn't true; she wouldn't have done it really, but I didn't know that. Second of all, I mean, it was super-manipulative and it was just a power play. So, what it doesn't take a genius to figure out is what that would do to my relationship with her. In fact it was very bad for quite a while.

Finally, fortune imposes upon the inherited the cost of calculating just how much to give away and how much to keep for themselves. The inherited are taught to be givers by their parents; but until they succeed on their own in business or investment they remain unsure of how boldly they should pursue philanthropy. For instance, Hirsch's first attempts to be generous turned out to be "very haphazard" and "really quite random." Setting out at first to be generous, Hirsch discovers quickly enough the relentless limits of fortune contained in the simple words "I couldn't": "I was giving away a lot and I sort of thought I was going to have more to give away and said, 'Oops I'm sort of running out of money here, you know, I can't give away as much as I thought I was going to be able to give away. What a shame.' But I couldn't." Coming full circle, even those who inherit must figure out how to manage their money. As Malcolm Hirsch honestly admits, the ultimate constraint is "not ending up broke myself."

So virtue and *virtu* come into play as the rich faithfully count and pay the costs of wealth. Like the alignment of vices and virtues across from each other on the wheel of fortune, each of the numerous and often contradictory facets of wealth calls for an equally diverse array of virtues summarized by Hirsch's phrase "paying the cost." What makes Hirsch and his peers self-consciously moral is their willingness to do "a lot of work of different sorts"—what others who are equally wealthy feel they don't have to do because they were born under different stars. According to Hirsch, wealthy Buddhists and Hindus are exempt from his dilemmas because they have already paid for their privileged status in a previous life. Also exempt are his doctor friends who "have a throw of the dice that at least in some sense was very favorable to them." Most are "way more" wealthy than he, but they do not have to face the "particular guilt" that he confronts since they can claim to have earned their money. This bothers Hirsch because they really benefit from inheritance as much as he; after all, they "have the gift of being able to be born in the United States or go to medical school. Inheriting money is just a more sort of obvious kind of inheritance," he complains. In a society where the cultural scripture values those riches that come at a price, the inheritors learn to cite their costs. Because "it's a burden that most people don't have," heirs must "start figuring these things out from the time [they are] really young." As they figure them out, they make them the centerpiece of their personalized gospel of wealth.

"To justify our very existence." In contrast to Hirsch, who feels the burdens of fortune having to do with the productive duties and responsibilities of money, are other inherited who suffer, ironically enough, from the under-imposition of other aspects of the laws and duties of money. Especially (but not exclusively) among inheritresses who grew up before the 1960s, there is a tendency to complain about being quite underprepared to enter the productive world of money, despite a rigorous and even stringent personal incorporation into the familial duties and social responsibilities of wealth. If inheritor men lament being thrust into adulthood at too young an age and with too little room for personal life, inheritresses lament being imprisoned too long in an adolescence with too little knowledge and skill about how to deal with money in a financially productive and personally efficacious manner.

Janet Arnold experienced all the guilt and self-doubt imposed by the inheritance of wealth. Fortune weighed especially heavy upon her because she came from one of the most celebrated wealthy families on the West Coast. At fifty-three, Arnold can now speak of her difficult journey from debutante to professional woman with more dispassion than she first experienced. Two aspects of fate impelled Arnold upon the path of virtue. The first was the highly visible public profile of her family and its wealth. The embarrassment of having to "lie down in the bottom of the car when we were driven to school by the chauffeur" as well as the "anger," "envy," and "curiosity" expressed by others were intensified by the controversial status of her family. As she says, "There were people who were angry because of the robber baron image and there were people who were angry because they weren't [members of our family] and didn't have this imagined social status."

Clearly, Arnold felt imprisoned by the cultural scripture of wealth. "Even as a child I felt awkward and odd," she reports. "I didn't like having that kind of specialness." It proved more an "obstacle" than an advantage especially in the areas of "self-expression and for being able to operate freely." The existential guilt of inheriting money is exacerbated by her coming of age in the 1960s—"a time of great social upheaval" when the prerogatives of power were being vigorously challenged. The result, says Arnold, is that she and her generation "had to justify our inheritance and our very existence in light of that social change." Inheritance is such a burden that marrying into wealth captures her imagination as the alternative that would have spared her pain. At least "if you acquire it by marriage," she suggests, "then you are not embarrassed, you could hardly wait to use it or be seen as having it."

There are two paths by which Arnold overcomes the obstacles of "being underprivileged by privilege." The first, the rehabilitation of her family history, provides insight into how unearthing hidden virtues from the past helps in the construction of a moral biography. She works to counteract the "imaginary" status of her family legacy as robber barons and exploitative leaders of the power elite. She talks about her intensive exploration of the family record and her confrontation with the less than favorable images of her family when she was in high school. The mythology of the robber baron in her mind becomes replaced by her memory of her father as a "lovely" man and an "extraordinary" philanthropist who was dedicated to help what she calls the "little people." She also cites both his virtue in business ("he made his profession") and the belief that her father did just what others on the ladder of success were doing: "The more I read the more I saw that he wasn't any different than dozens of other men, some of whom made it and some of whom didn't." Finally, Arnold counters the assumption that the successful must necessarily lack virtue and that only the unsuccessful can be virtuous. The fact is, she says, that those who "didn't make it weren't . . . any better or virtuous—they just didn't make it."

The second path of virtue by which Arnold deals with the shadow side of inheritance is through striking out on her own in family and career. It is easier for entrepreneurs to describe their lives as careers with their risks and choices building into an ordered sequence of steps on the road to success. But the inherited, too, understand their lives as an orderly and progressive unfolding of virtuous acts of agency. "My career began in prep school" and continued in the navy, says Thomas Cooke, fifth-generation heir of a prominent Boston family. Janet Arnold's career involves sharing in the welfare commitments of her husband. Against the wishes of her family, she married a social worker and lives among the poor on the east side of Detroit. Like Hirsch, she is willing to pay the costs of being wealthy. This period of Arnold's life, approximately ten years in duration, is by her own definition the most intense period of "struggle" with her wealth.

Although her inheritance "was pouring in," she disguises her wealth, declining to spend it on herself and refraining from conventional philanthropic involvements. She dissolves her public identity, immersing herself in the inner space of the domestic family, raising her children, and communing with other women in the "urban slum" community. "I lived very, very simply for years," she says, pointing to one of the most commonly reported tests of virtue among the inherited. Her parents taught her "by word and deed . . . that you were stewards of the money," that she is to be productive and avoid indulgence.[25]

In her new life as a secret heiress, Janet Arnold becomes productive— even entrepreneurial. The growth of her wealth creates new responsibilities rather than increased leisure. The activist ethic of stewardship requires that money be used productively in philanthropy as well as in business. "I didn't know what to do with it so I gave it away," Arnold recounts. But being willing to give money is only the first condition for demonstrating character. The second is that the money be put to a socially redeeming use. Thus Arnold lends moral stature to her life by telling how she targets her gifts for particularly important causes:

I gave in civil rights and I gave in the arts. And roughly my arts [giving] was connected to civil rights and human rights somehow or other. In other words I didn't give to the symphony orchestra. I gave to struggling young artists or I gave to black artists or I gave to the Dance Theater of Harlem, you know all those kinds of things. . . . I gave to things that were around civil rights and I gave to black schools that were springing up.

The experience of traversing the worlds of the rich and poor was central to the transformation of Arnold's conception of self. Entrance into the world of the poor "confirmed something that I had secretly thought for years but had no way of confirming." The "potential" of human beings to be creative, virtuous, and moral has nothing to do with their class position or wealth. The most valuable possession is a strong set of ethical values and morals which emphasize the dignity of human beings and their intrinsic worth: "Beyond survival, money has very little to do with satisfaction or happiness or sense of purpose or direction or anything." Even though we have already seen that, by her own account, money really does have a lot to do with her "sense of purpose" and "direction," her point is to stress the continuity between her own account, money really does have a lot to do with her "sense of purpose" and "direction," her point is to stress the continuity between her own inner life and that of the poor. Ironically, she bolsters the moral stature of being wealthy by highlighting what she shares in common with the poor.

Making a Narrative Space

A common thread woven through each narrative is a retrospective account of the construction of a moral personality—a self responsibly shaping the world rather than simply being shaped by it. This is the dialectic of fortune and virtue: the recurring interplay between what is given and what we make of it. The starting points of life—both good and bad—are transformed by industry and fortitude into something better.

It requires a quite definite kind of character, confidence, and moral rectitude to hold oneself, and not fortune, accountable for one's place in the world. Even the wealthy who start out blaming their stars invariably come to chorus Cassius' dutiful assertion that any fault for remaining an underling "lies not in our stars but in our selves." In the process of becoming, staying, and living as a wealthy person, our respondents become immersed and often baptized in the waters of self-sufficiency, empowerment, righteousness, and control over their own fate and the fate of others.

By devoting narrative space to recounting the challenges and hardships—as well as the blessings—of fortune under which they labored, the wealthy open a moral space for constructing their biographies. To acknowledge the Goddess Fortuna is to set an agenda for virtue: to confront resolutely the obstacles of bad fortune, to recognize gratefully the blessings of good fortune, to avoid squandering opportunities, to advance the productive use of money as a social investment, and to resist the dual temptations of materialism and self-aggrandizement. This makes life moral. What also makes it moral is that the wealthy employ archetypal motifs to frame the progression of their lives. They locate the dialectic of fortune and virtue within a broader symbolic context in which biographies become morality plays. Suffering under fate is death; overcoming obstacles is rebirth. Structurally, personal accounts of wealth become dramatic texts. Thematically, the unfolding of personal development coincides with the unfolding of economic life.

BIOGRAPHY AS DRAMA OF TRANSFORMATION; MAKING MYTH OUT OF THEIR LIVES

A second way the wealthy make myth out of their lives is by telling their stories as a series of personal transformations within a framework of moral symbols. They flag the turning points or benchmarks that separate one stage of their lives from the next, and then link the events into a thematically coherent narrative in which sufferings and obstacles eventuate in learning and progress. Each biography becomes a morality play or dramatic text in the literary sense of an integrated narrative that unfolds in a series of acts or chapters and that describes periods of transformation within the imagery of initiation, learning, forgiveness, and healing.

The Dramatic Structure of Biography: *Nomos* and Liminality

I refer to each of these unfolding biographies as a *nomos* and to the periods of self-transformation that take place within each nomos as *liminality*. The term *nomos*, taken from the Greek meaning "law" or "ordering principle," denotes a dramatic progression through identifiable phases of self-development. There are a number of possible etymologies for the word but a likely one is the verb *nemein*, meaning "to distribute." *Nomos* is the "pasture" or "that which is in habitual practice, use, or possession," and hence "usage," "custom," and "habit." Consequently, *nomos* is everything that derives from traditional usage and habit and becomes established as custom, law, and institution. As a *nomos*, each biography is described by a coherent language, tone, and imagery and ordered into a law of progression in which events become organized into a meaningful sequence. Each life is in fact a "pasture" to be reaped, a terrain that is harvested and shaped by discourse into a thematically unified account.[26]

There are numerous such *nomoetic*, or dramatic, patterns, but each reflects a basic tripartite movement from an initial condition through a phase of transformation, or *liminality* (discussed in the next section), to a new plateau of identity that constitutes the starting point of a subsequent phase of self-development. At that point the dialectic of fortune and virtue becomes worked out anew. According to Porter, the most encompassing formulation of the tripartite movement is at the archetypal level. Some biographies, like some rituals and literary texts, can be adequately described in these fundamental terms. However, most stories contain enough particular details to make it fruitful to specify what Porter calls the "cultural" and "mythic" levels of the *nomos*, with the latter representing specific variations of the former.[27]

As the wealthy move through *nomoetic* progressions, they arrive at various points of transition. Drawing again on insights from anthropology and literary criticism,[28] I refer to such phases of transition as periods of *liminality*. This term is derived from the Latin *limens* meaning "threshold," and denotes the boundaries between and passage through different stages of life, as in purgation and initiation rites. In such liminal periods the exercise of virtue becomes especially crucial for the wealthy, for it is here that they confront and transform those aspects of fortune that impose conditions of life and aspects of identity that have ceased to be acceptable. By focusing on these periods of liminality, we can discern the intricate process of change by which the wealthy undergo self-transformation at the same time as they move to a new stage in their relation to money. For instance, many prospective entrepreneurs undergo an intense period of liminality as they leave the shelter of a secure job to strike out on their own. In a similar way, many inheritors undergo liminality as they separate themselves from the expectations of wealth imposed by their families and search out more personally enriching uses for their money. Sometimes these are rather brief periods of learning. At other times there are extended and intense periods of tension, uncertainty, and self-testing marking major transitions from one phase of life to another. In either case, the wealthy recount numerous such experiences, integrating them into their narratives by describing them with the same *nomoetic* imagery with which they describe other aspects of their lives. At the archetypal level, liminality is expressed in terms of death; at the cultural level, in terms of separation, purgation, questioning, and illness. Although this symbolic interpretation goes well beyond how our respondents would spontaneously characterize themselves, it nevertheless remains congruent with the rich imagery and meanings the wealthy attribute to their lives.

Table 1 outlines my working model of the tripartite *nomos* patterns at the archetypal and cultural levels and, in selected ways, at the mythic level. The archetypal pattern follows the calendrical and cosmogonic sequence of life-death-rebirth that occurs in the seasonal and biological regeneration of life. Applying this to biographies of the wealthy, I find that each account begins with a description of the circumstances of fortune initially faced by the narrator; reports a liminal phase of death in which the narrator undergoes a personal transformation; and concludes by setting forth the conditions of rebirth that endow the narrator with new conditions of life and a new identity. This denouement constitutes both a positive resolution of struggle and the initiation of a renewed phase of life-death-rebirth. In analyzing the interviews I found four cultural patterns of *nomos* and liminality that bridge the archetypal and mythic levels: *gnosis* (coming to insight), *purgation* (obtaining reconciliation), *healing* (restoring health), and *initiation* (becoming incorporated). At the next most specific level, the biographies contain mythic patterns evincing themes of harvest, odyssey, journey, war, sport, construction, vocation, awakening, courtship, hunt, race, game, and so forth. There is no hard-and-fast correspondence between specific cultural and mythic patterns, but there is a tendency for certain

Table 1
Archetypal, Cultural, and Mythic Patterns of Dramatic Progression

Level of Analysis	Pattern	Structure		
		initial condition	*liminality*	*denouement*
Archetypal	*Calendrical-Cosmogonic*	life	death	rebirth
Cultural	*Initiation*	union	separation	reunion
	Purgation	sin	purgation	reconciliation
	Gnosis	experience	questioning	insight
	Healing	health	illness	restoration
Mythic (examples)	*Courtship*	attraction	tribulation	marriage
	Vocation	being lost	call / transformation	mission
	Horatio Alger	arrival	trial	success
	Journey / Odyssey	home	adventure / test	establishment of new home
	Agricultural	planting	growth	harvest
	Sport / War	engagement	combat	victory
	Business	investment	risk / failure	profit
	Awakening	confusion	self-scrutiny	revelation

mythic themes to occur in association with particular cultural patterns. For instance, mythic patterns of awakening and odyssey tend to occur in conjunction with the gnosis pattern, just as mythic themes of journey and courtship tend to occur in conjunction with the initiation pattern. One caution is that neither the cultural nor mythic patterns I have identified comprise an exhaustive list. It is possible to add other patterns to both lists as well as to make a case for moving one or more of the mythic patterns "up" to the cultural level. One such candidate, for instance, would be the journey motif (life at home, travel to new situations of testing, and establishment of a new home).

How do the notions of *nomos* and liminality contribute to understanding the narratives of the wealthy as moral biographies? First, the themes of initiation, purgation, healing, and learning are inherently moral in content and structure. By framing events as the movement from separation to union, sin to forgiveness, illness to health, and ignorance to knowledge, the wealthy pronounce a positive verdict about the direction their lives have taken and, more importantly, attest to the efficaciousness of the steps they have taken to get there. They have become personally fulfilled and financially successful; and they have reached these milestones by practicing virtue. Second, the struggles and hard-won transformations depicted in the various passages of liminality also contribute to the portrayal of the wealthy as moral. The mere existence of ordeals demonstrates that the rich do not get everything they want and are "acquainted with grief." But the fact that they use their material resources to face and overcome, rather than simply avert, such trials suggests that the wealthy have moral fiber and not just moral opportunity.

THE MORAL DRAMA OF *NOMOS* AND LIMINALITY

I discuss the role of *nomos* and liminality in the creation of moral biography by focusing on the lives of four respondents, one representing each of the cultural patterns of *nomos*. The analysis will exemplify how the four *nomoetic* patterns are used in the construction of moral biographies. It will also demonstrate what is distinctive about the way the wealthy incorporate these triadic patterns into their accounts. Third, not only do the wealthy turn their biographies into morality plays by incorporating the moral themes of the *nomoetic* patterns, they mold them into specifically *American* morality plays by making successful resolutions of financial aspects of their lives a major component of what they mean by reunion, reconciliation, insight, and healing.

Initiation: "Tom, we're in business . . . and I want you to be my partner"

"I didn't do it for women's liberation or for financial reasons. We were financially fine. I didn't want to show up my husband. I just felt, like the doctor told me, 'You have to do something for June, for Mrs. Radkey. You *have* to, to save your sanity.' " With these words, June Radkey summarizes the impetus of fortune that impels her along the path of personal growth and entrepreneurial success. Radkey is a married woman with three grown children who starts up an exceptionally successful company that makes calzones based on a family recipe. She dramatically transforms her identity from passive homemaker—in which her children were her whole life and she deferred all decisions to her husband—to confident entrepreneur. Her story is mainly one of initiation, but also reflects elements of healing, gnosis, awakening, and odyssey. As she builds her calzone company, Radkey undergoes a radical separation from her customary family relations, takes up a new persona as a vibrant entrepreneur, and reconstitutes her family and her place within it. At the same time she speaks about "saving" her sanity, awakening to unanticipated revelation, gaining self-knowledge, and undertaking an uncharted journey of risk and adventure.

Radkey also frames her liminal crisis in the imagery of family relations. The crisis begins as her children get set to leave home and her relations with her husband of forty years have soured: "I was having some problems in my life," she confides, "as almost every family does. Both of my sons had finished school. And my daughter [Alice], in the meantime, got married to a very nice boy and moved to Philadelphia. . . . And I thought, 'Geez, before you know it, Tommy and Kenny will be out of the house. What's going to happen to me?' " The "worst thing" for Radkey, is that "I just didn't have my husband. That was very hard. He is very sorry that neither of his sons became engineers. And I can understand that feeling. I respect that feeling. But by the same token, I was down here, and I had to lift myself up. I was very insecure." For years she harbored the idea that starting a business might help, but her husband remained intransigent. "Every time I'd bring this idea up, the boys would get excited, but not my husband. He'd say, 'Those kids should go to school and become engineers like me.' "

At the depth of her liminal suffering, Radkey is on the "verge of a nervous breakdown." Then comes "that fateful day" that begins with a visit to her family doctor. After listening to her symptoms of depression he tells her that she must do something for herself. But what? As she drives home with tears blurring her vision, she receives illumination. "Suddenly it came back to me," she says, referring to her long-deferred ambition to start the calzone store. That afternoon she locates a site for her store and initiates the first of many assertive steps she would take that day and over the next three years. "What are you going to put in here?" challenges the property owner to whom she goes to rent space. " 'This place is so small, you can't put hardly anything in here.' And I said, 'For what I'm going to do, this spot is perfect.' 'There are already two food stores in this mall,' he challenges again. I says, 'That doesn't make any difference,' " reports Radkey in her distinctive manner, " 'nobody has ever had what I'm going to introduce to the market.' " She goes to a banker friend, convinces him to grant her a loan on her own and not her husband's signature, and makes him promise not to inform her husband about the loan. As she strives for transformation, she rearranges family relations. She brings her son Tommy into her scheme. She makes him her partner and advises him, to his—and her—surprise, to hide her plan from his father, for whom Tommy now substitutes as help-mate and confidant:

That fateful day, in comes my son. He was working at a Volkswagen dealership. He'd come home greasy and so forth. He walks in, and I said, "Hi, Partner." He looks at me and says, "What do you mean, 'Partner'? What are you talking about?" I says, "I did it, Tom! Tom, we're in business, we're going to open up, and I want you to be my partner." He says, "Ma, you know I haven't got any money." "Hey, Tom," I says, "I don't either." "But, Ma," he says, "we're never going to make it." I says, "Tom, you just have faith in me. I promise, we're not going to fail. We're going to make it."

She rents an oven and refrigerator and sets up an "eleven-by-ten counter with a garbage can on each side of it." Concluding her account of the genesis of her business she says, "And that's the story of the beginning of all this." It is of course also the beginning of Radkey's emotional and familial rehabilitation.

Radkey goes on to detail the rave reviews of her calzones, the adventures of rapid expansion, and the implications of her success for herself and her family. At every turn she works hard, takes risks, and produces a quality product. She caters parties, expands her original store, opens new ones, and, just as importantly, gradually rebuilds the family around her. Through it all, her husband remains distant and disapproving, but her children actively support her. Tommy becomes a partner, and Alice and her husband fly in from Philadelphia to help out with a breakthrough catering opportunity. Eventually Radkey accepts a friendly buy-out offer arranged by a long-term customer. Today she remains personally active in the company and is happy with her limited role "doing the promotion and the PR."

The central *nomoetic* pattern of initiation as well as the complementary patterns of gnosis, awakening, odyssey, and healing all reach positive resolution. Ten years earlier, as she works through liminality, Radkey agonizes over catering a party for three hundred: she worries through more than one "sleepless night," because, as she confides, "I didn't know nothing." Now she is a millionaire with her sanity and family intact. Economic attainment proves salutary for rebuilding Radkey's self-conception and her troubled relationship with her husband. It is not accidental that she undergoes a name change as she moves out of liminality into her new life: "They start calling me 'June.' No more 'Mrs. Radkey.' Everything was June . . . I'd hated my name all my life. But when we needed a name for the company, my attorney said, 'It's a great name,' . . . so we named it *June's* after me":

And this is a shot in the arm every time I go into one of those *June's*. And I don't mean it as being conceited or anything, but it's a wonderful feeling, an absolutely wonderful feeling . . . but it was meant to be. And God was on my side—that's the only thing I can think of. I don't know the words to say it, but I guess in my lifetime this had to be for me. Because I think if it was anybody else, they wouldn't have been as determined as I was, especially when you have your husband against you. And by the way, it's going on forty years that we've been married. And we're still married. It's just that we've had our ups and downs.

It is not all sweetness and light with her husband, but they have worked out a modus vivendi that resolves the initiation motif. Her husband takes credit for being long-suffering, an attitude June publicly tolerates but privately resents.

You know when we're at a function, people come up to him and complement him and say, "Oh, Robert, that's wonderful what your wife has done." And he says, "Yeah, boy, I hung in there. If I wasn't as stubborn as I was and told her she couldn't do it—my telling her that encouraged her to do that." I just listen and I just smile very nicely, and I say, "Only God above knows what I went through. And me."

Radkey also demonstrates a major theme in the moral biographies of the wealthy: the denouement of the *nomoetic* patterns comes about in conjunction with favorable economic developments. In Radkey's initiation story, personal restoration and family reunion coincide with her entrepreneurial achievements. This is not because riches can buy happiness, but because the virtue that makes her wealthy also enlightens her, strengthens her emotional health, and restores her home. Her happiness is the consequence of virtue, her biography a personal triumph, her wealth a badge of courage:

And so now, I'm very happy. The money is good. It could have been better if I stayed in. But I felt, at my age, the fact that I did this, and that I succeeded, was important, with God's help and with their [my children's] help, because I could not have done it myself. I wish that I did some things different. I mean we could have taken pictures of certain things that happened. But I still remember them, so it's the same thing."

Purgation: "To save the world and atone"

For Norman Stryker, the fifty-nine-year-old scion of an industrial fortune, the dominant theme of his narrative is the burden of being born into wealth and fortune, a burden he views quite explicitly as a sin for which he has had to spend his life in atonement through philanthropic and political good works. "I think the worst thing [wealth] has done for me is to make me feel as though I had to atone—for what sin, I don't know—but there needn't be anything much more than having money I didn't earn. And being more fortunate than others for reasons I didn't have the least to do with." Raised in Houston, where his father was a trust officer, Stryker's wealth derives from his maternal grandfather, who was one of the principal founders of Randolf Petroleum. "And so," he continues, wealth "has always made me frantic about making use of every golden moment to save the world and atone."

If Radkey's story is one of initiation revolving around the entrepreneurial assent to wealth, then Norman Stryker's is one of purgation concerned with undoing the psychological burden he inherited along with his wealth. Like Radkey, he recounts a *nomoetic* story of moral progression. But in contrast to Radkey, Stryker's liminal struggle involves working through to a new understanding of money rather than working to obtain it in the first place. For Radkey, entering into the world of wealth is the path to restoration; for Stryker it is a transgression that requires rectification.

Stryker became cognizant of the moral burden, or "sin," of being wealthy at a very early age. His liminality began upon entering elementary school as he reached what traditional Roman Catholic confessional discipline calls "the age of reason"—the point around seven years of age when children are said to become able to distinguish right from wrong:

One only had to look at our house, the gardens, I mean, versus the houses of all the other people in my class. It created huge guilt, you know. I shared the experience of an enormous number of inherited wealth people—I had a chauffeur drive us to school, and I would insist that he drop us several blocks from the school. I like to say that being different in money is no different than having a harelip or clubfoot or green hair, except that wealth makes people envious of you or resent you, instead of sympathetic. And I don't want to overdo the poor-little-rich-boy thing, but a person in my position has to carve out every goddamn day of his life.

Stryker's realization of sin took a high psychological toll, putting him "through much agony" and giving him "low self-esteem" for "a long, long, long time." "Who am I to deserve all this good fortune?" he recalls asking himself, coming away from his youth feeling "paranoid": "I felt, with considerable justification, that people liked me to a greater or lesser extent because of my money; that everybody that looked at me secretly had a dollar sign in their eyes."

As intensely as he feels the guilt of his wealth, Stryker pursues its expiation. He does this by transforming himself from a passive recipient to an active producer of beneficience. Again, a moral biography emerges— both by exercising virtue to rectify the preconditions set by Fortuna and by becoming engaged in specific productive enterprises. In effect, Stryker takes up a job, albeit, self-supported, in which he can earn his way to moral righteousness. Radkey, we recall, achieves the restoration of her world by forging a new self as she earns her wealth. Stryker achieves the expiation of his sin also by forging a new self; but he does so not by earning wealth but by using it to make himself an "earner."

In his liminal quest for purgation, Stryker takes up an ethic of good works, no less than the most ambitious entrepreneur. In doing so he finds two ways to atone for the sin of wealth: "I have taken great pride in a few things. Those things I'm most proud of are the books I've written. And second, the social inventions—the organizations that I've helped bring into being." First, easing the pressure "to carve out every goddamn day" requires him to find a trade. Fusing his need to work with his social interest, he becomes a radical newspaper reporter and goes on to author five books on socially progressive issues, including, significantly, two important books on the unfair privileges of the rich. These works are very well received and provide the ethical confirmation for which he so long yearned. Once plagued by the guilt and shame of privilege, he now enjoys the pride of accomplishment:

The books I'm proud of because I know that the merit of those has zero to do with the amount of money I have. Zero! The quality of those books was purely mine and I—people say, "Oh, are you the Stryker that wrote this or that book?" I take enormous pride in that because I did that as a profession. Two of my books have been on the best-seller list. Not at the top, but they've been successful, especially critically.

Stryker's second path of expiation is through philanthropy. From his childhood his family had been seriously engaged in philanthropy, through a family fund. But again, simply administering a family fund is not enough. Philanthropy, like writing, must be a trade, and it must be productive and focused on empowering the less well-off. "I think I'm good at inventing new institutions," he says, describing his efforts to create a fund to support investigative journalism. Picking up the complementary *nomoetic* pattern of rags to riches as well as the transformation of guilt into pride, Stryker extols his entrepreneurial accomplishments: "I pride myself with—this is going to sound immodest, but if I don't blow my horn, who will?—I think I'm a pretty good or a very good social inventor. I get a big kick out of creating or making something possible, making something happen that wouldn't have happened."

The denouement of Stryker's purgation *nomos* results in his being reconciled with his money, himself, and society. Continuing the religious motif of sin, guilt, and expiation, Stryker describes what, again, confessional discipline calls "a firm purpose of amendment" by making the future better for others:

My father was not a religious man—nor am I in the conventional sense—but he believed that each human being had a hereafter. And it is not amorphous or in heaven. It is tangible, palpable, measurable. And it consists of all the people who live on, who you've touched in your life, for better or for worse, who live after you. And that is as good a precept for daily living as I can think of.

In the end, Stryker too evinces the nexus of *nomos* and wealth. His sin is due to the unearned privileges of inheritance, his purgation is to become a productive worker, his peace lies in using his wealth to advance the Fortuna of the exploited. "I found out I was just very happy being an activist," he says, especially concerning that "favorite subject of mine—money and politics." His wealth sets the terms of his moral biography. It defines the nature of his sin and the means for his atonement:

The worst thing it [wealth] did was to make me have less self-respect than I ought to. 'Cause I'm really not such a bad guy, and I'm really quite a good guy. . . . And it has until recently given me a less than usual capacity to enjoy myself. . . . [Now] I'm getting more relaxed about spending it on myself and giving it to others.

Gnosis: "You have to learn things all the time"

While Radkey's successful dealings with wealth coincide with the reintegration of familial relations and Stryker's provide an avenue of redemption, Benjamin Ellman's revolve around the themes of learning and knowledge. This Chicago manufacturer, part inheritor and part entrepreneur, repeatedly enjoins the gnosis imagery of experience, questioning, and insight to describe the dialectic of search and success that marks his financial journey. Building and maintaining a business is an enterprise made moral by knowing and learning. The 64-year-old native of Chicago grew up very comfortably, his father owning a chain of dime stores. The bulk of his wealth, however, was made, and remade, in the hotel supply industry, on his own. Looking back on the ups and downs of a long and largely successful business and philanthropic career, Ellman notes that "it hasn't always worked out," but nevertheless "it's important to know that the older you get, the more you find out what you don't know."

Numerous liminal quests mark Ellman's search to fulfill his destiny, each of which is marked by an identifiable period of "not knowing" or "confusion" that motivates his personal and economic growth. He is restless and unsure rather than settled and certain:

When I graduated college with a degree in business administration, the Korean War was on. I did not want to go into my father's business. . . . And I really didn't know what I wanted to do. In college I'd joined the Naval ROTC and the summer of my junior year they sent you to summer camp at a naval air station in Pensacola, Florida. And they took me for a ride in a jet trainer and I fell in love with flying. It seemed like a good opportunity, so when I graduated college, I signed on for active duty and went immediately to pilot-training school. I served two and a half years as a fighter pilot, and after coming back to the States, I was still looking around for something to do. . . . I started to travel the United States myself because I'd always been a pretty good salesman.

For Ellman, being a salesman is to discover and apply information—to be ahead of others in locating growth areas and producing products to meet an emerging demand. In a contemporary example of a vision quest, Ellman describes his journeys around the United States in the early sixties as attempts "to see more and more what was going to be happening in the food service industry, to discern what we take for granted today." He determines that this industry "was made up of many small companies and that there would be an opportunity for someone to build a larger company, that this was a field where restaurants were going to grow, and that people were going to eat their meals outside the home." For an entrepreneur such market analysis is always more than an interesting research finding; it is also a recognition of opportunity for action. "The difference between successful people and very successful people, I've always felt, is . . . a

unique ability to take advantage of opportunities. Everybody gets opportunities but most people don't recognize them as opportunities."

Ellman's account of the convergence of journey, gnosis, and awakening
in his own recognition of opportunity resembles a literary tour de force.
Like Jay Gatsby, he spies and is drawn to the green light—"all lit up and
gorgeous"—of fertile expectation. The vision quest leads him to the Emerald City of the Holiday Inn, where he stays up all night learning of
marvelous new horizons. It is worth quoting Ellman at length in order to
capture the imagery of travel, light, a sleepless night, and a counselor
unlocking the secret to the last leg of the journey:

I was traveling across the state of Iowa toward Des Moines, sometime in 1961. It's
a long drive out there, and it was late at night. And in those days, they didn't have
any motels or nice hotels. You either had the old hotel in the downtown area or a
bunch of grungy little rooms you used to stay at around the outskirts. And I couldn't
afford the hotel, so I used to stay in these grungy little rooms all over the country. I
pull into Des Moines and I saw a Holiday Inn. I had never seen one before. It was
beautiful. It had a great big green sign. It was all lit up and it was gorgeous. I couldn't
believe this place. It had carpets on the floor. It was air-conditioned. Had a nice
restaurant. I had never seen anything like this. And I went and introduced myself
to the manager and I asked him what kind of place this was. Well, the manager
happened to be the franchisee and he talked to me. We sat up half the night talking
about Holiday Inns and about this fella Kemmons Wilson who started Holiday Inns
and what he was and everything else.

This new knowledge literally turns Ellman around, pointing him east-
ward into the rising sun. After another "long drive" he arrives at the
fountainhead of a new business and a new life:

And I got so excited that the next morning instead of continuing on out West to
Omaha, I turned around and drove to Memphis, Tennessee. It's a long drive. And
I went up to Holiday Inns headquarters and introduced myself to Kemmons Wilson
who was the chairman of the board of Holiday Inns. . . . And we spent about three
hours where he talked to me about the future for people. . . . All of the things we
take for granted today, he told me about in 1961. He then turned me over to their
director of purchasing and they specified for use at Holiday Inns coffee shops a light
fixture of mine. I never forgot that conversation, and of course used that [informa-
tion] to plan my business according to what was going to happen in this industry.

The consequence, recalls Ellman, is that "I started to get national and
eventually international recognition for my product." He is not just lucky,
although Fortuna does smile upon him; what brings him success is his
willingness to pursue a journey to its end, to discern and take "advantage
of opportunity."

From that point on, Ellman's business expanded and grew more profitable each year. That is, until 1981, when he faced a second liminal crisis

as his business faltered—due mainly to what he identifies as a failure of insight—both by the man he hired to take over the management of his company and by himself for allowing this to happen. As always for Ellman, such events are instructive; new knowledge induces new directions. This time the learning emerges from the threatened demise of his firm. Ellman's account of the crisis is replete with gnosis imagery. He describes his faulty "assumptions": how he overestimates the competence of the new president he brings on board, and how he underestimates his own abilities. He regrets being seduced by business school reports and book knowledge, characterizes his business troubles as resulting from an "error in judgment," and criticizes the failure of the new management to make proper "decisions":

I *felt* the company was as big and as strong as I could take it, and that I needed to bring someone in from the outside who would add organizational strengths that I did not have. . . . And so, I brought this fellow in to be the president—the chief operating officer, because he had operated a 900 million dollar division for a Fortune 500 multibillion dollar company. I made the *assumption* that he would bring to the company the kinds of maturities and organizational and management skills that I didn't have because I really—I had built this company from scratch and was very much an entrepreneur. That's a classic *syndrome*. In fact, Kellogg Business *School* put out a program on emerging companies and I fell in love with that program. It said that the successful emerging companies—companies that successfully go from 10 million dollars to 100 million dollars—are the ones where the individual who starts the company, the entrepreneur, the owner, can *get around his ego* and bring in somebody from the outside who can make the company grow in a more third-party way, someone who has not been as personally involved as an entrepreneur is. Well, I *believed* that, and without going into a lot of detail, he arrived in '81 and took over in fiscal '82. The company had never lost money in its 25-year existence. And in two years the company lost seven and a half million dollars. The *answer* was that I made—I made a very serious *error in judgment*. Brought these people in who had never been involved in a smaller company. They were only involved in multibillion dollar companies where they had many committees that made many *decisions*. Basically, they couldn't make *decisions*. Couldn't make *decisions*. And the company fell apart under his management. [Emphasis added.]

It was not a failure of will or his negligence that led to the problems. After all, insists Ellman, "I felt that I was doing the best thing for this company." It was just that he was misinformed, trusting abstract knowledge instead of his instincts. "I'd read too many books put out by various business schools who really had no practice in being in business. And I made a serious error of judgment," he confesses again.

But just as the liminal period is couched in the discourse of mistaken knowledge, the rebirth is framed in a language of lessons learned. As Ellman remarks, "So what I've learned from all of this, really, is to go with more my gut feeling about what's happening than with what someone else tells me to do or what some other would advise me to do." And as we have seen in the cases of Radkey and Stryker, the resolution of liminal struggles coincides with positive financial outcomes. In the first instance, insight provides the impetus for Ellman's manufacturing enterprise to take off; in the second, insight gets "the company back to profitability":

I had to come back into the company in 1983—'84 rather. Take it over again and get the company back to profitability, which I did in 1984 and '85. So what I learned from this experience was that (a) I was probably a better manager than I thought I was; and (b) that necessarily coming from large, well-managed companies does not mean that someone can succeed in a different kind of atmosphere. So the major thing I've learned in this business is that I had been very successful in my major decisions over all these years, and I was terribly unsuccessful in this one. And that you're just not always right. You just got to learn. You have to learn things all the time.

By couching his story within the gnosis progression of experience, questioning, and insight, Ellman makes his life moral. He searches for knowledge, applies it forthrightly, becomes misinformed, suffers the consequences, and learns and applies the lessons. The lessons translate into business success, and business success translates into personal fulfillment. What reunion is for Radkey and reconciliation is for Stryker, knowledge is for Ellman. It helps him establish a good business and make it better; it also helps make him a better person. First, profitability and financial success are the fruit of insight: "Today the company's a publicly owned company and we do about 37 million dollars in sales. And we have factories in Indiana and Nebraska and Chicago and in Edmonton, Ontario. And we're very much of a manufacturing, vertically integrated company." At the same time, his business success defines him as an ethically successful person:

This company was built around me. Everybody in the United States thinks about this company as me personally. [For a while] I felt that that was wrong, and that there was no way you could be successful in business if things revolve around one individual and you want to grow larger. But that's not necessarily true. Look what's happening today with Lee Iacocca and many other people. Individuals who are heading up businesses are becoming more connected with their businesses.

Healing: "Finding out who you are and coming from what is inside you"

"I was brought up in a very, very narrow-minded atmosphere and I did everything I was told to do," laments Laura Madison, 63, who grew up in Chicago in what she describes as a stereotypical blue-blood family. "I was going by the book, not thinking for myself," she reports, "yet I was always a rebel." Her life was impaired, "like a total contradiction," filled with bruised feelings and combative disputes with her parents.

I was always thinking: Why did I have to wear gloves to go to town? Why does my father talk about people as "top drawer" and "second drawer" and stuff like that as if those people are worth knowing and other people aren't. And the very first person that I had a crush on was the plumber's son. I mean, you know I just didn't want—I just never accepted that any people were really any different from any other people.

From early on she recognized that what her parents required of her "was not what I wanted in my life." A case in point was her debutante ball. "I like parties but don't think you're doing it for me," she told them. "I know why you want me to do it and that is to make me a puppet on strings and put me out there for all your friends to see."

Yet what she faced and resisted by way of Chicago social customs was only a metaphor for the encounters with death and infirmity, including her own, which she endured throughout her life and from which she emerged in a restored spiritual state to use her money and her energies for "the health of humanity." The drama of health, illness, and restoration began when Madison was ten years old and continues through to the present, intermingled with the themes of family separation, travel, and gnosis, as the following passage demonstrates:

When I was ten years old, I got double mastoid and I was sent out to an Arizona boarding school because they didn't think I was going to survive. And while I was out there my older brother died. We were all there was for each other because our parents were always going out and doing things and really not relating to us at all. . . . He got mastoid. There were no antibiotics and it turned into spinal menin-gitis. And they couldn't do anything. So he died while I was at boarding school in Arizona and they knew somebody in the town in Arizona and asked them to come up and take me out for lunch and tell me my brother died. Which they did; and I couldn't believe it. And I got home and my mother had changed his room into a girl's room. She'd done this dressing table all up in pretty colors and glass things, and about half his things were still in the room, and she turned the room into my room. Yea. And, and when I tried to talk about my brother, she told me how terrible it was for her. Which is the way it's always been. If I'm sick, she says, 'I've been sicker.' If I say I'm tired, she says, 'You're not—you're too young to be tired.' I mean, this is the way that it's always been with me for my mother. . . . It forced me out in a way. It forced me to take care of myself. But I think lack of love is a very hard thing to deal with and if you become a loving person in spite of that, you've come quite a ways.

Before Madison comes "to take care" of herself and evolve her philoso-phy of healing love, she suffers through intense periods of liminality revolving around the emotional and physical turmoil of sickness and death.

Encounters with affliction become personal crises of identity and purpose. Her father becomes "terribly ill" and whenever her mother "didn't like something I did, she'd threaten to tell my father and upset him and I knew he was too sick to be bothered with that kind of thing." In order to escape the "awful situation of being at home" with her mother, she marries a man who "was crippled emotionally as well as physically, which was really a humdinger. I thought I was Florence Nightingale," she quips, explaining her self-sacrificial posture.

And so I married him to take care of him and that's just what I got. And at the end of twenty years of marriage or something like that, I knew I was going into the loony bin if I didn't get out. So I picked up with my youngest child and moved to New York. And I spent two years here kind of on the verge of suicide, just thinking every day, how am I going to end it.

For two years Madison goes through "total despair." But one day the cloud of liminal suffering lifts: "One morning I woke up and I heard words, just as clearly as if somebody walked in the room and spoke to me. And the words were something I never would have thought of: 'Nobody is going to rescue you.' " After being "paralyzed for years and years," it "suddenly dawned" on her that no one, not even "some knight on a white charger," could "make it work" for her. And so the message "was like a rocket under me and I started to move."

At first "I didn't do anything very exciting," Madison recalls, who for a while was content simply to sift through and "throw out most of the values I'd been trained in." Content, that is, until the day she heard a second voice:

I walked in the alley one day and again I heard a voice and the wind almost blew me down as I came into the alley and the voice said, "If you really believe what you think you believe, you've got to let go." And that's what I mean when I say you've got to let go of your ego. Life is all letting go of your children, letting go of your ego—letting go of everything that you think is contributing to you, rather than finding out who you are and coming from what is inside you which is everything you need. The message was, "You've got to let go." And I walked into the house and I realized that all that time I'd been trying to control everything, trying to keep everything together because I felt like . . . it was all up to me."

This is immediately followed by a third voice that ushers in her rehabilitation. This time the voice comes via telephone and is referred to by Madison literally as "the Call."

I've just come in from hearing these words, "You've got to let go," and the telephone rings. And this guy says, "I'll pay your way to Colorado and back and put you up for three or four days if you'll come out to see something I know you'll be interested in." And I say, "What is it?" And he says, "I'm not going to tell you." And this was something I would never in the world have done before, but I thought, "You've got to let go. If that's true, what have I got to lose? This is a good way to find out what letting go is like."

From that point on, Madison becomes restored and moves from healing herself to healing the world. At the same time, as we have seen in the three previous cases, a successful and satisfying use of wealth accompanies and helps define movement from liminality to rebirth. "The ticket came the next day," recounts Madison who then journeys to Colorado for a meeting with environmentalists wanting her "to put money into" geothermal steam as an alternative source of energy. "I put it in," she reports, "and it quadrupled into quite a large amount of money, quadrupled in about four or five months." From here Madison next moves on to her mission of advancing the "health of humanity":

And I just had one great thing happen after another. Just from that one time of letting go. And from then on, I have let anybody, who wants to, come in. I listen and I go where I think I'm needed, when I hear it seems to be working toward helping humanity. That's my prime goal. The only thing I'm interested in is the health of humanity. And I mean, human beings having an opportunity to be truly human, which very few people are. They don't even know what it is to be human, which is to be a spiritual person as well as a physical one—not only an emotional person— and to really relate to other human beings, whatever they are, wherever they are, and to make a oneness that's there, but isn't seen by most people. Healing the earth, healing the rifts between people—that's what I'm really interested in. And when-ever I see any chance or see that I'm supposed to be doing something about it, I do it . . . because being human isn't dependent on being poor or rich to my mind. It's dependent on being aware and caring and conscious and responding to whatever you can respond to when the need arises. . . . What it means, basically, is being totally loving.

As we have found in the previous three narratives, the resolution of liminality brings a new moral identity associated with a new relation to money. Being totally loving explicitly entails for Madison a new and more conscientious orientation toward wealth. The physical and emotional heal-ing that brings her from despair and depression to active engagement also moves money from an embarrassment of consumption to an instrument for creating "balance" in the world:

I will do my utmost to see that it [money] really goes to the places where it will do something worthwhile for people. And so that's been what I've done. I've really bitten off a huge bite. . . . The thing about money that I found more than anything else is that a lot of people think money is love, for instance, or they think that money can get you whatever you want, or can help you to change somebody else's mind, instead of seeing it as a tool to make some kind of balance.

CONCLUSION: THE CULTURAL SCRIPTURE OF HYPER-AGENCY

The existence of individual moral biographies of wealth is the condition for the reproduction of the cultural scripture of wealth, and visa versa. Individual story and social discourse are mutually constitutive. They depend on each other's viability for their own continuation. Together and in interaction they form what Michel de Certeau calls "the scriptural economy" with "rules" and "instruments" for guiding the reciprocal insinuation of micro and macro discourse.[29] On the one hand, the cultural text requires the existence of an individual text. The "normative discourse" at the cultural level, says de Certeau, " 'operates' only if it has already become a *story*, a text articulated on something real and speaking in its name, i.e., a law made into a story and historicized (*une loi historée et historicisée*), recounted by bodies. Its being made into a story is the presupposition of its producing further stories and thereby making itself believed."[30] In a word, "There is no law that is not inscribed on bodies," says de Certeau.[31] "The *credibility* of a discourse is what first makes believers act in accord with it. It produces practitioners. To make people believe is to make them act." At the same time, the individual text requires a cultural text. "By a curious circularity, the ability to make people act—to write and to machine bodies—is precisely what makes people believe. Because the law is already applied with and on bodies, 'incarnated' in physical practices, it can accredit itself and make people believe that it speaks in the name of the 'real.' It makes itself believable by saying: 'This [cultural] text has been dictated for you by Reality itself.' "[32]

How the mutually constitutive micro and macro discourses of individual story and cultural text come together around the specific topic of wealth can be shown by exploring what the moral biographies of the wealthy reveal about the underlying cultural scripture of wealth. First, I will discuss how the elements of fortune, virtue, *nomos*, and liminality are woven together to form coherent moral biographies. Second, I will explore how the moral biographies of the wealthy point toward an underlying social text of wealth. It turns out that like all scripture, the scripture of wealth is a complex array of often contradictory moral justifications and challenges comprising the consciousness of the rich. Still, it is possible to designate the content of this scripture and how the existence of contradictory consciousness is itself both a legitimating and challenging presence.

The Moral Biographies of the Wealthy

What the wealthy have to say about *nomos* and liminality—and the way they say it—is, of course, intimately connected to what they have to say about the interplay of fortune and virtue. While all our respondents work out their moral biographies within one or another tripartite dramatic pattern, and within the terms of liminality, fortune, and virtue, they vary considerably in the degree of dramatic intensity and type of narrative they employ.

In biographies where the road to success is less strewn with obstacles, we hear a modulated and sometimes undramatic account of a gradual, evolutionary ascent. Here the opposition between fortune and virtue is less pronounced. The imagery of construction, career, and harvest dominate accounts of both the disposition of inheritance and the building of businesses. As always, we are made to witness the exercise of virtue. But it is virtue in service of fortune, not in opposition to it. It is the virtue of consistency, humility, and attentiveness rather than that of bravery, courage, strength, and cunning. Fortune is gratefully acknowledged and virtue humbly recognized. In this discursively subdued model, fortune creates the opportunity for virtue; breaks create the context for efficacious personal effort. Despite childhood hardships, a disadvantaged youth, or later business obstacles, the world given by fortune is accepted as a friendly ally rather than a harsh foe. For these wealthy—entrepreneurs and inheritors alike—virtue is perceived as playing out the opportunities of fortune rather than overcoming its constraints.

In other biographies the path from being controlled by to controlling wealth requires staving off enemies, reversing setbacks, conquering opponents, taking risks, and beating the odds. Here we hear dramatic narratives couched in the imagery of war, sports, odyssey, sex, and labor. The language of virtue dominates these narratives—not to the exclusion of fortune, only to the exclusion of a tame fortune. In fact, those who endure a more treacherous psychological journey to material wealth always remember to honor the workings of fortune.

In either case, fortune is virtually always Janus-faced, first appearing as a captor to be eluded and then as a guide to be befriended. Positive fortune, in the form of breaks, leads, and unsolicited assistance, arises only as virtue overcomes the obstacles and impediments comprising the shadow side of fortune. "Diligence," counsels Poor Richard, "is the mother of good luck, and God gives all things to industry." Although related in some distant way to the notion of "making one's own breaks," it is more accurate to say that disciplined effort transforms obstacles into opportunities. Fortune is first a nemesis, requiring the prospective entrepreneur or discontented inheritor to cultivate and execute such active virtues as cunning, bravery, courage, and fortitude. Virtue's first task is to extricate these neophytes from the nether world of imposed conditions. Once in tow or tamed, fortune can them come to serve as an ally calling forth the gentler virtues already described. Regardless of whether the wealthy describe their alignment to the workings of money as an unfolding career or a tumultuous storm, to work out a life of wealth is to work out a moral identity. It is also a way to reproduce the broader cultural discourse.

The Cultural Scripture of Wealth

The cultural scripture of wealth is the general environment of conscious-ness and conscience within which the wealthy live and which they repro-duce as they live and work in the world. In the terms I have used here, the cultural scripture of wealth is part of the Fortuna that they encounter as they make and deal with their money. As Anthony Giddens insists, culture and social structure are not reifications that have lives of their own. Rather, they exist like grammar or, as I say, like a genetic code. They occur and exert their effects only when embedded in discourse or incarnated in a living being—to continue the analogy. The same is true for the cultural scripture of wealth. We know it only as it exists in the consciousness and activity of the wealthy. But that is still to know a lot.

How does the analysis of moral biographies contribute to understanding the cultural scripture of wealth? Each moral biography is a personalized version of a more universal story about the relationship between wealth and transformation of identity. At a low level of abstraction, each story is a set of experiences unique to a specific individual. But when analyzed through the conceptual framework of fortune, virtue, *nomos*, and liminality, these individual stories become grouped into a limited number of more general accounts. At this intermediate level of abstraction, the level at which I have worked thus far, each story appears as a particular variation on a set of common themes. I now turn my attention to describing these common themes, what I refer to as the cultural scripture of wealth. Since each story is tied to and grows out of a shared text about the meaning and purpose of wealth, then what we have learned about the moral biographies of the wealthy should provide the basis for discerning the major contours of this shared text.

My purpose is to extract the "class" traits or "cultural logic" that under-gird the moral biographies of the wealthy. By "cultural logic" I mean the set of socially given rules and ordering principles that designate certain categories of events as important and stipulate the causal relations that link these events together. It is the set of socially shared assumptions and expectations according to which the wealthy single out certain events as benchmarks in their lives, attribute meaning to these events by describing them with a coherent cluster of imagery, and sequence them so as to highlight a moral progression. Cultural logic exists in the realm of socially determined, normatively oriented sentiments rather than syllogistic rea-son. There is no syllogistic necessity, for instance, for separation to be followed by reunion, searching to be followed by revelation, trials of courtship to be followed by marriage, or the risks of investment to be followed by economic success. There is, however, a cultural "necessity," in the sense that these sequences are what "make sense" according to the way we have learned to feel about things. In the previous two sections of this chapter I examined how the wealthy create moral biographies by narrating events in terms of the dialectic of fortune and virtue and the triadic patterns of *nomos* and liminality. I now generalize from these findings to draw out the major lines of the cultural scripture of wealth.

The major lesson to be learned about the cultural scripture of wealth from the biographies of the wealthy is that it is a moral scripture. The fact the wealthy make so much of virtue, envelop their stories in moral themes such as learning and purgation, and tell of their quests for self-transformation—all this means that living with wealth is a test of character. The scripture of wealth is moral because wealth—like mana—has a moral valence. Of course, this is true of money in general. But what makes wealth more highly charged is the fact that in addition to being a resource for existence, it is a resource for transition and transformation. It is, as Giddens says, both enabling and constraining. On the one hand, wealth is a call in the form of an attraction. It elicits a commitment among entrepreneurs to search it out and among the inherited to make it work for them. Once obtained or satisfactorily organized, wealth provides a resource of empowerment for accomplishing one's desire. On the other hand, wealth is a burden and obligation binding the rich to forms of consciousness and ways of life that are imposed rather than chosen. In both cases, however, the challenge is to learn and apply a personal asceticism of virtue to make wealth work for them and to justify its possession.

In the broadest terms, then, the cultural scripture of wealth dictates that both the earned and the inherited wealthy view their lives as moral or spiritual careers. They advance from what the Jesuit theologian Karl Rahner calls a life of "having-to" to one of "wanting-to." If the Enlightenment and Calvinism combine to embed in all Westerns the aspiration, indeed the expectation, to move from being subjected to life's limits to becoming a subject capable of overcoming those limits, it is the wealthy who are most imbued with the opportunity of doing so, at least in the material realm.

In this way, the cultural scripture of wealth is about agency—hyperagency. The wealthy are not restricted simply to finding a reasonably compatible place in the world. They enjoy the additional capacity to create an institutional and organizational environment in the world—be it at work, at home, in politics, or in philanthropy—compatible to their will. What takes a social movement among the general citizenry to accomplish, the wealth can accomplish relatively single-handedly. This is precisely the point that real estate magnate Graham Reynolds makes when he declares that wealth gives him the "power to get through time and red-tape barriers." As he boasts, "I can pick up the phone and call a congressman who's heard my name and I can have the impact of one million votes on the issue with a phone call. You always have the upper hand in negotiating, and it allows you to do in one-tenth the time what it would take somebody else ten times the time [to do] because of the credibility you have to develop." In the dialectic of fortune and virtue, the exercise of virtue by the wealthy creates an institutional environment in which the rules of the game are eventually tailored to the will of the rich. In the dramatic progression of life represented by the motifs of *nomos* and liminality, the wealthy are those who eventually prevail in recording a personally and financially successful transformation to initiation, learning, healing, and purgation.

In the course of their encounter with money, the wealthy graduate from being disposed over to disposing over the rules and regulations of institutional life. In the interplay of fortune and virtue, or what can be called the dialectic of socialization and social construction, the wealthy are masters of social construction. In the dialectic of structure and agency, the wealthy are hyper-agents. This applies, we find, not just to gaining control over the external world but over their money and their selves. This is the freedom and empowerment bestowed by wealth, and it constitutes the central moral fact that the cultural scripture of wealth provides and justifies. Progressive activist and millionaire Allison Randall accurately captures this constructive capacity of hyper-agency: "I'm free, you know. I'm free of financial restrictions. It's wonderful. What more could I want? I have money that I can do things with—for myself and for the causes I feel are important. My next career could be anything. I have that freedom and I'm not afraid to sort of think, 'Well, maybe you *could* do that.'"

It is not accidental that one of the three monastic vows connects worldly treasure to personal salvation. It reflects the conviction that economics is as spiritually charged as sexuality and power. In European feudalism, the morality of money focused on the distributional duties connected to each social station. Economic probity meant spiritual disengagement for ascetics, surrendering of rent for the serf, and compliance to the code of noblesse oblige for the rich. Around the time of the Puritans, the new economic and cultural dispensation of capitalism led to the emergence of a new doctrine of economic responsibility summarized in the activist ethics of stewardship. In this "world turned upside down," to borrow Christopher Hill's apt phrase,[33] the cultural scripture of wealth became reoriented. Financial asceticism now became oriented toward the quality of engagement with money as a factor of production, whereas previously it focused on the quality of disengagement from money in undertakings of consumption or charity.[34] The precepts of stewardship offer nothing less than a vocation, says Weber.[35] For the wealthy the call is to expand the productive capacity of money as a measure of their social contribution and metaphysical worth.

Much has been written about this stewardship—as either a biblical virtue or an earthly responsibility. Yet much remains to be learned about its daily manifestations, especially in regard to the moral sentiments and self-understanding that shape the thinking of the wealthy on a daily basis. With a few exceptions like Benjamin Franklin's *Autobiography* and Andrew Carnegie's *Gospel of Wealth*, works on the inner life of wealth end up being written "from the outside." They register principles for right living without examining the actual practice of money in the lives of the rich.[36] In this chapter, my aim has been to shed some new light on the lived morality of wealth by examining the normative structure within which the wealthy recount their lives. This normative structure is the cultural scripture of wealth. It has direct implications for how the wealthy relate to the world, conceptualize money, and regard themselves.

In regard to the world, the wealthy are in some respects quite like all people. They work out a place in the world by living out the dialectic of socialization and social construction, of being disposed over and disposing over. Many strive with disciplined effort and some with enduring suffering to transform what was given by fortune into something more productive, more satisfying, or more rewarding. In other respects, as we have seen, the wealthy are quite different. Empowered by their wealth, they retain the potential of hyper-agency not only for establishing their place within the world but for transforming the institutional or structural shape of the world itself. Each carves out a more or less elaborate, but always quite individualized, domain of influence that I term a "principality."[37] The wealthy construct businesses, establish foundations, initiate social and political campaigns, adopt inner-city classes, build hospital wings, endow university professorships, and—more in the same vein than may first be apparent—have their clothes tailor-made, their offices distinctively decorated, and their homes personally designed.

In regard to money, however, the wealthy become even more distinctive in the exercise of hyper-agency. Here, they move from being under the influence of the demands of making and using money to taking charge of it; from conforming to its workings to conforming it to their wills; from being consumed by it—as one respondent put it—to consuming it in accord with their interests and desires. Entrepreneurs recount being consumed by the insecurity of not having money, and later by their efforts to make money in their businesses. Many inheritors report being consumed by the weight of obligation, privilege, or burden associated with their legacy. Rather than abandon either the quest for money or the search for its meaning, both groups eventually bend money to their wills, subordinating its lure and its power to what they want to do with their lives in the realm of consumption, family, philanthropy, further investment, or self-development.

Not surprisingly, then, the third realm in which the cultural scripture of wealth dictates a moral vocation of hyper-agency is in the promotion of an independent and confident moral self. This moral self, or individuality,[38] is both source and outcome of worldly and monetary control. The path of getting and dealing with money is a moral quest that entails not just the transformation of objective materiality but of identity as well. We hear in each narrative one or another version of how current success is not just a matter of the quantity of money but of the quality of self. Whether in quiet tones of sincere humility or apologetic tones of defensive legitimation, each recounts a story of moral triumph in which the wiles and blessings of fortune are transformed by some positive quality of character. In this regard, every transcript is at least in some small way a contemporary *Poor Richard's Almanac* and a gospel of wealth.[39]

NOTES

I am grateful to the T. B. Murphy Foundation Charitable Trust for supporting the research reported here and to Ethan Lewis, who graciously and competently assisted in the preparation of this chapter.

1. For a discussion of the research methodology and a description of the sample, see Paul G. Schervish and Andrew Herman, *Empowerment and Beneficence: Strategies of Living and Giving Among the Wealthy*, Final Report on the Study on Wealth and Philanthropy (Chestnut Hill, Mass.: Social Welfare Research Institute at Boston College, 1988).

2. For a discussion of the spatial, temporal, and psychological empowerment afforded by wealth, see Paul G. Schervish, "Wealth and the Spiritual Secret of Money," in *Faith and Philanthropy in America: Exploring the Role of Religion in America's Voluntary Sector*, ed. Robert Wuthnow and Virginia A. Hodgkinson (San Francisco: Jossey-Bass, 1990).

3. "The Priest of Spring," in Chesterton, *A Miscellany of Men* (New York: Dodd, Mead and Co., 1912).

4. Although the decision to entitle Carnegie's two essays "The Gospel of Wealth" was made by Carnegie's editor, and although some aspects of the essays are more theoretical than evangelical, the term is appropriate. Like Benjamin Franklin over a century earlier, Carnegie fashions a practical economic course for those who hold dual citizenship in the city of God and the earthly city, and who pursue what Weber calls the vocation of worldly asceticism. As such, Carnegie provides more than a gospel in the general sense of an instructive narrative describing the moral path he followed and wants other to imitate. He offers a gospel of wealth delineating the distinctive discipleship associated with the (ethical accumulation and) socially productive use of wealth. Andrew Carnegie, *The Gospel of Wealth and Other Timely Essays*, ed. Edward C. Kirkland (Cambridge: Harvard University Press, 1962).

5. Durkheim's notion of culture revolves around his notion of "collective representation," or commonly held meanings and behaviors that bind a society. When speaking in a more limited way about collective cultural meanings, Durkheim employs the term "conscience collective." Although translated variously as collective conscience and collective consciousness, Durkheim's term really combines the two, indicating the convergence of existential consciousness and normative conscience. Emile Durkheim, *The Elementary Forms of the Religious Life* (New York: Free Press, 1915).

6. Quoted by Tom Wolfe in "Stalking the Billion-Footed Beast," *Harper's*, November 1989, 51.

7. See David S. Landes, "Why Are We So Rich and They So Poor?," *The American Economic Review* 80, no. 2 (May 1990): 1–13. In his Richard T. Ely Lecture, Landes says that answers to the question posed in his title fall into two lines of

explanation. One is that "we are so rich and they so poor because we are so good and they so bad; that is,we are hardworking, knowledgeable, educated, well-governed, efficacious, and productive, and they are the reverse." The other explanation is that "we are so rich and they so poor because we are so bad and they so good: we are greedy, ruthless, exploitative, aggressive, while they are weak, innocent, virtuous, abused, and vulnerable" (1).

8. This does not mean that it is unimportant for others to discriminate between those modes of consciousness that appear substantively humanitarian or ethical and those that do not. The point is only that here too there is much controversy and that such an effort faces many of the same hermeneutical issues that confront the study of my autobiographical narratives. Even where there is consensus on values, it is possible for specific behavior that appears principled to one observer not to appear so noble to another. The implication is that competing theories of positive ethics, like the autobiographies of the wealthy, can themselves be searched for their common underlying currents of logic. In one way or another, all sociology is biographical investigation. See, for instance, Norman K. Denzin, *Interpretive Biography*, Qualitative Research Methods Series, vol. 17 (Newbury Park, Calif.: Sage Publications, 1989). It has also always been concerned with uncovering the normative foundations of social life: the central problematic of both Durkheim and Weber, as well as of all who have come in their wake.

9. As quoted in the *Boston Globe*, February 3, 1990, 9.

10. James Olney, "Autos*Bios*Graphein: The Study of Autobiographical Literature," *South Atlantic Quarterly* 77 (Winter 1978): 118.

11. Erving Goffman, *The Presentation of Self in Everyday Life* (Garden City, N.Y.: Doubleday Anchor Books, 1959), 66. In an accompanying footnote, Goffman suggests that positive aspects of a narrative tend to be presented as unique performances while negative aspects tend to be presented as common.

12. Schervish, "Wealth and the Spiritual Secret of Money."

13. The fact is that as interviewers we prompted the respondents to address certain categories of topics. It is thus more accurate to refer to the narratives as "interactive autobiographies" or "interactive memoirs."

14. Robert Coles, *The Spiritual Life of Children* (Boston: Houghton Mifflin, 1990), 21.

15. Thomas Bastard, *Epigrams* ii, 35, as quoted in Howard R. Patch, *The Goddess Fortuna in Mediaeval Literature* (Cambridge: Harvard University Press, 1927), 2.

16. Emile Durkheim, *The Rules of Sociological Method* (New York: Free Press, 1938).

17. Anthony Giddens, *The Constitution of Society* (Berkeley: University of California Press, 1984).

18. Patch, *Goddess Fortuna*, 3.

19. Ibid., 16.

20. Ibid., 42–46.

21. Ibid., 13.

22. Gordon Rattray Taylor, *The Angel-Makers: A Study in the Psychological Origins of Historical Change, 1750–1850* (London: Heinemann, 1958).

23. Niccolò Machiavelli, *The Prince*, trans. George Bull (1514; reprint, Baltimore: Penguin Books, 1961), 130–31 (chapter XXV).

24. Patch, *Goddess Fortuna*, 24–25.

25. Entrepreneurs tend to accuse inheritors of not knowing the meaning of hard-earned money, and the inheritors accuse the new rich of immodestly pampering themselves and their children. Yet both of these criticisms come down to the same thing: wealth is never to be lavishly displayed or inordinately consumed. The inheritors repeat more frequently than I can count one or another version of the disclaimer: "I do not have a yacht," or "I drive a Toyota."

26. Henry George Liddell and Robert Scott, *A Greek-English Lexicon* (Oxford: Clarendon Press, 1940).

27. I have worked with this notion of *nomos* in my sociological work for so long that it is hard for me to know exactly which aspects of this framework I have developed and which I have learned from others. It is clear, however, that I owe my greatest debt to Thomas E. Porter who, as my teacher and in his writing, introduced me to this framework in the study of drama. See Thomas E. Porter, *Myth and Modern American Drama* (Detroit: Wayne State University Press, 1969).

28. In addition to Porter I am indebted to the anthropological and philosophical writings of Arnold Van Gennep, *The Rites of Passage*, trans. Monika B. Vizedom and Gabrielle L. Caffee (Chicago: University of Chicago Press, 1961); Victor W. Turner, *The Ritual Process: Structure and Anti-Structure* (Chicago: Aldine, 1969); Johan Huizinga, *Homo Ludens: A Study of the Play Element in Culture* (Boston: Beacon Press, 1969); and Bernard F. Lonergan, *Insight: A Study of Human Understanding* (New York: Philosophical Library, 1958).

29. Michel de Certeau, *The Practice of Everyday Life*, trans. Steven F. Rendall (Berkeley: University of California Press, 1984), 131–32.

30. Ibid., 149.

31. Ibid., 139.

32. Ibid., 148.

33. Christopher Hill, *The World Turned Upside Down: Radical Ideas during the English Revolution* (London: Temple Smith, 1972).

34. Peter Drucker, for instance, implicitly attributes the economic doldrums of the United States to its postwar tendency to move too far away from the productive ethics of stewardship and too close to the redistributional ethic of noblesse oblige. "We also know that a consumption driven economy does not 'spread the wealth.' There is far more equality of income in investment-driven Japan than in consumption-driven America or Britain. In addition, though the Internal Revenue Service still refuses to accept this, tax revenues are higher within a few years when saving is favored." Peter F. Drucker, "Japan's Not-So-Secret Weapon," *Wall Street Journal*, January 9, 1990, A14.

35. The usual citation for Max Weber's thinking on economic asceticism is of course his *Protestant Ethic and the Spirit of Capitalism*. However, important less familiar material on this topic can be found in *Economy and Society: An Outline of Interpretive Sociology*, ed. Guenther Roth and Claus Wittich (New York: Bedminster Press, 1968), chap. 6, sections viii–xv.

36. For the most part, however, such formulations tend to be either trite or contentious. Ironically, commentaries that go beyond rehearsing established moral arguments often become occasions for dispute by one side or the other in the class war of words between the rich and poor.

37. Principality is defined "as the sum total of social activities, organizations, and property through which individuals extend their empowerment in time and space." Schervish and Herman, *Empowerment*, 51.

38. Individuality is "the distinctive psychological attribute of a person's identity characterized both by a sense of entitlement to shape the world in accord with one's desires and by the confident drive to do so." Ibid., 49.

39. In addition to the structural aspects of moral biography I have discussed here, there are a number of further considerations that can be added concerning the content of the moral sentiments voiced by the wealthy. One such substantive component of the moral biography of wealth is the process by which the wealthy—often simultaneously—move toward and away from asserting control over the lives of others. In the course of their everyday activity, the wealthy are able to exercise social agency. They construct a worldly domain of principality and build a confident and efficacious inner domain of individuality (see notes 38 and 39) by which they graduate from being disposed over by the demands of daily life to disposing over the world as active subjects. But in addition, the wealthy have the special opportunity to act as hyper-agents or demigods. As respondent Benjamin Ellman says, it is a matter of developing another individual as an extension of oneself: "I anticipate that five years from today, the company will be doing $100 million in volume. I will operate as the chairman of the board and the chief executive officer and in five years I will have developed an individual who will in time be the executive vice president of the company or the president and chief operating officer of the company. [For now] I still want to do that but I want to bring someone into this company or develop one of the junior executives of this company that will eventually be that." Being a demigod means that the wealthy can create the limits within which others must live while easing the constraints within which they live. At the same time, as part of their moral quest, some wealthy come to eschew such hyper-agency as a betrayal of the spiritual secret of money. This is an alternative mode of psychological empowerment generated by wealth in which the wealthy turn their attention to the quality of their pursuits, especially by taking into account a reciprocal rather than a determinative relationship with those in the purview of their agency. (See Schervish, "Wealth and the Spiritual Secret of Money.") A second substantive aspect of the modern discipleship of wealth that deserves attention is the conduct of philanthropy as a spiritual exercise. For Carnegie the vocation of philanthropy requires the wealthy to contribute their surplus unsparingly on behalf of the public good. But in addition to the degree of their generosity, the wealthy vary in the extent to which they strive to forge a reciprocal relation with the beneficiaries of their gifts. In fact, the most important criterion for defining various strategies of philanthropy and for differentiating among them is the type of engagement donors have with the recipients of their gifts. See Susan A. Ostrander and Paul G. Schervish, "Giving and Getting: Philanthropy as a Social Relation," in *Critical Issues in American Philanthropy*, ed. Jon Van Til et al. (San Francisco: Jossey-Bass, 1990).

8

Scripture, Moral Community, and Social Criticism

LISA SOWLE CAHILL

The problem of interpreting Scripture for ethics has been posed from many angles in the work of the seminar on culture and economics from which this volume is derived.[1] We have seen, for instance, that Christians offering moral views of social relationships, including the economy, characteristically defend their assessments as consistent with the Bible as "Scripture," that is, as authoritative for the faith and life of the community. But the meaning of biblical authority continues to be debated in theory and ambiguous in practice. The argument of this contribution is that (1) the Bible is not useful for ethics primarily as a source of "rules"; (2) following recent scholarship, it is useful primarily in forming communities whose relation to society is analogous to that of the New Testament communities; and (3) it yields "inclusion of the marginalized" and "solidarity" as ideals of Christian community.

At the same time, it is important to keep in mind several qualifications. In regard to point (1), the Bible does contain concrete moral rules or specific action guides, which mediate between Christian identity and the practical context for a given time and place. Thus, it is appropriate for Christian ethics or religious leadership to offer specific recommendations about economic arrangements, though these must remain open to continuing reconsideration and revision. Moreover, in regard to points (2) and (3), the New Testament communities formed identity interactively with culture, not wholly over against it, and they experience occasional tension and failure in the realization of their ideals. Therefore, in the contemporary context, we should not be surprised to find that a Christian moral view of wealth will take part of its shape form cultural values and practices, even as it criticizes them. The readings and discussion that have furthered our common project on wealth have served to confirm the insight of contemporary hermeneutics that, while social context is potentially the condition of misinterpretation of the Bible, it is also the condition of possibility of any biblical interpretation at all.

SOME EXAMPLES

Dayton Haskin has indicated both the assets and the debits of culturally nuanced interpretation in Chapter 4, on the parable of the talents (Matt. 25:14–30). The parable's meaning has always been shadowed by obscurity, and its interpretation has become quite diversified in accord with the circumstances and interests of interpreters. Haskin suggests "a dynamic concept of making 'meaning,' " which excludes the possibilities both that the full value of the parable lies in a reconstructed original meaning and that anyone can legitimately make the parable mean whatever they want it to mean. After noting that, historically, a thread in specifically economic interpretations of the parable has been stewardship, Haskin resists the reappropriation of the parable in the service of "capitalist ideology." He observes that the hermeneutics of the parable have not infrequently focused on socially responsible conduct, especially in response to the emergence of capitalism in the early modern period.

In Chapter 6, Carol Petillo calls attention to the fact that individual biographies, in addition to cultural outlooks, influence one's construal of the biblically based Christian themes that give shape to moral identity. She shares her history of growing up in a small-town Baptist community committed to the proposition that "all were equal under God." She also details some of the life of Jane Addams, whose father's admonition not to wear a showy new cloak to Sunday school suggested to the young Jane that religion presents challenges to "the inequalities of the human lot." Many of the contemporary wealthy Americans interviewed by Paul Schervish (Chapter 7) also use religious themes, especially stewardship, to make moral sense of their advantages and to direct them toward social service. The heiress called "Janet Arnold" tells us that her parents taught her that family members were "stewards of the money" and that she ought "to be productive and avoid indulgence." For many years, she lived simply, marrying a social worker and living among the poor of Detroit. Later, turning more deliberately to philanthropy, she supported human rights and civil rights causes.

Haskin, Petillo, Schervish, and many of their subjects speak of concern for the less well-off and take religion to encourage aggressive redistributive efforts to enhance the opportunities of the poor to better their economic position. In the words of Jane Addams, confronted with the effects of industrialization on the immigrant population of Chicago, "private beneficence is totally inadequate to deal with the vast numbers of the city's disinherited."[2] All imply or directly forward a critique of "unbridled" capitalism, suggesting that the market alone cannot guarantee a just society. Of course, they write from a historical perspective in which the national and international shortcomings of laissez-faire capitalism are increasingly evident, and in which, in fact, attempts at "pure" capitalist systems would be considered obsolete. Thus, much of what they say would be acceptable both to those who believe a transformed market system can be rescued (and can rescue) and by those whose basic economic commitments are socialist rather than capitalist in character. Nonetheless, it is fair to say both that the authors cited above are profoundly critical of capitalism, even if not absolutely so, and that they judge Christian religious and biblical themes and models to be on the whole critical of it also.

Other Christian groups and authors have taken a different approach. In *The Embarrassment of Riches*, Simon Schama illustrates how the seventeenth-century Dutch Calvinists use a biblical Zion metaphor to build a sense of privileged identity and mission, a nationalism grounded in their confidence in divine favor.[3] "In keeping with a nation sired of David's stock, and obedient to Moses' law, they should combine God-fearing resolution with courage, resourcefulness and a hearty appetite for life, the better to indulge it according to classical canons of moderation and scriptural commandments of prudence."[4] But the Dutch sense of providential entitlement (as well as the fundamentally hierarchical view of the universe inherited from medieval Christianity) apparently inhibited their ability to ask the following critical questions: Should wealth be so unevenly distributed among groups and classes? And should "godly" social action be directed toward the creation of new social relationships, rather than toward ad hoc remedial efforts to remove the most evident sufferings of the needy?

The harnessing of biblical and religious warrants to pull disparate social programs confronts us with the question of the controls to which such warrants may be subject, and particularly whether the biblical materials advance a "message" about economic relationships that is in any way culturally transcendent. In other words, who is "right"?

Pheme Perkins's chapter speaks to this question. She concludes that the New Testament does not endorse any particular patterns of economic exchange, but does deal with "the social, communal, and personal relationships expressed by" such patterns. In fact, it is not wealth as such that appears as the primary moral problem, but power. Wealth is often associated with power, but the misuse of power can exist at all socioeconomic levels.

The egalitarian ethos and ideal of solidarity in the early Christian communities especially challenged the benefactor-client traditions in which the wealthy could wield great power over the lives of those who depended on them. Although the rich were not necessarily expected to give up all possessions, they ceased to benefit from the unequal relationships their wealth would customarily create. In particular, Christianity challenged patterns of distribution in which wealth was accumulated by a few who deprived many of the necessities of subsistence. Although the New Testament manifests "a fundamental suspicion of wealth," it "is not concerned with economic conditions for their own sake. The questions it raises concern the social and religious attitudes expressed in the economic exchanges that occur between persons." But the bottom line is that greed, drastic inequities, and exploitative economic relationships can never be consistent with the neighbor love and solidarity the New Testament enjoins. Particularly in a world in which—increased productivity notwithstanding—resources will be finite, the requirement of minimal equality sets a limit on acquisitiveness. Moreover, the New Testament emphasis on assisting those in need subverts any "entitlement" view of wealth, and holds up instead an ethos of sharing, sacrifice, and of not looking for a return on beneficence.

The practical and radical importance of this perspective, even in the absence of any specific New Testament instructions about economic institutions, is quite clear when it is compared with alternative worldviews. An ancient example is provided in David Gill's study of class privilege in classical Greece (Chapter 2). "Guilt feelings about wealth and privilege are not something we find in classical literature and philosophy. Nor do we even find much sign of pity or sympathy for the poor. . . . To depend on another economically was to be unfree, i.e., to be in some sense a slave, and hence to some degree less than fully human." In contrast with the Greek mentality, Christianity raises a noticeably distinctive consciousness in regard both to the moral status of the rich and to the duties owed the poor, extending even to the broad redistribution of resources. The New Testament does not set a specific economic agenda, but it urges an egalitarian view of human relationships and establishes on this basis a sharp critical approach to any and all sociocultural institutions, including the economy.

APPROACHES TO INTERPRETATION: FUNDAMENTAL CONSIDERATIONS

Few biblical scholars or ethicists today view the Bible as a simple source of concrete directives for moral decision making, rules that can be transposed without translation from the biblical world to our own. As James Gustafson indicated in a now classic essay on the subject, the "great variety" of Scriptural contributions must be recognized, as well as the fact that they are addressed to particular historical contexts; and Scripture must be appropriated within a process of discernment by the ongoing historical community itself.[5] This means reinterpretation. In the process, Scripture is not a sufficient or solely authoritative source of judgments, though it is deeply informative of them. Biblical scholars such as Perkins agree. She notes that even if we assume a "permanent validity" for the Bible, we still "cannot interpret without bringing the text into dialogue with situations, categories, methods of analysis, and visions of the world that are external to the text itself."[6] Moreover, Scripture and other sources, such as tradition, experience, the empirical sciences, and philosophy, are not even fully distinguishable from one another. Especially when the emphasis is on community formation and practice, the ethicist or biblical critic is apt to recognize that all these shaping factors are "already" at work when the explicit reference to any one is made.

Today, the tools of sociology, social history, and cultural anthropology are available to understand better how the New Testament narratives interacted with their original environment and functioned in the creation of communities that were not only of religious significance, but of integral social, political, and economic import too. New Testament communities in specific social situations gave meaning and content to the Christian life as discipleship; and it is present-day communities, forming their own moral identities in faith and action, that mediate the biblical witness and make it their own.

Lively current discussions of biblical authority—including its functions in ethics—as located in community reflect tacitly the postmodern context of theological inquiry. Over against the modern, Enlightenment confidence in the power of critical reason to unmask hidden interest and transcend biased points of view in favor of objective, universal knowledge (a standpoint reflected in the first wave of historical criticism), postmodern thought does not necessarily give up truth claims, but "is more likely to see truth served by divesting oneself of the conviction that we possess unshakable foundations on which to adjudicate claims to truth."[7] Hence the crucial importance of community as the context of dialogue, as affording continuity to the interpretation of texts, and also as testing dialogue in action.[8]

To summarize: (1) Both because of diversity in the specific moral instructions contained in the Bible, and because modern historical criticism has highlighted the fact that they are directed to cultural settings very different from our own, "biblical" ethics today does not focus on deriving from Scripture concrete moral rules. Instead, it elucidates general themes (equality, solidarity, concern for the excluded) and, above all, seeks to understand the implications of these themes for the basic shape of communal life. (2) Three principles guide the hermeneutics of biblical materials: appropriation, suspicion, praxis. Christians turn to the Scriptures as the original and defining source of their identity, offering continuity over time to self-understanding and life (hermeneutics of *appropriation*). But the critical consciousness of contemporary Christians does not permit a simple transposition of the cultural values and action norms of the early Christians. Some biblical materials are not useful or are even oppressive ("Slaves be obedient to your earthly masters" [Eph. 6:5]), and have to be reexamined in the light both of contemporary experience and of the most central themes or messages of the gospel itself (hermeneutics of *suspicion*). There is no simple or clear formula for the reconciliation of first-century ideals, values, and morality with our own. I hope the present discussion will show the importance in guiding the process both of understanding the main moral message of the Bible to be "love of neighbor and enemy" as compassion toward and inclusion of the excluded, and of patterning morality today in ways analogous to the moral life of the early Christians. But many authors, in both the Bible and ethics, emphasize that the final norm of adequacy is community formation itself and the type of inclusive and socially challenging life it enables (hermeneutics of *praxis*). (3) The primary task of Christian ethics is to define the sort of moral life Christians should live, given their specific identity. Yet recognizing that they are also members of other, overlapping communities, Christians often address the social order. The typically Roman Catholic approach has been to seek a "community of moral discourse" premised not on religious values and symbols, but on generally human values (the "natural law") or at least values shared within the body politic by members of various religious and moral traditions. One example of a tradition-based attempt to influence the social order in these terms will be offered below: efforts of the Catholic Health Association to transform health-care institutions in ways consistent with a Catholic interpretation of biblical values.

RECENT CONTRIBUTIONS BY ETHICISTS

Undoubtedly the foremost advocate of the links among community, practice, and theory is Stanley Hauerwas, who from *Vision and Virtue* (1976) to *Resident Aliens* (1989)[9] has persistently and forcefully advanced the view that the Christian "narrative," grounded in the Scriptural accounts of the ministry and teaching of Jesus, gives shape and continuity to a community of character formation, and gives rise to forms of lived discipleship that are above all faithful witnesses to Jesus' preaching of the kingdom. For instance, "the Gospel is the story of a man who had the authority to preach that the Kingdom of God is present," and "Jesus did not have a social ethic, but . . . his story is a social ethic."[10]

Yet the profundity of the "turn to the community" in Christian ethics is evident in that it is not only more confessional authors who ground their approaches to the Bible in communal praxis and reflection. In their widely used *Bible and Ethics in the Christian Life*, Bruce C. Birch and Larry L. Rasmussen argue that use of the Bible in character formation will be more important than its function in explicitly ethical discourse, and insist that " 'the moral life' " is a "dimension of community" and of "community faithfulness."[11] In the same vein, Allen Verhey says that the use of Scripture is justified "in the midst of life,"[12] and Thomas Ogletree sees New Testament eschatological communities replacing the family as the basic social unit, providing a creative internal dynamic which shaped "the struggle of early Christian leaders to work out forms of common life appropriate to the gospel."[13]

Of vast importance in shaping a more praxis-based approach to Christian ethics has been the emergence of the liberation theologies, whose orientation toward concrete sociopolitical outcomes is deeply ethical. They begin in specific life experiences that provoke reinterpretations of both the Christian message and the function of Christian community as a catalyst in society. Deriving from the more theoretically and hermeneutically grounded concerns of Continental "political theology," liberation theology has taken root in Latin America and has expanded in the last twenty years to include feminist, black, Native American, African, Asian, and South Pacific expressions, both Roman Catholic and Protestant.[14] The Peruvian Gustavo Gutiérrez coined the phrase "theology of liberation" in 1968, publishing his view of all theology as "critical reflection on historical praxis" in 1971.[15] The theologically critical novel phenomenon in our century is the "irruption of the poor" as self-conscious active agents who respond effectively to their oppression.[16] Gutiérrez displays a typically Roman Catholic optimism about eventual approximations of justice within the historical order, and an expectation that the social reordering implied by the gospel will be consonant with a humanist commitment to justice.

Although contemporary ethicists recognize the importance of grounding moral agency and evaluation in community, they still have not reached precision about the ways in which the biblical literature functions as an authority for that community. Most ethicists have found historical criticism helpful in the ways suggested by Elisabeth Schüssler Fiorenza: it reminds us of the meaning of the original witness, over against later "usurpations"; it deters the assimilation of the text to self-interest; it challenges our own assumptions; and it limits the number of interpretations that can credibly be offered for a text.[17] Yet these crucial types of contributions retain a rather ad hoc character. Is it possible to generalize some definite and necessary role that historical criticism will have in the development of any ethical (or even any theological) perspective?

BIBLICAL SCHOLARS

Wayne A. Meeks anticipates the efforts of many scholars to marry their interest in critical research on the origins of biblical materials (in Krister Stendahl's terms, on what the bible "meant") to their interest in discovering some productive method for proposing a normative function for the Bible today (what it "means"). He also shows how hermeneutical and historical issues are inseparable from ethical ones. Indeed, Meeks calls for "a conversation between social historians of early Christianity and Christian ethicists." His thesis is that "the hermeneutical process has a social dimension at both ends": it should attend both to the cultural and social world of the author and first hearers and to the social setting in which the text is reappropriated." What the text "means" "entails the competence to act, to use, to embody" a capacity "realized only in some particular social setting."[18] In *The Moral World of the First Christians*, Meeks explains that the New Testament literature functioned in a process of "resocialization," in which new identities and new social relationships are established, even though members of the Christian community may live simultaneously in other communities with other values.[19] A "hermeneutics of social embodiment" investigates the patterns of interaction between biblical narratives and their generating environment, then seeks appropriate recapitulations of such patterns in the contemporary church. Meeks accepts that not all social interactions indicated by texts historically understood are ones we necessarily want to replicate. Hence, the notion of analogy (a word Meeks does not use) may be helpful.

Both the first Christian communities and latter-day ones are transformations and "resocializations" which sometimes challenge, sometimes reorder, but also sometimes incorporate the values and structures in which their members participate; the shape and reality of life in Christian community is constantly responsive to its actual circumstances.

Of potentially immense significance for the ethicist's work are several exegetical studies that use sociological and historical tools to illumine the originating environment of biblical materials and so disclose the interaction both of narrative and community and of community and society. Far from exhibiting an arcane interest in "past" meaning, this scholarship makes quite direct recommendations about the normative character of the radical social configurations embodied by the New Testament communities refracted through the Bible. Historical research thus becomes a necessary first step in the constructive ethical task, and the concrete social strategies of biblical narratives become components of their "normative" status. Many of these authors reflect a Marxist concern with production, consumption, and control of the means of production as basic to social relationships, particularly exploitative relations between poor and rich. In setting a specific context for such relations at the time of Jesus or of the genesis of the New Testament, they draw on history, sociology, and cultural anthropology.

Richard Horsley, Halvor Moxnes, Michael Crosby, and Ched Myers see historical research as crucial for discovering the ethical relevance of the Bible today, and all rely on the hypothesis of an ancient "embedded" economy. A common presupposition is that ancient Palestine exhibited an economy that was not a separate sector, but enmeshed in religious, political, and cultural institutions to a much greater degree than in modern societies.[20] Moreover, in traditional peasant societies, social goods (both material and nonmaterial) are perceived to be "limited," so that the welfare of all persons is thoroughly interdependent, and any improvement in the situation of one is thought to occur at the expense of another.[21] Obvious consequences for the subsistence-level economy of the peasant village are high levels of anxiety, subservience, resentment, envy, and competition, as well as in-group loyalty centered on the family.

In several books on the socially revolutionary nature of the Jewish Palestinian movement focused on Jesus, Horsley uses social history and sociology to examine "the salvation embodied in Jesus . . . in its historical context of concrete political, economic, religious relationships."[22] The communities of the Jesus movement, for which "kingdom of God" functioned as a symbol, renewed the social order, especially through local communities as new "families" which were nonpatriarchal, but "tight-knit and disciplined." A special feature was these communities' concrete cooperation and care for one another, expressed in the saying, "Love your enemies," which Horsley refers not to external political enemies but to renewed reciprocal generosity among households.[23] In *The Liberation of Christmas*, he explicitly draws "a modern analogy" to the exploitive relation of North America to Latin America, highlighting religiously inspired "base communities" as a powerful source of political and economic change.[24] Likewise, Moxnes sees in Luke a challenge to "empower the poor" to act on their experiential insights.[25]

Ched Myers argues that Mark's Jesus challenges the "powers" (1:21–3:35), presents an alternative eschatological community of compassion and inclusivity (4:36–8:9), and calls the disciple to servanthood and the way of the cross (9:30–10:52). Myers calls Mark's ideology "an *analogue* for our modern practice of revolutionary nonviolence."[26] Social science contributes, either by looking for "social indicators" within texts or offering historical information about the likely social worlds grounding texts. Grass-roots Christian communities constitute a "revolutionary strategy" against power and domination and establish a new social, economic, and political order.

The consensus here is that moral norms are justified not as transcriptions of biblical rules, or even as references to key narrative themes, but as coherent social embodiments of a community formed by Scripture. Moreover, a criterion of the "coherence" of Christian ethics must be analogous conformity to the paradigmatic social challenges the first Christian communities presented historically.

The recent orientation toward community makes the problem of verification harder and harder to resolve, because it tends to throw truth claims back on participation in shared experience. This approach works perhaps best for a community whose form as well as commitments are analogous to those of the New Testament, that is, the enthusiastic discipleship "household." Even "Christian community" is a term that now refers to realities beyond the "tight-knit and disciplined" local churches of the first century, for instance, national and international churches. And even if we set aside the multiple referents of "Christian community," how do we know that there are certain concrete practices (e.g., nonviolence or economic redistribution) which must always be replicated by a "faithful" community, if each community works out "embodiment" in its own sociopolitical context? Can there be meaningful cross-traditional conversations about morality, and even serious cultural challenges to the biblical tradition? Perhaps there lies at bottom an ambivalent relation in much theological theory between an incipient "postmodern" recognition of praxis as the sine qua non of all theoretical inquiry, and a persistent "modern" conviction that any truth worthy of commitment ought to transcend one's own (or one's community's) admittedly partial perspective.

In light of the scholarship reviewed, we may conclude that community and praxis are key in connecting Bible to ethics, and that the ethical "message" of the Bible has clear socioeconomic overtones: (1) As revealed by historical and sociological studies, the New Testament itself emerges from, makes sense of, and forms a community of discipleship and moral practice. (2) The contribution of the Bible to ethics is at the level of community formation, not primarily at that of rules or principles. (3) Both historically and normatively, the connection between the moral "meant" and "means" is the community, which seeks analogous expressions of its life. (4) Christian solidarity and equality challenge exploitative socioeconomic relationships whereby some are deprived of basic necessities of life. (5) Christian community overlaps and interacts with other communities both in identity formation and in social transformation.

BIBLICAL MODEL AND COMMUNITY PRAXIS: ONE ILLUSTRATION

A specific illustration of the biblical, communal, and practical aspects of Christian ethics, as well as its participation in a larger community of moral discourse, may be found in Catholic health-care ministry in the United States. It is possible to trace through this example several "tiers" of Catholic Christian ethics, demonstrating one way in which members of a large, Western, postindustrial Christian denomination redefine church "community" as a specific locus of praxis in communion with ideals of a "universal" church. Those ideals focus, for economic ethics, on inclusiveness toward the marginalized, currently expressed as an "option for the poor."

Tier 1. Roman Catholic Church Teaching about Economic Justice

The modern papal social encyclicals, beginning with Leo XIII's *Rerum Novarum* (*The Condition of Labor*) in 1891, emphasize the sociality of the person and the social interdependence of individuals and groups around a guiding notion of "common good." In contrast to the stress of liberal democracy and capitalism on individual freedom and rights, the encyclicals see rights and duties as correlative and emphasize common good as prior to individual rights. Government authority is important, and governments have a duty to intervene in order to protect the common good and the fulfillment of rights and duties within it. In contrast to Marxist socialism, however, and partly due to the influence on the Christian tradition of Western democratic ideals, the encyclicals not only insist on the transcendent origin and destiny of the person, but also conserve a right to private property, civil and political as well as material rights, and the limited autonomy of "subsidiary" groups within society. A response to the social injustice perpetrated on the working class by industrialization, *Rerum Novarum* has also been seen as in part an attempt to endorse moderate change in order to avoid the total social reorganization promoted by Marxism's incipient mobilization of the masses.[27] The encyclicals following it are characterized by somewhat ad hoc efforts to respond to what are perceived as the social crises of the day, and swing back and forth in their critiques of socialism and capitalism. In general, however, it can be said that, while earlier encyclicals were more favorable to democratic capitalism, popes since the 1960s have turned their criticisms increasingly toward the materialism and social inequities encouraged by (laissez-faire) capitalism. Particularly since the encyclicals of John XXIII and Paul VI, there is an expansion of the term "common good" to "universal common good," as the reality of a global community and the importance of "development" for Third World nations has been recognized. In other words, it is important to guarantee a greater level of social participation (and the material conditions permitting that) not only to the marginalized within local communities and nations, but also to support affirmatively and enable the cultural, political, and economic self-realization of all groups and states within the international community.

In a recent encyclical, *Sollicitudo Rei Socialis* (*Social Concerns*, 1988), John Paul II criticizes the competition between East and West blocs for contributing to the underdevelopment of other nations. He accuses both "liberal capitalism" and "Marxist collectivism" (21.) of a truncated view of the person, of undermining humanity's true interdependence, and of harming the common good. Above all, he commends the virtue of "solidarity" as a challenge to present "structures of sin." (38.). The pope sees the whole Christian tradition as affirming "the option or love of preference for the poor" (42.). "By virtue of her own evangelical duty, the church feels called to take her stand beside the poor, to discern the justice of their requests and to help satisfy them" (39.). Although he does not offer specific solutions, he does call for general reforms, especially the reform of the international trade system, which is mortgaged to protectionism and increasing bilateralism; the reform of the world monetary and financial system, today recognized as inadequate; the question of technological exchanges and their proper use; the need for a review of the structure of the existing international organizations, in the framework of an international juridical order (43.).

In honor of the one hundredth anniversary of *Rerum Novarum*, John Paul II issued *Centesimum Annus* (*One Hundredth Year*), an encyclical written after the beginning of the demise of communism in Eastern Europe. *Centesimum Annus* affirms democracy and gives support to market systems and private ownership, recognizing that competition for profit is not necessarily incompatible with social justice. The moral parameters kept in view by the pope are the spiritual and transcendent destiny of the human person, the nature of work as a vocation and the dignity of the worker, and the importance of access to meaningful work as a means of participation in society. He also appeals to government, labor unions, and international agencies as mechanisms for restraining the market in favor of more equal distribution of the goods capitalism produces (although he is not specific about exactly which extra-market measures should be taken).

Tier 2. A National Episcopal Conference

In the mid-1980s the Roman Catholic bishops of the United States were drafting a pastoral letter on the economy,[28] which, when eventually published, leveled fairly drastic criticisms against the capitalist system's tendency to marginalize large classes of the poor, though without demanding that the system be entirely dismantled. Other American (U.S.) Catholics expressed a much more affirmative attitude toward capitalism in a competing "lay letter," *Toward the Future*, produced by a commission chaired by William E. Simon and Michael Novak. Other members included Mary Ellen Bork, J. Peter Grace, Alexander M. Haig, and Clare Booth Luce. The essential theme of this letter is the commendability of the market as the most effective remedy for inequality. It would not be true to say that *Toward the Future* disavows the creation of any and all "safety nets," but it does adopt a quasi-messianic rhetoric in proclaiming the mission of free enterprise to further human dignity:

Only a market system allows economic agents regular, reliable, ordinary liberties. Only a market system respects the free creativity of every human person. . . . A market system obliges its participants to be other-regarding, that is, to observe the freely expressed needs and desires of others, in order to serve them. . . . A market system is validated because it is the only system built upon the liberty of its participants. . . . In no other economy does the worker command more social respect.[29]

Because the letter is addressed to the Catholic community primarily, especially the magisterial teaching authority, its major appeals are to the traditions of that church rather than to the Bible. Some biblical themes enter, such as love of neighbor as "other-regard" and "wise stewardship" (directed to productivity).[30] However, the thrust of the argument rests on the marriage of the North American political tradition (liberty, autonomy, privacy) with modern Roman Catholic social teaching (human dignity, common good, reciprocal rights and duties). Within this framework is advanced a sense of national salvific destiny not dissimilar to that of the Dutch Calvinists. "The testimony of our ancestors is clear, and to their voice we add our own. The . . . fundamental principles of Catholic social thought . . . have correlatives in the fundamental conception of the unalienable rights inhering in every single human person," and so on.[31]

But the final draft of the bishops' pastoral letter offered a less triumphalist evaluation of North American values. Still self-consciously indebted to the national political tradition, the bishops do not reject the U.S. economic system out of hand. Rather, they call for a "new American experiment" (295.–325.), in which the tradition of economic rights would be broadened to include previously excluded groups and also international accountability. Although they embrace no particular economic theory absolutely, nor offer their own proposals as definitive, they clearly intend to speak out of and to their own society, revising rather than replacing its present economic system. Yet, in a countercultural move, the pastoral letter makes central the biblically derived theme "preferential option for the poor" (52.). In trying to establish "a floor of material well-being on which all can stand" (74.), those who are presently marginalized and powerless will be served first.

The bishops do not derive specific proposals directly out of biblical themes. Rather, they test present economic institutions with a practical criterion: What are the concrete inequities and suffering the present system engenders? Is that system essentially inclusive or exclusive? How could it be improved in the former direction? "[T]he impact of national economic policies on the poor and the vulnerable is the primary criterion for judging their moral value" (319.). Among their recommendations are changes in the welfare system, the tax system, the health-care system, and education, as well as enhanced employment opportunities for women and minorities. Many children in poor families, they note, are not insured for medical care and receive inadequate prenatal care and immunization (177.).

It could be objected that the letter's radical implications are not consistently developed in the concrete proposals for reform,[32] that some of the proposals will not be effective in achieving the goals sought, or that the proposals need to be revised or supplemented. The bishops do not claim infallibility, only that Christian moral leadership must take specific forms that address specific problems in ways that mediate Christian values to the practical level within the relevant cultural settings. A specific and aggressive advocacy for the poor that gives them (rather than productive entrepreneurs) priority in the economic system is a direct challenge to the capitalist system in place in the culture for which the authors write. Without arguing that the pastoral letter is a flawless example of Christian social ethics, one can still credit it, first, with granting that the economic system it culturally presumes (North American democratic capitalism) is not demanded by Christian religious commitments, nor necessarily the best possible realization of them, nor hardly beyond reform; and, second, with fidelity to a biblical sense of "disorientation" and "resocialization" in regard to dominant cultural values.

Tier 3. The Catholic Health Association

Headquartered in St. Louis,[33] the CHA has existed (formerly as the Catholic Hospital Association) since 1915 to unite and guide religiously sponsored health-care facilities in the United States under a common sense of values and mission. In the 1940s and 1950s, it saw its mission largely in terms of ensuring that hospitals conformed to Vatican norms on contraception, sterilization, abortion, and euthanasia. Now the social justice aspects of health care take a much higher priority, while pluralism and the need for some flexibility in areas of application are recognized around issues it used to control. (Here the CHA reflects a shift in Roman Catholic ethics generally, as well as certain American cultural values such as liberty, practicality, and civil discourse about value conflicts.) The CHA is not an official arm of the institutional church, but it is financially supported by and serves facilities that are its members.

The CHA uses several strategies for creating "community" among a constituency only loosely defined as a geographical community (as in the United States) but which shares a communal sense of special identity, shared activity, and sense of purpose oriented around providing health care consistently with Catholic values, while still within the social institutions and cultural values of North America. In order to reach and serve members, CHA staff sponsors national conferences on health-care institutions and on moral issues (death and dying, reproductive technologies); researches, publishes, and disseminates reports on special problems (health-care access and distribution; marketing, joint ventures, and mergers; the elderly; AIDS); publishes a monthly magazine (*Health Progress*) and a semimonthly newspaper (*Catholic Health World*); produces videos on social and moral issues; and has staff available for telephone consultations with members seeking guidance on institututional or moral issues. The Division of Theology, Mission, and Ethics is an important reference point for many of the ethical initiatives of the CHA. The new moral imperative is not just to staff a "Catholic" hospital which follows traditional roles, but to embody in health care a commitment to the poor which goes beyond charity to envision justice as empowerment.

In 1986 a thirteen-member task force of the CHA published *No Room in the Marketplace: The Health Care of the Poor*.[34] Essentially building on the moral framework of the economics pastoral, the report endorses the "preferential option for the poor." It cites the "compassionate visions" the bishops grounded in Luke's gospel and cites Isaiah: "Justice will bring peace; right will produce calm and security" (Isa. 32:17). It describes the identity and purpose of Catholic health care in these terms:

Inspired by the life and gospel of Jesus, Christians historically have embraced the care and service of the poor, the sick, and the disenfranchised. This commitment is rooted in a biblical and theological vision of the transcendent worth—the sacredness—of human beings.

Christians have always seen the poor as special recipients of God's love and have organized facilities such as hospitals and nursing homes to provide health care for them.

Regardless of the setting, compassionate care of the sick, especially the poor, is the Catholic health care ministry's mission.[35]

But biblical themes and a general vision inspired by religious ideals do not amount to specific, consistent, practical guidelines for action. To move toward those, the task force turns to an analysis of health care as it actually exists in America, in the culture addressed here and now. To summarize briefly, the report states that there are at least eighteen million people under age sixty-five who lack health insurance completely and sixteen million more who lack coverage for part of the year. An ideal solution would be federally mandated, universal health insurance, which the report acknowledges will not be available in the short term. Some interim changes are recommended: expansion of Medicaid and state-mandated private insurance for the newly unemployed and working poor; government payments to hospitals that serve a disproportionate number of the poor; and more equitable and efficient allocation of present health-care services to the poor.

Tier 4. The Local Health-Care Community

No Room in the Marketplace is not an isolated academic document. It is an example of an activist view of Christian economic responsibility which has an analytic moment, but moves quickly to strategies that can mediate Christian social values into concrete communities. Part of the CHA's "outreach" includes conferences and accessible publications which give a practical and even personal texture to its agenda. *Health Progress* and *Catholic Health World* include numerous articles speaking to the social responsibilities of Catholic health care, reporting on experiences in various local communities, and offering concrete advice for actual challenges. Extensive coverage is also given to social and legislative aspects of health-care distribution. The theme of a recent issue of *Health Progress* was "The Balancing Act: Keeping Ethics in Business."[36] A story in *Catholic Health World* describes the People's Clinic for Better Health in Port Huron, Michigan, an enterprise formed by Mercy Hospital working with other community organizations "as part of its special initiative for the poor."[37] Another issue of the publication ran a feature on the closing in El Paso of a Daughters of Charity hospital which was one of seventeen in the city and was losing money.[38] The Daughters instead opened a primary care clinic to serve the poor of the city. "Many of the 70,000 people in the neighborhood are the working poor: blue collar employees without health insurance. Twenty-three percent of the population lives below the federal poverty level and unemployment averages just under 18 percent. Ninety-nine percent of the residents are Hispanic." As Sr. Joan Pytlik, one of the organizers of the project, commented, "The poor need bread and the rich need meaning. We feed each other."

But a particularly good illustration of "community creation" around poverty and health care were coordinated attempts in 1990 to personalize the statistics. A project featured over several months in *Catholic Health World*, "Portraits of the Healthcare Poor" ran a front-page picture and a vignette detailing the situation of one person suffering inadequate access for an acute health-care need: Doris, fifty, divorced, uninsured, and with a bleeding gallbladder, who in excruciating pain made the rounds of three hospitals (two Catholic) before a surgeon at a fourth (also Catholic) treated her without charge; Amanda, an infant permanently disabled from a prenatal uterine infection, because her mother could not afford cab rides to see the doctor (who also came to town only once a week); Brenda, a young, black, unmarried mother, who works as a hospital cook, but whose insurance does not cover the serious but "preexisting" asthmatic condition of her eight-year-old son. The CHA annual convention in July 1990 included a photo contest and exhibit of "the healthcare poor," to which members submitted entries. A subsequent issue of *Catholic Health World* in turn published the photographs, others of conference attendees contemplating the portraits, and a brief piece by the winner of the contest, testifying how her search for a subject among the homeless of Los Angeles had focused her concentration on their plight and also stimulated her compassion and respect.

These interrelated ventures are essentially attempts to extend a sense of community from the Christian middle class to persons outside the perimeters of their daily exposure, and to induce recognition of the "humanity" of those less well off. The effort also functions to strengthen a sense of immediacy and connection within a "community" that is geographically dispersed. CHA also subsumes, encourages, and magnifies initiatives at the local level by reporting on them, often with photographs: a health-care program for pregnant teens; medical support to a homeless shelter; a special consultation team for geriatric patients.[39] Thus it moves the "preferential option for the poor" to the local communities and facilities of subscribers, actually shaping community and character at the end point where medical practice takes place. Each religiously sponsored facility, in turn, typically has a "mission statement" and a series of internally and externally directed programs which serve its embodiment of "Catholic identity" (Christian values) and connect its mission with the purposes of the sponsoring religious order, with the expectations of the diocese in which the facility is located, and with the needs of the local community.

On the other side, CHA publications, even by means of the amount of attention devoted to social mission, also reveal that concretization of the "option for the poor" is not without its perils and failures. St. Mary's Hospital, run by the Poor Handmaids of Jesus Christ in East St. Louis, assumes the city's burden of non-reimbursed care for the poor population. (Ninety-five percent of residents are black, and over half are unemployed.) "So strapped financially is the facility that the sisters have, in recent months, seriously considered closing the . . . hospital."[40] In financially tight situations, other facilities have been faced either with discontinuing their ministry or with joint ventures in which it may be hard to protect their specific ethical commitments.

In summary, in its community-building activities, the Catholic Health Association, as a venture in Christian economic morality, (1) reflects and is analogous to the early Christian communities as their praxis is disclosed by the biblical texts and historical research on them (insofar as those communities worked out practical ways of life within their cultures, but still challenged cultural expectations by reorganizing hierarchical social relationships in favor of the marginalized); (2) locates the meaning of the Bible for ethics primarily at the level of community formation, rather than specific action-guiding rules; (3) considers concrete guidelines or specific exhortations to follow from a serious commitment to discipleship, but does not absolutize them; (4) tests the adequacy of rules and specific practices in terms of concrete effects on "the neighbor"; (5) joins with other moral, religious, and political groups in seeking to refine standards of justice in health care, and in seeking feasible modes of approximating those standards within a shared political and economic setting.

WEALTH, CAPITALISM, AND CHRISTIAN PRINCIPLES: SOME CONCLUDING REFLECTIONS

Joseph Quinn's chapter in this book, "Capitalism and Wealth Creation," sets out that economic system's key advantage, and also its moral problem. On the one hand, "a capitalistic economic structure does an excellent job of creating material wealth." But, on the other hand, individuals acting in their own best interests do not always "work in society's best interests as well." Above all, unregulated market economies cannot ensure an equitable distribution of goods, material or social. In other words, efficiency as a criterion of economic success must be combined with some principle of distribution in a full moral perspective. This is not to say that efficiency is either immoral or amoral; to produce goods that contribute to human well-being may be seen as a moral mandate in itself. But the moral problem arises with the question of access to those goods. In situations of enduring scarcity, or when bountiful goods and opportunities are so limited in their scope of distribution that some persons lack even the basic conditions of well-being and social participation, then equitable distribution of available goods becomes a moral task. To use philosophical categories, the principle of beneficence (maximizing good results or states of well-being) must be accompanied by a principle of justice (treating persons fairly). Quinn cites as a major threat to capitalism as a system "the internal tensions of the divergent standards of living that our version of capitalism generates at home," a threat that is of course magnified when capitalism's effects on the global economy are measured in terms of the world's poor. As Quinn rightly concludes, "Society may well be better off with fewer goods, if they are allocated more equally," as is accepted at least to some extent in modern capitalistic societies.

We will recall that the U.S. bishops' pastoral letter also endorsed a modified capitalist system. It argues that unequal distribution should be evaluated and adjusted to meet the basic needs of the poor and to increase social participation by all members (185.). The bishops defend their position religiously in terms of the biblical love command interpreted as "preferential option for the poor," but the position adopted is not uniquely Catholic. Protestant documents have applied biblical principles to the economy with similar results. Themes common to Protestantism and Roman Catholicism are the dignity of the person as entailing basic human rights (to food, work, and economic decision making); the necessity to change economic structures so as to alleviate poverty; recognition of "stewardship" of present resources and for future generations; the distancing of the church from endorsement of any one economic system as "divinely ordained"; acceptance of a positive but limited role for government; involvement of the church in moral formation, in adopting internal practices of justice, and in public policy debates.[41] Further, since the bishops ground their recommendations philosophically in terms of human dignity and social solidarity, their range of effectiveness can and should extend to the political, policy, and legislative communities.

According to David Hollenbach, S. J., the critical moral issue for the economy or for a Christian approach to wealth is not whether capitalism is most efficient in maximizing material goods, or whether it is in theory capable of being united with principles of just distribution. It is not even whether our society could come to an agreement on what constitutes human happiness, or on how "fairness" in determining access to goods should be defined in relation to that. The real moral challenge is prior to any of those. "The chief problem in explicating an adequate concept of justice in our society today . . . is that many would prefer not to reflect on what it means to say that these marginalized people are members of the human community and we have a duty to treat them as such."[42] In the face of that reality, the bishops perform a prophetic, but not a religiously narrow, function when they issue their fundamental principle: "Basic justice demands the establishment of minimum levels of participation in the life of the human community for all persons" (77.).

The special and even novel perspective on the problem of poverty today is the realization that one element in social justice is a basic level of self-determination as a condition of free and integral participation in society and its goods. Charity is not enough; structural change is essential. Dependency on charity or on structural "safety nets" which inhibit rather than secure meaningful future social participation only perpetuates exploitive power relationships. Insofar as capitalism or any other economic system permits the accumulation of wealth, it is a moral system only if it encourages systemically the "solidarity" that characterized New Testament communities, and hence allows enrichment of the few only if the basic needs of the many are secured by their social and economic participation. A just society will institutionalize channels of access to social and material goods that remain open to all members, even when general access is not compatible with the self-interested economic action of the advantaged.

NOTES

1. Portions of the present paper (now in revised form) appeared in "The New Testament and Ethics: Communities of Social Change," *Interpretation* 44, no. 4 (1990): 383–95.

2. Quoted in Petillo, Chapter 6, "In Another Time."

3. Simon Shama, *The Embarrassment of Riches* (Berkeley and Los Angeles: University of California Press, 1988), 104.

4. Ibid., 121.

5. James M. Gustafson, "The Place of Scripture in Christian Ethics: A Methodological Study," *Interpretation* 24 (1970): 430–55. Reprinted in James M. Gustafson, *Theology and Christian Ethics* (Philadelphia: Pilgrim Press, 1974), 121–45.

6. "Scripture in Theology," in *Faithful Witness: Foundations of Theology for Today's Church*, ed. Leo J. O'Donovan and T. Howland Sanks (New York: Crossroad, 1989), 122.

7. David E. Klem, *Hermeneutical Inquiry*, vol. 1, *The Interpretation of Texts* (Atlanta: Scholars Press, 1986), 21.

8. David H. Kelsey, *The Uses of Scripture in Recent Theology* (Philadelphia: Fortress Press, 1975); Darrell Jodock, *The Church's Bible: Its Contemporary Authority* (Minneapolis: Fortress Press, 1989), 74–75. See also David Tracy, "The Uneasy

Alliance Reconceived: Catholic Theological Method, Modernity, and Postmodernity," *Theological Studies* 50 (1989): 568–69; and Matthew L. Lamb, "The Dialectics of Theory and Praxis within Paradigm Analysis," in Hans Küng and David Tracy, eds., *Paradigm Change in Theology: A Symposium for the Future* (New York: Crossroad, 1989), 98.

9. *Vision and Virtue: Essays in Christian Ethical Reflection* (Notre Dame, Ind.: Fides Publishers, 1976); *Resident Aliens* (Nashville: Augsburg Press, 1989).

10. Stanley Hauerwaus, "Jesus: The Story of the Kingdom," in *A Community of Character: Toward a Constructive Christian Social Ethic* (Notre Dame, Ind., and London: University of Notre Dame Press, 1981), 37.

11. *Bible and Ethics in the Christian Life*, 2d ed. (Minneapolis: Augsburg, 1989), 20.

12. *The Great Reversal: Ethics and the New Testament* (Grand Rapids: Wm. B. Eerdmans Publishing Co., 1984).

13. *Hospitality to the Stranger: Dimensions of Moral Understanding* (Philadelphia: Fortress Press, 1985), 128.

14. Particularly germane to this survey is Elisabeth Schüssler Fiorenza's *In Memory of Her: A Feminist Theological Reconstruction of Christian Origins* (New York: Crossroad, 1983).

15. *Teología de la liberación (Lima, 1971)*; trans. as *A Theology of Liberation: History, Politics and Salvation* (Maryknoll, N.Y.: Orbis Books, 1973).

16. Ibid., xx.

17. *Bread Not Stone* (Boston: Beacon Press, 1984), 130–31.

18. "A Hermeneutics of Social Embodiment," *Harvard Theological Review* 79 (1986): 184.

19. *The Moral World of the First Christians* (Philadelphia: Westminster Press, 1986), 126.

20. See, for instance, Halvor Moxnes, *The Economy of the Kingdom: Social Conflict and Economic Relations in Luke's Gospel* (Philadelphia: Fortress Press, 1988),28–30. He and others draw centrally on Moses I. Finley, *The Ancient Economy* (Berkeley and Los Angeles: University of California Press, 1973). On this theme as well as those of reciprocity and redistribution, also note Richard A. Horsley, *Jesus and the Spiral of Violence: Popular Resistance in Roman Palestine* (San Francisco: Harper and Row, 1987), 152–53, *The Liberation of Christmas: The Infancy Narratives in Social Context* (New York: Crossroad, 1989), 68–70, and *Sociology and the Jesus Movement* (New York: Crossroad, 1989), 88–92; Ched Myers, *Binding the Strong Man: A Political Reading of Mark's Story of Jesus* (Maryknoll, N.Y.: Orbis Books, 1988), 47–53; and Michael H. Crosby, *House of Disciples: Church, Economics, and Justice in Matthew* (Maryknoll, N.Y.: Orbis Books, 1988), 102–4.

21. Individuals must rely on others to support their own needs, either through trading or loans. Local exchanges of goods and favors occur within a reciprocity system, primarily but not exclusively kinship-based. Existing simultaneously with reciprocity in the societies of the ancient Middle East was also a socioeconomic system of centralized redistribution, which in Palestine's case was centered both on the Jewish temple and on Rome, each of which extracted wealth from the peasant villages. Both modes of exchange—reciprocity and redistribution—were to a large extent governed by the institution of patron-client relationships, in which one party with greater economic and political resources can offer protection

to another who repays with loyalty and support. Since patron-client relations are characterized by hierarchy, asymmetry, and inequality, power and status determine the way in which resources are channeled. See Moxnes, *Economy of the Kingdom*, 36–47, and Bruce J. Malina, *The New Testament World: Insights from Cultural Anthropology* (Atlanta: John Knox, 1981), 75–80.

22. *Liberation of Christmas*, xii.

23. Ibid., 92, 122–23, 125.

24. Ibid., 127–43.

25. *Economy of the Kingdom*, 168–69.

26. *Binding the Strong Man*, 47.

27. John T. Pawlikowski, O.S.M., "Modern Catholic Teaching on the Economy: An Analysis and Evaluation," in *Christianity and Capitalism: Perspectives on Religion, Liberalism and the Economy*, ed. Bruce Grelle and David A. Krueger (Chicago: Center for the Scientific Study of Religion, 1986), 3–24.

28. U.S. Catholic Conference,"Economic Justice for All: Catholic Social Teaching and the U.S. Economy," *Origins* 16 (1986):409–55.

29. Lay Commission on Catholic Social Teaching and the U.S. Economy, *Toward the Future: Catholic Social Thought and the U.S. Economy* (New York: American Catholic Committee, 1984), 26.

30. Ibid., 12.

31. Ibid., 8.

32. Rebecca Chopp, "Making the Poor the Rich," in *Religion and Economic Ethics: The Annual Publication of the College Theology Society 1985, Vol. 31* ed. Joseph F. Gower (Lanham, Md.: University Press of America, 1990), 263–69.

33. 4455 Woodson Road, St. Louis, Mo. 63134-0889.

34. Available from CHA. A condensed version is "CHA Task Force Report on Health Care of the Poor," *Health Progress* 67, no. 6 (1986): 87–99.

35. Ibid., 88.

36. Vol. 71, no. 1 (1990).

37. "Last Chance for Healthcare," *Catholic Health World*, May 1, 1992, 5.

38. April 15, 1989, 4–5.

39. All and more in one issue of *CHW*: November 15, 1990.

40. "Making It Fly in the Face of All Odds," *Catholic Health World*, January 15, 1991, 4.

41. Charles P. Lutz, "The Poor in the Church's Backyard," in *God, Goods, and the Common Good: Eleven Perspectives on Economic Justice in Dialog with the Roman Catholic Bishops' Pastoral Letter*, ed. Charles P. Lutz (Minneapolis: Augsburg, 1987), 164–66. These themes unite the Catholic bishops with American Baptist Churches, the Church of the Brethren, Lutheran Church in America, Presbyterian Church (U.S.A.), United Church of Christ, and United Methodist Church, as well as the National Council of Churches.

42. David Hollenbach, *Justice, Peace, and Human Rights: American Catholic Social Ethics in a Pluralistic Context* (New York: Crossroad, 1988), 83.

Afterword

PAUL G. SCHERVISH

If there is one thing on which Karl Marx and Adam Smith agree, it is that capitalism is an engine of wealth. Indeed, the revolutionary capacity of capitalism to generate surplus is at the heart of how both Marx and Smith approach change in the configuration of institutions, the role of the state, the labor theory of value, the problem of monopoly, technological innovation, the class struggle, and the shape of consciousness. Moreover, both Marx and Smith concur that in the long term, the magnet of wealth rather than the push of impoverishment is the objective basis for the progressive development of modern society. The quality of human existence advances along with the quantitative growth of physical wealth. The relentless accumulation of wealth sets in motion organizational and attitudinal transformations that further unleash a society's wealth-producing capacities and raise the overall physical and moral quality of life.[1] As Marx and Engels put it, "The real intellectual wealth of the individual depends on the wealth of his real connections." Socialism and "true communism" represent more than an increment in the productive capacity of society. They also signify the "end of prehistory," as humans come to "acquire the capacity to enjoy th[e] all-sided production of the whole earth."[2] For Smith, capitalism provides a "universal opulence" such that "the very meanest person" in a "civilized and thriving country" exceeds the wealth of "many an African king."[3]

Notwithstanding the "transition to capitalism" now fashioning the world economy, it remains unclear whether capitalism will last to the "end of history" or just to the "end of prehistory."[4] I leave it to others to haggle about the historical trajectory of capitalism. But I do want to suggest that as we move closer to the next millennium, the countenance of wealth will shape social relations and cultural morality at least as much as the face of poverty. In believing that wealth will increasingly characterize economic life and set the spiritual agenda, I am not alone, or original.

In 1930 John Maynard Keynes issued a provocatively promising prediction in an essay entitled "Economic Possibilities for Our Grandchildren": "the *economic problem* [of scarcity] may be solved, or at least within sight of solution, within a hundred years." Moreover, according to this most influential descendant of Smith and Marx,

When the accumulation of wealth is no longer of high social importance, there will be great changes in the code of morals. We shall be able to rid ourselves of many of the pseudo-moral principles . . . by which we have exalted some of the most distasteful of human qualities into the position of the highest virtues. . . . The love of money as a possession—as distinguished from the love of money as a means to the enjoyments and realities of life—will be recognized for what it is, a somewhat disgusting morbidity, one of those semi-criminal, semi-pathological propensities which one hands over with a shudder to the specialists in mental disease. . . . [As a result] all kinds of social customs and economic practices, affecting the distribution of wealth and of economic rewards and penalties, which we now maintain at all costs, . . . we shall then be free, at last, to discard.[5]

The chapters in this book remain silent about such prognostications. But the growing literature on wealth and its moral implications—including our volume—do respond at least indirectly to the tendencies cited by Keynes.[6] If, in fact, by force of history or by principled choice, we begin to encounter the transformations predicted by Keynes, our book may prove valuable in pointing out several lessons. First, by no means is our epoch the first or most critical time in history that issues of wealth have come under scrutiny. There is a rich Western heritage of reflection about riches. Second, this heritage does not speak with one or even two voices. Numerous, even contradictory, traditions have shaped prior discourse and remain active in shaping discourse today. Third, the subject of riches is so vexatious a cultural issue that every era devotes considerable energy to framing, defending, and applying an ethical case for and against the workings of wealth and the advantages of the wealthy. Fourth, much of what one era considers the proper case for and against riches is subjected to critical reappraisal in a subsequent era.

The most important lesson here, however, is that the issue of riches is never simply a topic of economic organization or social policy. It is always also a matter of moral identity and public character. This volume shares with Smith, Marx, and Keynes the premise that wealth simultaneously determines history and biography. The quality of spiritual life is wedded to the quantity of economic life. There are many ways to express this association. As a sociologist, I might phrase it as the link between the sociology of money and the sociology of religion, or the link between the institutional and moral life of world capitalism. In nonacademic terms we might refer to this (on the social level) as the connection between economic culture and the culture of faith and (on the personal level) as the link between financial autobiography and spiritual autobiography.

Of course, there is no way short of a crystal ball to evaluate definitely the validity of the progressive assumptions of Keynes and his predecessors. Is it possible that Keynes is correct about the coming era—that with the growth of wealth "for the first time since his creation man will be faced with his real, his permanent problem—how to use his freedom from pressing economic cares, how to occupy the leisure, which science and compound interest will have won for him, to live wisely and agreeably and well"?[7] Although I can be persuaded that a dramatic growth of wealth may be on the horizon, I remain skeptical that such a breakthrough will readily spur a concomitant moral regeneration. I have no doubt, however, that a substantial growth of wealth on the world scale will transform the moral terrain. Hence, whatever wisdom we can distill—from the case for and against riches at various moments in Western thought—should help define that terrain. For, says Keynes, "it will be those peoples, who can keep alive, and cultivate into a fuller perfection, the art of life itself and do not sell themselves for the means of life, who will be able to enjoy the abundance when it comes."[8]

NOTES

1. G. A. Cohen, *Karl Marx's Theory of History: A Defense* (Princeton, N.J.: Princeton University Press, 1978), 197–207.

2. Karl Marx and Frederick Engels, The *German Ideology* (1846; reprint, New York: International Publishers, 1947), 27.

3. Adam Smith, *The Wealth of Nations*, ed. Edwin Cannan (1776; reprint, New York: Modern Library, 1937), 11–12.

4. The term "end of history" has recently been turned into a topic of controversy by Francis Fukuyama, who suggests that the Eastern European turn to capitalism marks the final transition in world economic development (*Have We Reached the End of History?* [Santa Monica, Calif.: Rand, 1989]). His position has been derided by academics and journalists who believe his ahistorical presuppositions are absurd even if statist socialism has reached its end. The term "end of prehistory" coincides with its obverse, "the beginning of history." In his famous 1859 Preface to *A Contribution to the Critique of Political Economy*, Marx says that the demise of capitalism brings "the prehistory of human society to a close." His notion is that with the transition to socialism there emerges the first flowering of real human freedom as the creative force of history.

5. John Maynard Keynes, "Economic Possibilities for Our Grandchildren," in *Essays in Persuasion* (London: Macmillan, 1933), 366, 369–370.

6. See, for instance, Peter L. Berger, ed., *The Capitalist Spirit: Toward a Religious Ethic of Wealth Creation* (San Francisco: Institute for Contemporary Studies, 1990); Peter F. Drucker, *Post-Capitalist Society* (New York: Harper, 1993); John C.

Haughey, S.J., *The Holy Use of Money: Personal Finances in Light of Christian Faith* (New York: Doubleday, 1985); Michèle Lamont, *Money, Morals, and Manners: The Culture of the French and the American Upper-Middle Class* (Chicago: University of Chicago Press, 1992). Jacob Needleman, *Money and the Meaning of Life* (New York: Doubleday, 1991); Richard John Neuhaus, *Doing Well and Doing Good: The Challenge to the Christian Capitalist* (New York: Doubleday, 1992); Michael Novak, *This Hemisphere of Liberty: A Philosophy of the Americas* (Washington, D.C.: AEI Press, 1990); Kevin Phillips, *The Politics of Rich and Poor: Wealth and the American Electorate in the Reagan Aftermath* (New York: Random House, 1990); and Robert Wuthnow, *Acts of Compassion: Caring for Others and Helping Ourselves* (Princeton, N.J.: Princeton University Press, 1991).

    7. Keynes, "Economic Possibilities," 367.

    8. Ibid., 368.

Selected Bibliography

Addams, Jane. *A Centennial Reader*. Edited by Emily Cooper Johnson. New York: Macmillan, 1960.
———. *Twenty Years at Hull-House with Autobiographical Notes*. New York: Macmillan, 1911.
Annotations upon the Holy Bible. 2 vols. London, 1683–85.
Augustine, Saint. "On Christian Doctrine." Translated by J. F. Shaw. In *A Select Library of Nicene and Post-Nicene Fathers of the Christian Church*. Vol. 2, *Saint Augustine's City of God and Christian Doctrine*. 1866. Reprint. Grand Rapids, Mich.: Eerdmans, 1956.
Austin, Michel, and Pierre Vidal-Naquet. *Economic and Social History of Ancient Greece*. Berkeley and Los Angeles: University of California Press, 1977.
Bauman, Zygmunt. *Legislators and Interpreters: On Modernity, Post-Modernity and Intellectuals*. Ithaca, N.Y.: Cornell University Press, 1987.
Baxandall, Rosalyn Fraad. *Words on Fire: The Life and Writing of Elizabeth Gurley Flynn*. New Brunswick, N.J.: Rutgers University Press, 1987.
Baxter, Richard. *A Paraphrase on the New Testament, with Notes, Doctrinal and Practical*, 1685. 3d ed. London, 1701.
Berger, Peter L. *The Capitalist Revolution: Fifty Propositions about Prosperity, Equality and Liberty*. New York: Basic Books, 1986.
———, ed. *The Capitalist Spirit: Toward a Religious Ethic of Wealth Creation*. San Francisco: Institute for Contemporary Studies, 1990.
Birch, Bruce C., and Larry L. Rasmussen. *Bible and Ethics in the Christian Life*. 2d ed. Minneapolis: Augsburg, 1989.
Bloor, Ella Reeve. *We Are Many, An Autobiography with introduction by Elizabeth Gurley Flynn*. New York: International Publishers, 1940.
Bourdieu, Pierre. "The Production of Belief: A Contribution to an Economy of Symbolic Goods." In *Media, Culture and Society: A Critical Reader*. Edited by Richard Collins et al. Beverly Hills, Calif.: Sage Publications, 1988.

Braudel, Fernand. *Civilization and Capitalism.* Vol. 2, *The Wheels of Commerce.* Translated by Siân Reynolds. 1979. Reprint. New York: Harper and Row, 1982.

Calvin, John. *Commentary on a Harmony of the Evangelists, Matthew, Mark and Luke.* 1563. Translated by William Pringle, 3 vols. Grand Rapids, Mich.: Baker Book House, 1981.

Carnegie, Andrew. *The Gospel of Wealth and Other Timely Essays.* Edited by Edward C. Kirkland. Cambridge: Harvard University Press, 1962.

Catholic Health Association, Task Force on Health Care of the Poor. *No Room in the Marketplace: The Health Care of the Poor.* St. Louis: Catholic Health Association of the United States, 1986.

Chopp, Rebecca. "Making the Poor the Rich." In *Religion and Economic Ethics: The Annual Publication of the College Theology Society 1985, Vol. 31.* Edited by Joseph F. Gower. Lanham, Md.: University Press of America, 1990.

Chrysostom, Saint John. *Discourses against Judaizing Christians.* Translated by Paul W. Harkins. Washington, D.C.: Catholic University of America Press, 1979.

———. Homily LXXVIII. In *A Select Library of Nicene and Post-Nicene Fathers of the Christian Church.* Vol. 10, *Saint Chrysostom: Homilies on the Gospel of Matthew.* Translated by George Prevost. 1888. Reprint. Grand Rapids, Mich.: Eerdmans, 1956.

Coles, Robert. *The Spiritual Life of Children.* Boston: Houghton Mifflin, 1990.

Cone, Orello. *Rich and Poor in the New Testament: A Study of the Primitive-Christian Doctrine of Earthly Possessions.* New York: Macmillan, 1902.

Cook, Blanche Wiesen, ed. *Crystal Eastman on Women and Revolution.* New York: Oxford University Press, 1978.

Copeland, Warren R. *Economic Justice. The Social Ethics of the U.S. Economic Policy.* Nashville: Abingdon, 1988.

Critici sacri. [Edited by John Pearson et al.] 8 vols. Amsterdam, 1698.

Crosby, Michael H. *House of Disciples: Church, Economics, and Justice in Matthew.* Maryknoll, N.Y.: Orbis Books, 1988.

Danziger, Sheldon, Robert Haveman, and Robert Plotnick. "How Income Transfer Programs Affect Work, Savings, and the Income Distribution." *The Journal of Economic Literature* 19 (1981): 975–1028.

Davis, Allen F. *American Heroine: The Life and Legend of Jane Addams.* New York: Oxford University Press, 1973.

de Certeau, Michel. *The Practice of Everyday Life.* Translated by Steven F. Rendall. Berkeley: University of California Press, 1984.

Dennis, Peggy. *The Autobiography of an American Communist: A Personal View of a Political Life, 1925–1975.* Westport, Conn., and Berkeley, Calif.: Lawrence Hill, 1977.

Denzin, Norman K. *Interpretive Biography.* Qualitative Research Methods Series, vol. 17. Newbury Park, Calif.: Sage Publications, 1989.

Dickens, Charles. *A Christmas Carol.* 1843. Reprint. New York: Airmont Publishing, 1963.

Donlan, Walter. *The Aristocratic Ideal in Ancient Greece.* Lawrence, Kans.: Coronado Press, 1980.

Dorr, Rheta Childe. *A Woman of Fifty.* New York: Funk and Wagnalls, 1924.

Drucker, Peter F. *Post-Capitalist Society.* New York: Harper, 1993.

Easterling, P. E., and Bernard M. W. Knox, eds. *The Cambridge History of Classical Literature*. Part 1, *Greek Literature*. Cambridge and New York: Cambridge University Press, 1985.

Engels, Donald. *Roman Corinth. An Alternative Model for the Classical City*. Chicago: University of Chicago Press, 1990.

Finley, Moses I. *The Ancient Economy*. Berkeley and Los Angeles: University of California Press, 1973.

Fiorenza, Elisabeth Schüssler. *In Memory of Her: A Feminist Theological Reconstruction of Christian Origins*. New York: Crossroad, 1983.

Flynn, Elizabeth Gurley. *The Rebel Girl: An Autobiography, My First Life (1906–1926)*. Revised edition. New York: International Publishers, 1973.

Foucault, Michel. "Nietzsche, Genealogy, History." In *Language, Counter-Memory, Practice*. Translated by Donald F. Bouchard and Sherry Simon. Ithaca, N.Y.: Cornell University Press, 1977.

Frank, Robert H. *Passions within Reason: The Strategic Role of Emotions*. New York: W. W. Norton, 1988.

Friedman, Milton. *Capitalism and Freedom*. Chicago: University of Chicago Press, 1962.

Garrison, Dee. *Mary Heaton Vorse: The Life of an American Insurgent*. Philadelphia: Temple University Press, 1989.

————, ed. *Rebel Pen: The Writings of Mary Heaton Vorse*. New York: Monthly Review Press, 1985.

Giddens, Anthony. *The Constitution of Society*. Berkeley: University of California Press, 1984.

Gill, David. "Aspects of Religious Morality in Early Greek Epic." *Harvard Theological Review* 73 (1980): 373–418.

Gilman, Charlotte Perkins. *Herland*. New York: Pantheon Books, 1979.

————. *The Living of Charlotte Perkins Gilman: An Autobiography, with Foreword by Zona Gale*. New York: D. Appleton-Century, 1935.

————. *Women and Economics: A Study of the Economic Relation between Men and Women as a Factor in Social Evolution*. 1899. Reprint. Edited by Carl N. Degler. New York: Harper and Row, 1966.

Goldman, Emma. *Living My Life*. Edited by Richard and Anna Maria Drinnon. 1931. Revised edition. New York: New American Library, 1977.

Gonzalez, Justo L. *Faith and Wealth. A History of Early Christian Ideas on the Origin, Significance and Use of Money*. San Francisco: Harper and Row, 1990.

Greene, Kevin. *The Archaeology of the Roman Economy*. Berkeley: University of California Press, 1986.

Gregory the Great. *Forty Gospel Homilies*. Translated by Dom David Hurst. Kalamazoo, Mich.: Cistercian Publications, 1990.

Gustafson, James M. "The Place of Scripture in Christian Ethics: A Methodological Study." *Interpretation* 24 (1970): 430–55. Reprinted in James M. Gustafson, *Theology and Christian Ethics*. Philadelphia: Pilgrim Press, 1974.

Gutiérrez, Gustavo. *A Theology of Liberation: History, Politics and Salvation*. Maryknoll, N.Y.: Orbis Books, 1973.

Hammond, Henry. *A Paraphrase, and Annotations upon all the Books of the New Testament*. 2d ed., enl. London, 1659.

Hauerwas, Stanley. *A Community of Character: Toward a Constructive Christian Social Ethic*. Notre Dame, Ind., and London: University of Notre Dame Press, 1981.

———. *Resident Aliens*. Nashville: Augsburg Press, 1989.

———. *Vision and Virtue: Essays in Christian Ethical Reflection*. Notre Dame, Ind.: Fides Publishers, 1976.

Haughey, John C., S.J. *The Holy Use of Money: Personal Finances in Light of Christian Faith*. New York: Doubleday, 1985.

Heilbroner, Robert L. *The Essential Adam Smith*. New York: W. W. Norton, 1986.

———. "The Triumph of Capitalism." *The New Yorker*, January 23, 1989, 98–109.

———. *The Worldly Philosophers*. New York: Simon and Schuster, 1953.

Heilbrun, Carolyn G. *Writing a Woman's Life*. New York: W. W. Norton, 1988.

Hesiod and Theognis. *Theogony, Works and Days and Elegies*. Translated by Dorothea Wender. Harmondsworth, England: Penguin, 1973.

Hill, Christopher. *The World Turned Upside Down: Radical Ideas during the English Revolution*. London: Temple Smith, 1972.

Hill, Mary A. *Charlotte Perkins Gilman: The Making of a Radical Feminist 1860–1896*. Philadelphia: Temple University Press, 1980.

Hollenbach, David. *Justice, Peace, and Human Rights: American Catholic Social Ethics in a Pluralistic Context*. New York: Crossroad, 1988.

Homer. *The Iliad*. Translated by Richmond Lattimore. Chicago and London: University of Chicago Press, 1951.

———. *The Odyssey*. Translated by Richmond Lattimore. New York: Harper Collins. 1975.

Horowitz, Daniel. *The Morality of Spending: Attitudes toward the Consumer Society in America, 1875–1940*. Baltimore: Johns Hopkins University Press, 1985.

Horsley, Richard A. *Jesus and the Spiral of Violence: Popular Resistance in Roman Palestine*. San Francisco: Harper and Row, 1987.

———. *The Liberation of Christmas: The Infancy Narratives in Social Context*. New York: Crossroad, 1989.

———. *Sociology and the Jesus Movement*. New York: Crossroad, 1989.

Huizinga, Johan. *Homo Ludens: A Study of the Play Element in Culture*. Boston: Beacon Press, 1969.

Hutchison, Terrence. *Before Adam Smith: The Emergence of Political Economy 1662–1776*. Oxford: Basil Blackwell, 1988.

James, Edward T., and Janet Wilson James, eds. *Notable American Women, 1607–1950: A Biographical Dictionary*. Cambridge: Belknap Press of Harvard University, 1971.

Jelinek, Estelle C. *The Tradition of Women's Autobiography: From Antiquity to the Present*. Boston: Twayne, 1986.

Jodock, Darrell. *The Church's Bible: Its Contemporary Authority*. Minneapolis: Fortress Press, 1989.

Josephson, Matthew. *The Robber Barons: The Great American Capitalists, 1861–1901*. 1934. Reprint. New York: Harcourt, Brace and World, 1962.

Kelly, Lori Duin. *The Life and Works of Elizabeth Stuart Phelps, Victorian Feminist Writer*. Troy, N.Y.: Whitston Publishing, 1983.

Kelman, Steven. *What Price Incentives? Economists and the Environment*. Boston: Auburn House, 1981.

Kelsey, David H. *The Uses of Scripture in Recent Theology*. Philadelphia: Fortress Press, 1975.

Keynes, John Maynard. *The End of Laissez-Faire*. London: Hogarth Press, 1926.

_____ . *Essays in Persuasion*. London: Macmillan, 1933.

Kidd, Reggie M. *Wealth and Beneficence in the Pastoral Epistles*. Atlanta: Scholars Press, 1990.

Kirk, G. S., ed. *The Iliad: A Commentary*. Cambridge: Cambridge University Press, 1985.

Lamb, Matthew. *Solidarity with Victims. Toward a Theology of Social Transformation*. New York: Crossroad, 1982.

Lamont, Michèle. *Money, Morals, and Manners: The Culture of the French and the American Upper-Middle Class*. Chicago: University of Chicago Press, 1992.

Landes, David S. "Why Are We So Rich and They So Poor?" *The American Economic Review* 80, no. 2 (May 1990): 1–13.

Lane, Ann J. *To "Herland" and Beyond: The Life & Work of Charlotte Perkins Gilman*. New York: Pantheon Books, 1990.

Lay Commission on Catholic Social Teaching and the U.S. Economy. *Toward the Future: Catholic Social Thought and the U.S. Economy*. New York: American Catholic Committee, 1984.

Lehmann, Hartmut. "Ascetic Protestantism and Economic Rationalism: Max Weber Revisited after Two Generations." *Harvard Theological Review* 80 (1987): 307–20.

Lewis, N. *Life in Egypt under Roman Rule*. Oxford: Clarendon, 1983.

Lindblom, Charles E. *Democracy and Market System*. Oslo: Norwegian University Press, 1988.

_____ . *Politics and Markets*. New York: Basic Books, 1971.

Livermore, Mary A. *The Story of My Life, or the Sunshine and Shadow of Seventy Years*. 1899. Reprint. New York: Arno Press, 1974.

_____ . *My Story of the War, A Woman's Narrative or Four Years of Personal Experience as Nurse in the Union Army. . . .* 1899. Reprint. New York: Arno Press, 1972.

Lonergan, Bernard F. *Insight: A Study of Human Understanding*. New York: Philosophical Library, 1958.

Lutz, Charles P., ed. *God, Goods, and the Common Good: Eleven Perspectives on Economic Justice in Dialog with the Roman Catholic Bishops' Pastoral Letter*. Minneapolis: Augsburg, 1987.

Machiavelli, Niccolò. *The Prince*. 1514. Reprint. Translated by George Bull. Baltimore: Penguin Books, 1961.

Malina, Bruce J. *The New Testament World: Insights from Cultural Anthropology*. Atlanta: John Knox, 1981.

Meeks, Wayne. *First Urban Christians*. New Haven: Yale University Press, 1983.

_____ . "A Hermeneutics of Social Embodiment." *Harvard Theological Review* 79 (1986).

_____ . *The Moral World of the First Christians*. Philadelphia: Westminster Press, 1986.

Miegge, Mario. *I talenti messi a profitto. L'interpretazione della parabola dei denari affidati ai servi dalla Chiesa antica a Calvino*. Urbino: Argalia, 1969.

Milton, John. *Complete Prose Works of John Milton*. Edited by Don M. Wolfe et al. 8 vols. New Haven: Yale University Press, 1953–82.

————. *The Poetical Works of John Milton*. Edited by H. C. Beeching. Oxford: Humphrey Milford, 1922.

Moxnes, Halvor. *The Economy of the Kingdom: Social Conflict and Economic Relations in Luke's Gospel*. Philadelphia: Fortress Press, 1988.

Murray, Charles. *Losing Ground: American Social Policy 1950–1980*. New York: Basic Books, 1984.

Myers, Ched. *Binding the Strong Man: A Political Reading of Mark's Story of Jesus*. Maryknoll, N.Y.: Orbis Books, 1988.

Needleman, Jacob. *Money and the Meaning of Life*. New York: Doubleday, 1991.

Neuhaus, Richard John. *Doing Well and Doing Good: The Challenge to the Christian Capitalist*. New York: Doubleday, 1992.

Neustadt, Richard E., and Ernest R. May. *Thinking in Time: The Uses of History for Decision Making*. New York: Free Press, 1986.

Nickelsburg, George E. "Riches, the Rich and God's Judgment in I Enoch 92–105 and Luke's Gospel." *New Testament Studies* 25 (April 1979): 324–44.

Noonan, John T. *The Scholastic Analysis of Usury*. Cambridge: Harvard University Press, 1957.

Novak, Michael. *This Hemisphere of Liberty: A Philosophy of the Americas*. Washington, D.C.: AEI Press, 1990.

————. "Wealth and Virtue: The Development of Christian Economic Thinking." In *The Capitalist Spirit: Toward a Religious Ethic of Wealth Creation*. Edited by Peter L. Berger. San Francisco: Institute for Contemporary Studies, 1990.

Oakman, Douglas E. *Jesus and the Economic Questions of His Day*. Lewiston, N.Y.: Edwin Mellen, 1986.

Ober, Josiah. *Mass and Elite in Democratic Athens*. Princeton, N.J.: Princeton University Press, 1989.

Odendahl, Teresa. *Charity Begins at Home: Generosity and Self-Interest among the Philanthropic Elite*. New York: Basic Books, 1990.

Ogletree, Thomas W. *Hospitality to the Stranger: Dimensions of Moral Understanding*. Philadelphia: Fortress Press, 1985.

O'Hare, Kate Richards. *The Sorrows of Cupid*. St. Louis: National Rip-Saw Publishing, 1912.

O'Higgins, Michael, Guenther Schmaus, and Geoffrey Stephenson. "Income Distribution and Redistribution: A Microdata Analysis for Seven Countries." *The Review of Income and Wealth* 35, no. 2 (1989): 107–31.

Okun, Arthur M. *Equality and Efficiency: The Big Tradeoff*. Washington, D.C.: Brookings Institution, 1975.

Olney, James. "Autos*Bios*Graphein: The Study of Autobiographical Literature." *South Atlantic Quarterly* 77 (Winter 1978): 113–23.

Origen. *Homilies on Genesis and Exodus*. Translated by Ronald E. Heine. Washington, D.C.: Catholic University of America Press, 1982.

Ostrander, Susan A., and Paul G. Schervish. "Giving and Getting: Philanthropy as a Social Relation." In *Critical Issues in American Philanthropy*. Edited by Jon Van Til et al. San Francisco: Jossey-Bass, 1990.

Parker, Gail, ed. *The Oven Birds: American Women on Womanhood, 1820–1920*. New York: Doubleday/Anchor, 1974.

Parch, Howard R. *The Goddess Fortuna in Mediaeval Literature*. Cambridge: Harvard University Press, 1927.

Pawlikowski, John T., O.S.M. "Modern Catholic Teaching on the Economy: An Analysis and Evaluation." In *Christianity and Capitalism: Perspectives on Religion, Liberalism and the Economy*. Edited by Bruce Grelle and David A. Krueger. Chicago: Center for the Scientific Study of Religion, 1986.

Perkins, Pheme. *Jesus as Teacher*. New York: Cambridge University Press, 1990.

————. "Scripture in Theology." In *Faithful Witness: Foundations of Theology for Today's Church*. Edited by Leo J. O'Donovan and T. Howland Sanks. New York: Crossroad, 1989.

Perkins, William. *Works*. Cambridge, 1605.

Phelps, Elizabeth Stuart. *Chapters from a Life*. Boston and New York: Houghton, Mifflin, 1897.

————. *The Silent Partner*. 1871. Reprint. Ridgewood, N.J.: Gregg Press, 1967.

Phillips, Kevin. *The Politics of Rich and Poor: Wealth and the American Electorate in the Reagan Aftermath*. New York: Random House, 1990.

Plato. *The Republic*. Translated by Richard W. Sterling and William C. Scott. New York and London: W. W. Norton, 1985.

Polanyi, Karl. "Our Obsolete Market Economy." *Commentary*, February 1947, 109–17.

Porter, Thomas E. *Myth and Modern American Drama*. Detroit: Wayne State University Press, 1969.

Preston, John. *The New Covenant, or The Saints Portion*. 2d ed. London, 1629.

Preston, William. *Aliens and Dissenters: Federal Suppression of Radicals, 1902–1933*. Cambridge: Harvard University Press, 1963.

Réau, Louis. *Iconographie de l'art chrétien*. 3 vols. Paris: Presses Universitaires de France, 1955–59.

Reisman, David A. *Adam Smith's Sociological Economics*. London: Croom Held, 1976.

Ringe, Sharon. *Jesus, Liberation and the Biblical Jubilee*. Philadelphia: Fortress, 1985.

Ste. Croix, G.M.E. *The Class Struggle in the Ancient Greek World*. Ithaca. N.Y.: Cornell University Press, 1981.

Sanger, Margaret. *Margaret Sanger, An Autobiography*. 1938. Reprint. New York: Dover Publications, 1971.

Schama, Simon. *The Embarrassment of Riches: An Interpretation of Dutch Culture in the Golden Age*. Berkeley and Los Angeles: University of California Press, 1988.

Schelling, Thomas. "Economic Reasoning and the Ethics of Policy." In *Choice and Consequence*. Cambridge: Harvard University Press, 1984.

Schervish, Paul G., and Andrew Herman. *Empowerment and Beneficence: Strategies of Living and Giving among the Wealthy*. Final report of the Study on Wealth and Philanthropy. Chestnut Hill, Mass.: Social Welfare Research Institute at Boston College, 1988.

Schervish, Paul G. "Wealth and the Spiritual Secret of Money." In *Faith and Philanthropy in America: Exploring the Role of Religion in America's Voluntary Sector*. Edited by Robert Wuthnow and Virginia A. Hodgkinson. San Francisco: Jossey-Bass, 1990.

Schottroff, Luise, and W. Stegemann. *Jesus and the Hope of the Poor*. Maryknoll, N.Y.: Orbis, 1986.

——, eds. *God of the Lowly. Socio-Historical Interpretations of the Bible*. Maryknoll, N.Y.: Orbis, 1984.

Smeeding, Timothy, Barbara Torrey, and Martin Rein. "Patterns of Income and Poverty: The Economic Status of Children and the Elderly in Eight Countries." In *The Vulnerable*. Washington, D.C.: Urban Institute Press, 1988.

Smith, Adam. *The Theory of Moral Sentiments*. 1759. Reprint. Edited by D. D. Raphael and A. L. Macfie. Oxford: Clarendon Press, 1976.

——. *The Wealth of Nations*. 1776. Reprint. Edited by Edwin Cannan. New York: Modern Library, 1937.

Spirituall Experiences of sundry Beleevers. Edited by Vavasour Powell. 2d ed. London, 1652.

Stevenson, Laura Caroline. *Praise and Paradox: Merchants and Craftsmen in Elizabethan Popular Literature*. Cambridge: Cambridge University Press, 1984.

Synopsis Criticorum. Edited by Matthew Poole. 4 vols in 5. London, 1669–76.

Taylor, Gordon Rattray. *The Angel-Makers: A Study in the Psychological Origins of Historical Change, 1750–1850*. London: Heinemann, 1958.

Taylor, Jeremy. *Ductor Dubitantium* (1660). In *The Whole Works*. Edited by Reginald Heber. 15 vols. London: Ogle, Duncan, 1822.

Thalmann, William G. "Thersites: Comedy, Scapegoats and Heroic Ideology in *The Iliad*." *Transactions of the American Philological Association* 118 (1988): 1–28.

Thucydides. *History of the Peloponnesian War*. Translated by Rex Warner. London and New York: Penguin, 1972.

Thurow, Lester. *The Zero-Sum Society*. New York: Basic Books, 1980.

Tilley, Christopher, ed. *Reading Material Culture*. Oxford: Basil Blackwell, 1990.

Tracy, David. "The Uneasy Alliance Reconceived: Catholic Theological Method, Modernity, and Postmodernity." *Theological Studies* 50 (1989): 568–69.

Turner, Victor W. *The Ritual Process: Structure and Anti-Structure*. Chicago: Aldine, 1969.

U.S. Catholic Conference. "Economic Justice for All: Catholic Social Teaching and the U.S. Economy." *Origins* 16 (1986): 409–55.

Van Gennep, Arnold. *The Rites of Passage*. Translated by Monika B. Vizedom and Gabrielle L. Caffe. Chicago: University of Chicago Press, 1961.

Veyne, Paul. *Bread and Circuses. Historical Sociology and Political Pluralism*. Abridged with an introduction by Oswyn Murray. Translated by Brian Pearce. London: Penguin/Allen Lane, 1990.

——. *A History of Private Life 1: From Pagan Rome to Byzantium*. Cambridge: Harvard University Press, 1987.

Vorse, Mary Heaton. *A Footnote to Folly: Reminiscences of Mary Heaton Vorse*. Edited by Annette K. Baxter. 1935. Reprint. New York: Ayer, 1980.

Wailes, Stephen L. *Medieval Allegories of Jesus' Parables*. Berkeley: University of California Press, 1987.

Weber, Max. *Economy and Society: An Outline of Interpretive Sociology*. Edited by Guenther Roth and Claus Wittich. New York: Bedminster Press, 1968.

——. *The Protestant Ethic and the Spirit of Capitalism*. Translated by Talcott Parsons. New York: Macmillan, 1958. [Weber's essays originally appeared in German in 1904–5.]

Weigel, George. "Camels and Needles, Talents and Treasure: American Catholi-
    cism and the Capitalist Ethic." In *The Capitalist Spirit: Toward a Religious
    Ethic of Wealth Creation.* Edited by Peter L. Berger. San Francisco: Institute
    for Contemporary Studies Press, 1990.
Wiebe, Robert H. *The Search for Order.* New York: Hill and Wang, 1967.
Wilson, Thomas. "Sympathy and Self Interest." In *The Market and the State: Essays
    in Honour of Adam Smith.* Edited by Thomas Wilson and Andrew S.
    Skinner. Oxford: Clarendon Press, 1976.
Wuthnow, Robert. *Acts of Compassion: Caring for Others and Helping Ourselves.*
    Princeton, N.J.: Princeton University Press, 1991.

Index

About the Contributors

LISA SOWLE CAHILL is Professor of Theology at Boston College and past President of the Catholic Theological Society of America. Her most recent book is *"Love Your Enemies": Discipleship, Pacifism, and Just War Theory.*

DAVID H. GILL, S.J., is Associate Professor of Classics at Boston College. His teaching, writing, and research are largely in the areas of ancient Greek literature and religion. He is currently working on a book-length project entitled *Revenge and Justice: A Study in Greek Ethical Thought.*

DAYTON HASKIN is Associate Professor of English at Boston College, where he teaches Renaissance literature in the English Department and comparative literature in the Honors program. He is the author of *Milton's Burden of Interpretation*, a commentary editor for the *Variorum Edition of the Poetry of John Donne*, and currently President of the John Donne Society.

PHEME PERKINS is Professor of Theology (New Testament) at Boston College. She has been President of the Catholic Biblical Association and of the New England Region of the American Academy of Religion. Professor Perkins has written fifteen books and currently has two in press, *Peter in the New Testament and Early Christianity* and *Gnosticism and the New Testament.*

CAROL MORRIS PETILLO, Associate Professor of History at Boston College, specializes in U.S. military history and in biography. She is the author of *Douglas MacArthur: The Philippine Years* and editor of *The Ordeal of Elizabeth Vaughan.* Currently she is writing a history of U.S. army wives since 1850.

JOSEPH F. QUINN is Professor and Chair of the Economics Department at Boston College. His research focuses on the economics of aging, with emphases on the economic status of the elderly, patterns of labor force withdrawal, and the determinants of the individual retirement decision. He has published articles in numerous journals, and recently co-authored a book entitled *Passing the Torch: The Influence of Economic Incentives on Work and Retirement*.

PAUL G. SCHERVISH is Associate Professor of Sociology and Director of the Social Welfare Research Institute at Boston College. Currently he is directing the interdisciplinary study, "The Contradictions of Christmas: Troubles and Traditions in Culture, Home, and Heart." He has published in the areas of philanthropy, sociology of money, labor markets, and sociology of religion. He is completing work on *The Modern Medicis: Strategies of Philanthropy among the Wealthy*.